A

HISTORY OF THE HOLY SHRINE OF SRI VENKATESA

IN

TIRUPATI

A HISTORY OF THE HOLY SHRINE OF SRI VENKATESA IN TIRUPATI

S. KRISHNASWAMI AIYANGAR

GYAN

Published by

Gyan Publishing House
5, Ansari Road
Daryaganj, New Delhi-110002
Phone: 011-47034999, 9811692060
E-mail: books@gyanbooks.com

Distribution Network
gyanbooks.com
India, USA, Canada, UK, Australia

ISBN: 978-93-6780-119-2 (PB)

First Published, 1940

2nd Impression 2024

Printed at: Gyan Press, Delhi.

A HISTORY OF THE HOLY SHRINE OF SRI VENKATESA IN TIRUPATI
Author: S. KRISHNASWAMI AIYANGAR

For the statements made and the views expressed the author alone is responsible.

A HISTORY OF THE HOLY SHRINE OF SRI VENKATESA IN TIRUPATI

தேனோங்குசோலைத் திருவேங்கடமென்றும்
வானோங்கு சோலைமலை யென்றும்—தானோங்கு
தென்னரங்கமென்றுந் திருவத்தியூரென்றும்
சொன்னவர்க்குமுண்டோ துயர்.

CONTENTS

LIST OF ILLUSTRATIONS.

PREFACE

THE cluster of hills which goes by the name Vēnkaṭāchalam hills, and the small group in it called the Tirupati hills, have long been the most famous pilgrim spots in South India and the latter has enjoyed an eminence equalled but by a few even up to the present time. It is in the fitness of things that the management, recently constituted for carrying on the administration of the affairs of the temple on the hill and its large properties and income, should have thought of getting a history of the shrine written for the information of the public. The first Committee had this question before them for consideration. Śrī Dewan Bahadur T. A. Ramalingam Chettiar's suggestion that I be invited to write the history was readily accepted by the Committee. The Committee's invitation was quite acceptable to me, as it has long been my wish to bring to a conclusion the enquiry, in regard to the history of the temple, which I started so long ago as 1904 in writing a life-history of Rāmānuja, which publication came in for important public consideration in connection with the Gōvindarāja shrine in Chidambaram. The time was rather propi-

collected by the Dēvastānam Department of epigraphy during the last decade had at last been printed and was likely to become available to the public. The history of the shrine in the following pages is based upon these inscriptional records for the latter period, as they furnish an amount of information for that period, not inferior to that of any other important shrine for the corresponding period. This period has reference to that following the life activity of the Vaishṇava teacher, Rāmānuja, whose connection with the temple and his actual services to it had long been a fruitful subject of controversy.

For the period relating to Rāmānuja himself and his active work of reorganising the temple worship and ritual and putting these on a footing of permanence, we are driven to such information as the material for his life-history would provide. That material is hardly ample enough to give us any detailed information in regard to the details of his organisation. But luckily for us, we have a Sanskrit work composed just a few generations after Rāmānuja which bears specifically upon this work. The Committee was so good as to sanction the republication in good form of a critical edition of this work, of which there was an unsatisfactory Telugu edition, and even that had for some time been out of print. The then Commissioner, Śrī A. Ranganatha Mudaliar, deserves all thanks for having enabled me to bring out the edition, in Devanagari characters, of the work, *Śrī Vēnkaṭāchala Itihāsa-māla*, which gives a detailed account of what took place under Rāmānuja, and how that arrangement was allowed to continue since then.

For the period anterior to Rāmānuja, the sources of information are not as ample as for the period following. For about three centuries preceding Rāmānuja's activity in Tirupati, we have some inscriptions, not many, though some of them do throw much light upon the history of the shrine and the locality surrounding it. For the period before the 8th century, we have to depend entirely upon other sources of information, of which the dominent sources are literature, Tamil and Sanskrit, bearing upon the temple. The classical literature of the Tamils, the so-called Śangam works, have just a few references to Vēngaḍam, which formed the northern boundary of the Tamil land according to them, and just a few which would support the existence of the temple at the time, and even of the establishment of the annual festivals for worship in the temple. Proceeding therefrom we have the work of the twelve Vaishṇava Āḻvārs, whose age and active work occupied the period from the most brilliant period of the Śangam age on to the last years of the 8th century. These works necessarily have a great deal to say about the temple, as it was one of

yet made open to the public. What is more, the Government have declined to give me access to the records for the purpose. In the circumstances, I could do no more than to leave it as it is.

I must in the first instance acknowledge my obligation to my friend, Śrī T. A. Ramalingam Chettiar and the other Members of the first Dēvastānam Committee, as also the succeeding Dēvastānam Committee with its Chairman Śrī Venkata Ranga Rayaningaru. The two Commissioners, Messrs. Sitarama Reddiyar and Ranganatha Mudaliar were no less helpful in regard to the matter, as also the staff of the Dēvastānam Office on the occasion of my visit to Tirupati in the course of the work. I acknowledge with particular pleasure the assistance rendered in the course of my writing the book to *Sāhitya Śirōmaṇi* Pandit S. Rajagopalacharya and Dr. P. Srinivasacharya, M.A., Ph.D., in the earlier stages of the work. The index to the book is the work of Śrī T. V. Mahalingam, M. A., till recently University Research Student, who offered to do the work with alacrity. My grateful thanks are due to all of them for the assistance. The printing work has been entrusted to the Ananda Press. I am very much obliged to its Proprietor, Śrī B. Madhava Rau, M. A., for much accommodating assistance in the course of printing the work, which, as will be seen, has been excellently done. The illustrations are taken, about one half from the Dēvastānam Archæological photo negatives, and the other from photographs taken by Messrs. G. K. Vale for the Dēvastānam Committee.

I am really gratified that I have been able to carry the work to completion without break through the grace of Śri Venkaṭēśa, to whom I dedicate this in token of my devotion.

THE DASARA 1939,
Mylapore, Madras. } S. KRISHNASVAMI AIYANGAR.

A HISTORY OF THE HOLY SHRINE OF SRI VENKATESA AT TIRUPATI

CHAPTER I

GENERAL GEOGRAPHICAL FEATURES

Tirupati, or far rather the group of hills lying in a confused coil called the Tirumalai hills, forms a feature of the region of South India between the 13th and 14th degrees of north latitude. The Eastern Ghats which, from the northern extremity of the Presidency, run close to the coast, turn into the interior after passing the river Krishna, and then break up into a number of parallel ranges of hills of which, in the region south of the Krishna and extending southwards to the latitude of Madras, say roughly 13th degree of north latitude, three parallel ranges are distinguishable. The range nearest the coast runs more or less straight in one single range. The second range is an irregular group starting similarly from the Krishna well below Kurnool, and runs down in a semicircle into the Cuddapah District scattering about in a cluster, one group of which is called Śēshāchalam hills; the main range however runs southwards till it makes a further approach to the coast, coming down as far as Ponneri a few miles north of Madras. Another range more irregular and much lower in point of height, proceeds northwards from the foot of the Mysore plateau and scatters itself through Anantapur and Kurnool districts. The central group is what is called Nallamalais in the Kurnool District, and, as it proceeds southwards from there, it becomes more definitely something like a single range, and meets the Eastern range round about the group of hills at Tirupati, Kāḷahasti, etc. These hills therefore form a feature of the frontier half a degree to the north of Madras, extending the whole length from the Mysore plateau and stretching eastwards to almost near the coast at Ponneri, and thus constitute a prominent feature of the northern extremity of the Tamil land. Hence it is that, in defining the boundaries of the Tamil country, they mark Vēngaḍam, a prominent feature of this cluster of hills, as the northern boundary, the eastern and western boundaries being formed by the sea, and the southern boundary marked by the promontory of the Western Ghats, ending in Cape Comorin. The earliest Tamil grammar Tolkāppiyam defines the boundary of the provenance of Tamil as such. Some of the Purāṇas dealing with the holy shrine at Tirupati liken the range of hills, the Nallamalais and their continuation, to a huge cobra lying about at ease, of which almost

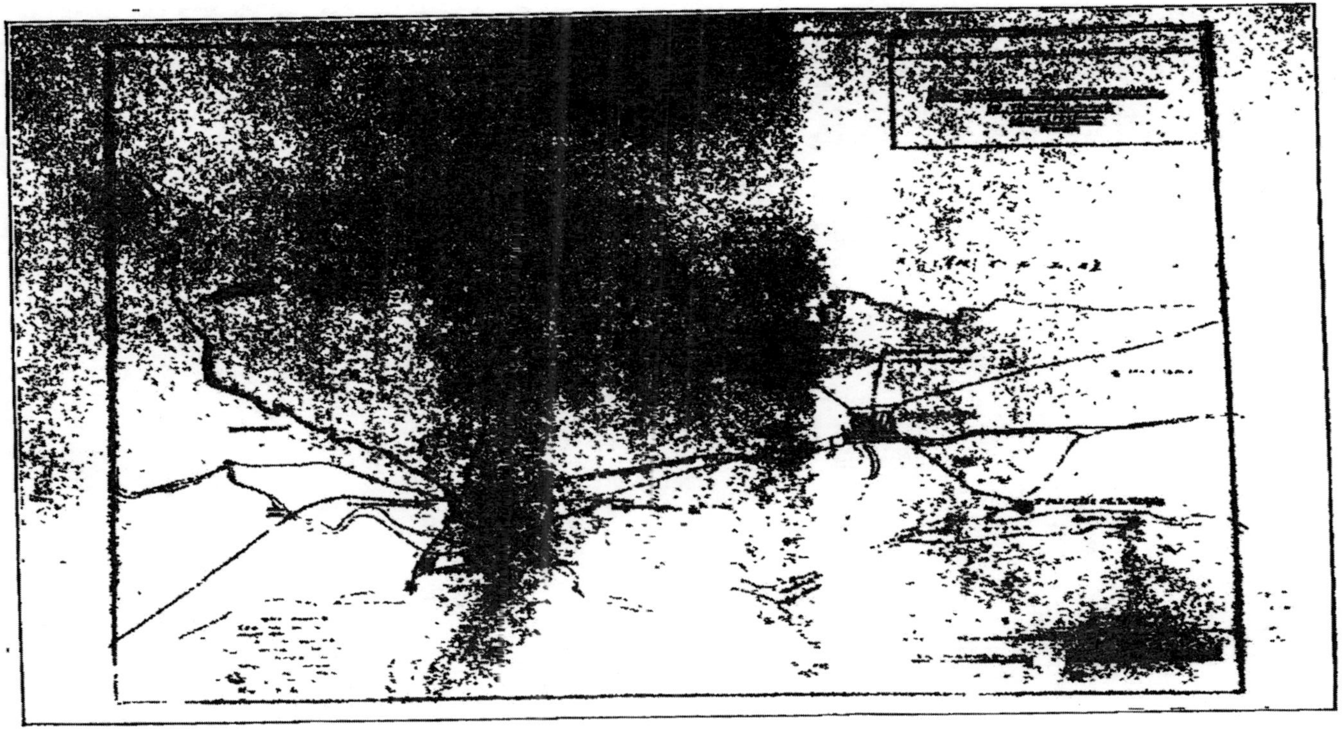

TIRUPATI HILL AND SURROUNDINGS

(To face page 3)

the end of the tail is marked by the great Śiva shrine of Śrīśailam not far from the Krishna river, beyond the 16th degree of north latitude and a considerable way down the river from Kurnool. Coming up on the back of this huge snake one next strikes the Vishṇu shrine of Ahōbalam which is at the beginning of the trunk of the snake. At the back of the hood stands the hill of Tirupati, and almost at the opening of the mouth again the great Śiva shrine of Kāḷahasti. This Paurāṇic description is rather graphic and accurate, although the features marked happen to be only the four holy places of Kāḷahasti, Tirupati, Ahōbalam and Śrīśailam. We mentioned already the cluster to the west being called Śēshāchalam hills, probably the name is given from this feature of the whole group lying about like a snake, or rather a cobra lying at ease in the sun. This curious feature probably had its own share in creating the peculiar impression upon people journeying from a distance, and is probably responsible for the names given which, at first sight, may seem fanciful.

THE ACTUAL NAME OF THE HILL. Tirupati which is a Vaishṇava sacerdotal name for the shrine there, is generally known to Tamil literature by the name Vēngaḍam, which is one of the alternative names in holy parlance as well. Vēngaḍam is generally referred to as a hill, though often the reference is as much to the territory surrounding it, and, when it happened to be the capital, the territory dependent upon it. In Tamil secular literature it figures as the northern borderland of the Tamil speaking country of the south. Tolkāppiyam, the classical grammar of the Tamils, popularly believed to be one of the oldest pieces of Tamil literature extant, defines the boundary of Tamil provenance as between the hill Vēngaḍam and the southern Comorin (Kumāri) as marking the northern and southern boundaries. In those days the seas marked the extent and the prevalence of Tamil on the other two sides. Therefore northern Vēngaḍam (Vaḍa Vēngaḍam) is the style in which it is most referred to. To make the position clear, it is possible to quote references in which it is stated quite unmistakably that when one passed Vēngaḍam from the south, he passed the bounds of Tamil on the one side and gets into a region where the language actually is different. That is usually referred to as 'Vēngaḍam passing which the language changes.' Numbers of instances could be quoted for that from Tamil classical literature. So we might take it that Vēngaḍam for Tirupati, is the name of the hill, so familiarly known to the Tamils, more or less as a landmark which characterised the northern border of the Tamil land passing across which one got into a region where the Tamil language was not spoken.

VENGADAM, BOUNDARY MARKING OFF TAMIL FROM VADUKAR. The language that was spoken beyond Tirupati was known to the Tamils as Vaḍuku, and the chieftains who ruled even over Tirupati and the regions to the west of it, were generally known as princes of the Vaḍukas (*Vaḍukar Perumakan*) in classical Tamil. This *Perumakan* evolves into *Perumān* in later Tamil which, in the sense of the great one, prince or king according to circumstances, is used as a title of dignity. Accordingly the language which they spoke is known as Vaḍuku which, in modern parlance, means Telugu. But, in the early centuries of the Christian era, the term *Vaḍuku* for the language, and Vaḍukar for the people, applied to all the people along the northern borders of the Tamil land extending from the east coast far into the peninsula, perhaps reaching even to the west Coast. At least there is one chieftain in the interior, the ruler of Erumai, who is referred to as *Vaḍukar Perumakan*, and the indication is that he held rule in a part of the country which is northern

Mysore now, and the territory adjoining it. Certain points in this long boundary, in fact the points on the highway of communication between the north and the south, seem marked off as *Vaḍukar-munai*, the frontier posts of the *Vaḍukar* land, that is, the outposts of the Tamil country, where one came into contact with the *Vaḍukar*, the contact in respect of *Vaḍukar-munai* being generally contact hostile. This term *Vaḍukar* seems merely to represent the linguistically analogous *Baḍagas* of the Nilgiris of to-day, and it is possible that that happened to be the common name, at least so far as the Tamils were concerned, for Telugu and Kanarese together, before perhaps the two languages differentiated. We have to go to the 11th or the 12th century for a distinctive reference describing the prevalent language in these regions as *Vaḍuku*, and locating both the Telugu and the Kanarese behind this *Vaḍuku* land. That distinction obtained in the days of Nacchinārkiniyar, the great commentator. So then, the whole northern borderland of the Tamils was *Vaḍuku*, and hence the road leading there to the north was described as *Vaḍukavaḷi*, which may mean only one great trunk road leading into the Vaḍuka-land, although from some of the expressions used in the inscriptions of a later date, it may be possible to infer more than one road, as had sometimes been done. Hence the Tamil land was bounded on the north, across almost the whole length of the peninsula, by the land of the *Vaḍukar*. A prominent landmark in this northern boundary was undoubtedly Vēngaḍam, and Vēngaḍam, according to references in classical Tamil literature, should have lain on the highway leading north from the Tamil land, as it happens to be even now.

TIRUPATI IN EARLY CLASSICAL TAMIL LITERATURE. The body of literature generally known as the Śangam literature consists of a number of collections of poems which at one time must have been more generally current in the Tamil land. These seem, from their nature, poems composed on occasions, exhibiting various modes of composition as a mere exhibition of poetic skill by their respective authors. Some time later it was apparently felt that these fugitive pieces of composition were in danger of being lost, and, as a practicable effort, some one was set to collect the most excellent of such pieces to provide typical illustrations of the various modes of composition. Presumably therefore the collections which have come down to us are composed of pieces considered the most excellent at the time that the collections happened to be made. There is one particular author who is reputed in Tamil literature as one who wrote the Bhārata in Tamil, and therefore was generally distinguished as Perundēvanār who composed the Tamil poem Bhāratam. Perundēvanār being a common name in Tamil literature, this distinction was considered necessary as, even in this comparatively narrow field of literature, there were a number of Perundēvans. But this Perundēvan who made the Bhāratam must be distinguished from the Perundēvan, the author of the Bhāratam in *Veṇbā* verses, whose time we know precisely. This Perundēvan must have been an earlier author. To the well-known eight collections he composed the verses in invocation, and these poems in invocation relate to all the well-known deities of the Tamil land at the time, and not confined to one or the other of these exclusively. A late copper-plate charter datable in the tenth century ascribes the "doing of the Mahābhārata in Tamil" to the Pāṇḍyan ruler well-known in this class of literature as the Pāṇḍyan "who won the victory at Talaiyālangānam." In this famous battle the young Pāṇḍya is said, in this literature itself, to have won a victory against his two rival contemporaries, the Chōḷa and the Chēra, assisted by a number of chieftains of the Tamil land, seven of whom are mentioned by name. It is probably therefore that, it was in his reign or immediately after that, the collections of these poems were made, and the poems in invocation to these collections composed by Perundēvanār, the author of the poem, the Mahābhārata. The collections which have been made therefore must all relate to a period anterior to this Pāṇḍyan, victor at Talaiyālangānam. References in this literature therefore must be regarded as having relation to the period before the date of Perundēvanār or the Pāṇḍya, victor at Talaiyālangānam.

THE CHARACTER OF THESE REFERENCES. These references collected from various pieces in two or three of these collections refer to Tirupati by the name Vēngaḍam, and generally to Tirupati as being on the northern borderland of the Tamils, as is made in the Tolkāppiyam. In the actual circumstances in which the references do occur, Tirupati is indicated as in a region passing across which one passes from the land of the Tamils into a land where the language spoken was different from Tamil. Among the authors referring to Tirupati we can distinguish two authors contemporary with the Pāṇḍyan of of Talaiyālangānam, Kallāḍanār and Nakkīrar. Poem 83 of the Ahanānūru refers to the chieftain Pulli of the region surrounding Vēngaḍam. He is described in this poem as *Iḷaigñar*

Perumakan; the latter word *Perumakan* is a Tamil equivalent of prince which later became Perumān, meaning king. The whole expression therefore would mean the prince of *Iḷaigñar*, and this latter term is generally used to indicate hunters by profession. Another attribute which he uses is the Tamil term *kallā* which would mean uncultivated; in other words, in a comparatively savage state of civilisation. In another poem 209 of the Ahanānūru, this same author describes the same Pulli and his Vēngaḍam, and mentions the peculiar feature that there was a narrow passage across the hills, described as a tunnel, through which one had to pass to emerge from the territory of the chieftain Pulli into the land to the northward of the region. Nakkīrar does not refer to Vēngaḍam as such. But he is undoubtedly referring to the territory dominated by Vēngaḍam, where he speaks of Tiraiyan and his capital Pavattiri, Reḍḍipālem in the Gūḍūr Taluk of the Nellore District. In another poem of the same collection, namely, poem 253, Nakkīrar speaks of *Vaḍukar Perumakan, Ērumai.* This Ērumai comes under reference in a number of other poems, and by various authors, as the chieftain of the *Vaḍukar*; but, in this poem, Nakkīrar indicates clearly that the territory of this *Vaḍukar* chieftain lay in the region of the river which he calls *Ayiri*, and, passing that river, one passes from the Tamil land into the land of the Vaḍukar. Ayiri seems to be the Tamil equivalent of the well-known Mysore river, Hagari, passing near Kadūr and through the Chitledrug District, falling into the Tungabadrā, a well-known frontier region in later history between the Tamils and powers to the north of them. Another poet by name Kaṇakkāyanār, probably the father of Nakkīrar, as he is often described as Nakkīrar son of Kaṇakkāyanār, refers to the northern Vēngaḍam in Aham 27, and of the breed of elephants infesting its forests in the course of a description of a Pāṇḍya and his famous port, the pearl-producing Korkai. Other authors referring to Vēngaḍam are Tāyām Kaṇṇan, otherwise Tayangaṇṇan, who refers to Vēngaḍam as belonging to Toṇḍaiyār, and refers to the country of the Vaḍukar across the region. Similarly another poet Kaṇṇan son of Kāṭṭūr Kiḻār, refers to Vēngaḍam as belonging to Tiraiyan, and gives a peculiar feature that the elephants there were being fed with the tender shoots of the bamboo. The last but the most important poet of them all, and, perhaps even the oldest among them, Māmūlanār, has seven poems in this collection in which he might be held to refer to Vēngaḍam directly or indirectly. In poem 61 he refers to Vēngaḍam as belonging to Pulli, the chieftain of the *Kaḷvar*, and another feature of Vēngaḍam which he notes, and which is noteworthy, is that Vēngaḍam was famous for its festivals. In two other poems 115 and 281, he does not refer to Tirupati. In the first he refers to Ērumai of Kuḍanāḍu, the chief Ērumai being the ruler of the western country *(Kuḍanāḍu)*. The other piece refers to the Vaḍukar, and to a hill where there was a tunnel for passing in and out, and these features come under reference in the course of a statement that the Mauryas invaded the south, pressing the Vaḍukar forward before them, passed this tunnel in the hill. In poem 295 however he refers undoubtedly to Tirupati as *Pullikuṉṟam*, the hill of the chieftain Pulli, and refers to the country across as the region of the Vaḍukar entering which the language changes. In other words passing into the region of the Vaḍukar, the language changes from Tamil into another language, obviously *Vaḍuku*. In poem 311 he refers to the good country of Pulli and the desert past it, and describes the feature that the people were accustomed to eating the rice prepared with tamarind, on teak leaves. In poem 359 he refers to Pulli liberal in gifts. In poem 393 Pulli comes under reference again, and Vēngaḍam, and here Pulli is described as one the words of whose speech are long, that is, the words are drawn out, as is the characteristic of some of these languages. There are other references by other authors which would confirm one or other of these features, though they do not specifically refer to Vēngaḍam as such.

TIRUPATI, NOT REFERRED TO AS A HOLY SHRINE AS IT IS. It will be noticed that although a number of authors of eminence in this collection actually refer to Vēngaḍam, and give some details of features which in those days were regarded as characteristic of the hill and the region of which it was a prominent feature, there is no reference to the great shrine which now-a-days is almost synonymous with the place name. Tirupati now-a-days means first and foremost, perhaps even almost exclusively, the shrine at Tirupati. The change of word to Vēngaḍam, a synonym, does not make much of a difference. That prominence of the shrine does not appear to be given to Vēngaḍam in the references quoted above. There is however one reference in poem 61 of the Māmūlanār which seems unmistakable in regard to this. Speaking of Vēngaḍam in this poem, Māmūlanār refers to it as Vēngaḍam of great prosperity, prosperous because of its having festivals. This may be regarded as an unmistakable reference at least to the celebration of festivals there during the year, and of the place being much resorted to on that account, thereby contributing to its prosperity. This may justify our presuming the existence of the temple there, and the series of festivals which had early been inaugurated in connection with it. But it falls short however of the actual mention of the temple as such. The more so as it gives no indication even inferentially of the character of the temple or of its deity. During the period of the Śangam literature therefore we may take it that the temple may have existed, but it had not quite attained to the importance or the prominence that it attained to in the period following.

NOTEWORTHY FEATURES OF THE PLACE FROM THIS CLASS OF LITERATURE. There are certain points however in connection with the region which are worth noting with a view to the position of the territory in the age of the Śangam literature. The first point to note is that it is the borderland separating Tamil from a northern language which goes by the name *Vaḍuku*. The modern equivalent of this *Vaḍuku* would be Telugu. The people who are on the northern borderland of the Tamil country, almost the whole way across the peninsula are referred to as *Vaḍukar*, and their rulers as *Vaḍukar Perumakan*, prince or chief of the *Vaḍukar*. The region here referred to would answer to the modern division called Rāyalu-Sīma to distinguish it from the Āndhra country proper, so far as the eastern half of it is concerned. In the earlier period, however, it is not merely the eastern but perhaps even the western half is equally distinguishable, the region of the *Vaḍukar* having behind it the block of territory which, early in South Indian History, went by the name Karṇāṭaka (Tam. Karu-nāḍu for the land, and Karunaḍam for the language), that is, in the period following the age of the Śangam, and judging from the information so far available to us. The distinction is made by certain commentators, at least by one commentator of the Tolkāppiyam. Expounding one of the Sūtras of the Tolkāppiyam itself, the commentary notes that the region we are concerned with was the region of the *Vaḍukar*; and behind it were the territories where the languages current were Telugu in the east and Kannaḍa in the west. The next point that comes out from the references is that the people across the border spoke a language different from Tamil. It was, in the judgment of the Tamils at any rate, a language as yet not much cultivated, and, according to them again, the pronunciation of words was drawling at least to the Tamil ear, which, from the point of view of the Tamil, would be true of the Telugu spoken in the Āndhra country as distinct from the more southern region. The next point is that the natural character of the region, which was a forest country more or less, made the profession of the inhabitants hunting and cattle rearing. Elephants seem to have been abundant in the forest region, and had been tamed and brought into service. The next point is that the region was under the government of a chieftain by name Pulli ruling over a people who are described as *Kaḷvar*, possibly with the variant form *Kaḷavar*. Subsequently to him it seems to have come under the authority of a chieftain called Tiraiyan with a capital at Vēngaḍam, and perhaps an alternative capital at Pavattiri, a little further north. The next point again is that the territory was included in the region of the Toṇḍaiyar; in other words, it was regarded as a part of what was called in brief Toṇḍai-maṇḍalam, or popularly Toṇḍamaṇḍalam in Tamil. The last point of importance to note from these references is that, at one time, the Chōḷas extended their conquests northwards to bring these *Vaḍukar* under their authority. A defeat of the *Vaḍukar* in the north and of the Paradavar, the fisher-folk, in the south happened to be mentioned in connection with a Chō̤la ruler; in another poem he is said to have inflicted a defeat on the *Vaḍukar* at a place called Pā̤li. It becomes clear therefore that the region dependent upon Vēngaḍam was inhabited by a people called *Vaḍukar* who were under their own chieftains, and became subsequently subjected to the authority of the Tiraiyan chieftains perhaps after the defeat inflicted upon them by the Chō̤la, and the Tiraiyan chieftain referred to here is called Tiraiyan without a qualifying attribute, who had his capital at Pavattiri, and not Iḷam Tiraiyan associated with Kānchi as his capital, a famous character in the Śangam literature itself perhaps of a subsequent generation.

CELEBRATION OF FESTIVALS, A FEATURE OF TIRUPATI IN EARLY TIMES EVEN. Before passing from these texts, there is one particular passage in the poems of Māmūlanār which calls for a few remarks. The passage actually occurs in poem 61 of the Ahanānūṟu. * Freely rendered the passage means that " the chieftain of the Kaḷvar

---

* கழல்புனை திருந்தடிக் கள்வர் கோமான்
மழபுலம் வணக்கிய மாவன் புல்லி
விழவுடை விழுச்சீர் வேங்கடம் பெறினும்
பழகு வரா தலோ வரிதே.

Aham. 61.

who are in the habit of handing over elephant tusks, bartering them for liquor prepared from paddy, and who wore anklets characteristic of warriors, was Pulli famed for the conquest of the land of the Maḻavar, and for great gifts to those who went to him. (Your lover) it is rarely possible will reconcile himself to stay away even if he got thereby Vēngaḍam, the capital of that Pulli which is prosperous *because of the festivals celebrated in it.*" The actual sense of the passage is that an imaginary lover who had departed from his sweetheart and travelled away in quest of wealth to distant parts, has tarried a little longer than he promised, and the consolation is offered to the heart-broken damsel that he might have delayed, but that he would not stay away under any circumstances. To add emphasis to this statement, it is set down that even if, in his desire for the acquisition of wealth, he got possession of such a prosperous city as Vēngaḍam, he would not stay behind. The point for notice here is that the fame of Vēngaḍam in the estimation of Māmūlar was due, at least in part, to the great festivals which were celebrated in the place from time to time, meaning obviously the annual festivals which are now a feature of the great temple-city. The casual statement of this feature has its own tale to tell. According to almost all the Purāṇas which make references to this shrine at Tirupati, it was a Toṇḍamān ruler who unearthed the shrine, built a temple for the God thus discovered by digging up an ant-hill, housed the God in a shrine and instituted a certain number of festivals to that God. The evidence of the Purāṇas therefore is that Tirupati became a human institution with a shrine and all its appurtenances only from the days of the Toṇḍamān. The identification of this Toṇḍamān would give us the clue to the actual period in which the temple came into being as a human institution. As a matter of fact, the Purāṇas state it that the shrine itself was not a human creation, but is regarded as the divine abode itself come on to the earth by the will of the God abiding there, that is, Viṣṇu. We noted already that, in these poems alone, we note a change of rulers of the locality, the chieftain whose territory it was, is Pulli, the chieftain of the Kaḷvar, a section of the Vaḍukar, and from him it becomes included in the territory of the Toṇḍaiyār. Three poets, Tāyam Kaṇṇan in Aham 213, Kāṭṭūr Kiḻār Makan Kaṇṇan in Aham 85, Nakkīrar in Aham 340 speak of the ruler as Tiraiyan instead of Pulli. If these poets were later than Māmūlar we could take it that the territory dominated by Vēngaḍam passed from the Kaḷvar chieftain

Pulli of the Vaḍukar people to the Tiraiyan chieftain. This Tiraiyan is referred to as having for his capital Pavattiri, identified with the village Reḍḍipāḷem in the Gudur Taluk. The extent of the territory is further indicated by Māmūlar himself who refers in poem 11 included in the *Kuṟum-togai* to the territory as on the borderland of the Vaḍukar (*Vaḍukar-munai*), and the district is referred to as Vērkkāḍu Nāḍu where language changes. This Vērkkāḍu is no other than the latter part of the name Paḻa-Vērkkāḍu, now anglisised into Pulicat. The territory therefore forming part of the modern Chingleput, North Arcot and Nellore Districts, constituted the hilly country dominated by Vēngaḍam and contained other cities like Pavattiri and Vērkkāḍu; it was in the territory of the people Vaḍukar ruled first by the Kaḷvar-chieftain Pulli, and then passing from him under the authority of the Tiraiyan chieftain, who at one time had his capital at Pavattiri. The question now would arise as to who this Tiraiyan is and whether he is the same as Iḷam Tiraiyan of Kānchi, or different from him. Literary evidence is not quite decisive. The Ahanānūṟu contains a number of poems relating to a Tiraiyan, and the fact that the more famous person associated with Kānchi and the hero of the Tamil Classic *Perumbāṇ-*

āṛṛupaḍai is always referred to as Iḷam Tiraiyan would support the view that the Tiraiyan was an older chieftain; and because of his existence the more famous chieftain coming after him has been called Iḷam Tiraiyan, so that the two personages may have to be regarded as distinct from one another. That they were distinct seems to be the view of the venerable scholar MM. Dr. Swaminatha Aiyar. The fact that Kānchi is referred to as Toṇḍamān Kānchi in an old quotation, and that, in another similar passage, the chieftain addressed is called Tiraiyan held to be Iḷam Tiraiyan, would support this latter view. It is rather strange, however, that in a poem composed to celebrate Iḷam Tiraiyan in particular and his capital Kānchi, such as the Perumbāṇ-āṛṛupaḍai is, there is no reference to his northern territory or to any one of the cities which seem to be special features of that territory. This omission would perhaps be held to go against the identification. However, for our present purpose we may take it that the various literary references are all of them to one and only one Tiraiyan, Iḷam Tiraiyan of Kānchi. That the organisation of festivals in connection with temples we see in his time is in evidence in lines 410 and 411 of the Perumbāṇ-āṛṛupaḍai, which, in substance, states, that Kānchi attained to greater fame than the other old cities comparable with it, because of various festivals celebrated there for the spiritual benefit of many peoples, rendered by the commentator, people of various communities in religion. In the days of Toṇḍamān Iḷam Tiraiyan therefore festivals associated with temples had become an ordinary feature in towns like Kānchi. When the Purāṇas state, as they do, that it was a Toṇḍamān who inaugurated festivals in Tirupati, one could very well take it that probably the Toṇḍamān of Tirupati fame is no other than the Toṇḍamān associated with Kānchi. Tirumaḷiśai Āḷvār has a similar reference in verse 41 of his Nān-Mukhan Tiruvandādi where he has a specific reference to the festival of *Ōṇam* called *Ōṇa Viḷavu.* This festival of *Ōṇam* (Sans. *Śravaṇa*) was the earliest festival inaugurated in Tirupati by no less a person than Brahmā himself and is as yet the principal festival, the *Brahmōtsava* in Tirupati. The advent of the Toṇḍamān to power therefore, we may take it, marks the beginning of temple festivals, and we could well believe the Purāṇas when they state it that it is a Toṇḍamān chieftain, generally called Toṇḍamān Chakravarti in Vaiṣṇava parlance, that instituted these festivals in Tirupati in his time.

TONDAMAN ILAM TIRAIYAN. Toṇḍamān Iḷam Tiraiyan is a great celebrity in Tamil literature, and is celebrated in the poem Perumbāṇ-āṟṟupaḍai, forming one of the collection called "the Ten poems" (Pattuppāṭṭu). The author of this poem is described as Kaḍiyalūr Rudran Kaṇṇan, which would mean Kaṇṇan, the son of Rudran of Kaḍiyalūr. From what is known of him, he seems to have been a Brahman, but the place from which he came has not so far been satisfactorily located. Though Iḷam Tiraiyan is described as a ruler of great influence and importance, he is still not regarded as a crowned monarch, and is placed in a rank inferior to that of the three crowned kings of the south, Chōḷa, Pāṇḍya and Chēra. Such rulers are called *Kuṟunilamannar*, which literally translated would mean kings or rulers who ruled over land of a smaller extent or of inferior character. In other words it would simply mean kings or rulers of a smaller degree. The Tolkāppiyam, the authoritative work on matters like this, classes them as of royal descent, but not of monarchical standing. As described in the poem of Rudran Kaṇṇan, he was the ancient ruler of Kānchi ruling over what, in Tamil literature, is generally described as Toṇḍamaṇḍalam, which included the vast region between the Telugu frontier, the 14th degree of north latitude on the eastern side, extending southwards to the river Pālār, sometimes extending as far south as the northern Veḷḷār. We may take it roughly that the northern Peṇṇār and the northern Veḷḷār constituted its boundaries north and south. It extended westwards from the coast to take into it all the territory down to the foot of the hills bordering the plateau of Mysore, and from there going across through the middle of the present-day district of Salem. He is regarded as the son of a Chōḷa ruler, generally described as *Kiḷḷi Vaḷavan*, which is more or less a generic name for the Chōḷa, but is probably identifiable with *Neḍu-Muḍi-Kiḷḷi* whose name figures in the Śilappadikāram and Maṇimēkhalai. The Perumbāṇ-āṟṟupaḍai describes him as descended of the royal family of Ayōdhyā, in fact specifically mentioning *Tirumāl*, generally taken to be Rāma; but it carefully distinguishes him at the same time as coming of a younger branch of the family, because the Chōḷas claim to belong to the family of Ikṣvāku, and, among their warrior ancestors, figure names like Śibi, etc. The actual passage under reference is "descended from one, the brother who came after him, who has the colour of the sea, who carries on his chest the goddess of prosperity, and who measured out the great earth.* " This would mean that the prince was descended of a younger brother of Vishṇu, and therefore equated with the family of the Chōḷas who made a similar claim. He bore the name Tiraiyan (belonging to the sea), because he was brought over by the sea and lashed ashore on the Chōḷa coast, to be taken and brought up by the Chōḷa ruler as his son. The story in connection with this is that the Chōḷa ruler in one of his solitary meanderings along the banks of the backwaters of the sea in Kāverip-pūmpattinam saw an extraordinarily beautiful damsel, and fell in love with her at sight. The damsel responded in her turn, and they carried on a love affair which extended to his visiting her in her underground residence as the commentators call it. This was because she was a Nāga princess, and the Nāgas usually live in the underworld. We shall see that it perhaps means no more than her parents were living in a place access to which could be obtained only by passing through a cavern or a tunnel across the hills. When she became enceinte as a result of this liaison, she expressed

* நீயிரு
மிரு நிலங்கடந்த திருமறு மார்பின்
முன்னீர் வண்ணன் புறங்கடை யந்நீர்த்
திரைதரு மரபினுர வோனும்பல்.

Perumbāṇ-āṛṛuppaḍai ll. 29-31.

her concern in regard to the child to be born. The Chōḻa king advised her to put the baby carefully in a box and send it afloat on the sea with a twig of the creeper of the Toṇḍai (coccinia indica) tied round his ankle. If the baby should reach him safe, he would bring him up as a prince and make him king as becoming a prince. Some time after, the baby was born, she did as she was directed, and the baby meeting with an accident on the sea somehow reached the shore, and was brought to the Chōḻa monarch. The king brought him up as his own child and appointed him to the viceroyalty of Kānchi when the time came. This story figures of course in a Buddhist setting in the Maṇimēkhalai. We shall come to that detail a little later. He was ruling over the whole of Toṇḍamaṇḍalam with his capital at Kānchi. The poem *Perumbāṇ-āṟṟuppaḍai* describes him in the conventional style which demands the description of the four classes of land of which one's territory must be composed, the seashore, the forest land, hilly country and agricultural land; and a fifth class has also to be marked in this, as some of these lands had a tendency to become desert land by frequent droughts and by the heat of the sun. This is described as desert land transformed into such either from forest land or from agricultural land. A port is described under the name *Nīr-Peyartu*, from which the *Pāṇ* or musician, expert in playing on the greater musical instruments, such as the Tamil *Yāḻ*, and hence called *Perum-Pāṇ* as opposed to the *Śiṛu-Pāṇ*, one who played on the smaller musical instruments, passes through various classes of land till he reached the town of Kānchi, the headquarters of Iḷam Tiraiyan. This particular poet describes the Vishṇu shrine in Kānchi called *Veḥ-Kā* or *Yadōkta-kāri*, and that is the only shrine, of all the multitudinous shrines that one finds now in Kānchi, which finds mention in this poem actually. Kānchi is described in this poem as having attained to reputation as already an ancient city where religious festivals were celebrated for various classes of people, to each according to its own conviction. Since the author of this poem Rudran Kaṇṇan has also celebrated the great Karikāla in another poem of the same collection called *Paṭṭinappālai*, describing particularly the city of Kaverippūm-paṭṭinam, the capital of the Chōḻas, and is said to have received a very liberal reward from the great Chōḻa ruler Karikāla, and since this poem is of almost the same character and must have been presented to the ruler whom it celebrates, we have to take it that Iḷam Tiraiyan came in the same generation as the great Chōḻa Karikāla.

As a matter of fact we have reason to regard him as coming in the second generation after Karikāla and may possibly be even in the third. He was contemporary with the Adiyamān chieftain specifically known by the name Adikan, and the poetess Avvai is said to have gone from him, who was her patron, to the court of Iḷam Tiraiyan on an ambassadorial mission and persuaded the monarch into peaceful ways. This would bring him into contemporaneity with the Adiyamān of Tagaḍūr, another celebrity in the Śangam literature. There are a number of fugitive pieces of poetry in which he comes under reference either as merely Tiraiyan, or as Toṇḍamān, neither of which could be described as a specific name. But these have been held to refer to Iḷam Tiraiyan generally, particularly one stanza which is quoted as composed by a Poygaiyār, identifiable with Poygai Āḻvār as we shall see later. He was himself an author, and a few poems are ascribable to him in the collections which have come down to us. He is supposed to have been the founder of a town or city which went by the name Tiraiyanūr. There is a tank which goes by the name Tiraiyanēri to the south of Kānchi; and the locality where the Mission Hospital and the adjacent buildings are now, is pointed out as the place where the Tiraiyan's palace and other buildings were found in ruins.

This locality may be considered distinct from the fortress of Kānchi, the part now-a-days called Big Conjeevaram. It may be that this suburb of Kānchi was called Tiraiyanūr. We shall see therefore that he is identifiable through and through with Kānchi, and we do not come upon any reference to Vēngaḍam, or Pavattiri, or even Vērkkāḍu which we find referred to as in the territory of Pulli first and the Toṇḍamān chieftains afterwards, as we have already stated before. There is however the fact that the whole of the territory under reference in these poems is included in the Toṇḍamaṇḍalam, or as it is sometimes called Toṇḍaināḍu.

CHAPTER II.

FOUNDER OF TIRUPATI—A TONDAMAN.

THE TONDAMAN AND THE EARLY ALVARS. From what has been stated above, it is clear that the Toṇḍamān Iḷam Tiraiyan was undoubtedly ruling over the Toṇḍamaṇḍalam so-called which included the territory dependent upon Vēngaḍam, and therefore we may take it that he came after the cheiftain Pulli referred to in the Śangam literature, particularly in the poems of Māmūlar. This should be quite in keeping with the trend of evidence in the Śangam literature itself which would bring Iḷam Tiraiyan into some kind of a chronological connection with the famous Pāṇḍyan, victor at Talaiyālangānam, and the contemporary of Nakkīrar. The names of both this Pāṇḍyan and the poet Nakkīrar are intimately associated in tradition with the third Śangam at Madura. Iḷam Tiraiyan therefore comes in at a time when we should expect him from his relationship, again chronologically, with Karikāla, and this is confirmed by Nakkīrar's poem Aham 340 where he associates Tiraiyan with Pavattiri, the capital of that part of Toṇḍamaṇḍalam dependent upon Vēngaḍam. It thus becomes clear that Iḷam Tiraiyan of

Kānchi was probably the Tiraiyan who is referred to in the other poems of the Śangam collections by various authors, and he came in the generation, not very remote from that of the Pāṇḍyan victor at Talaiyālangānam. The importance of this position consists in this, that the Vishṇu shrine at Veḥkā finds prominent mention in the poem actually dedicated to him. This is among the oldest shrines of Kānchi, if not actually the oldest. It is mentioned frequently along with Vēngaḍam or Tirupati in the poems of the earlier Āḻvārs, and is regarded as a shrine of the greatest importance. What is more, the names of two Āḻvārs get associated with the place, namely, Poygai Āḻvār and Tirumaḻiśai Āḻvār. In the Vaishṇava tradition Poygai Āḻvār is said to have come and worshipped at Kānchi, which is made just possible by the fact that this Āḻvār is taken to refer to Tiraiyan in one of the fugitive stanzas already referred to. That particular stanza is quoted as the work of Poygaiyār, not Poygai Āḻvār. But a contemporary commentary on a work of the eleventh or twelfth century, Yāpparungalakārikai, quotes a few stanzas from Poygai Āḻvār including the one already referred to. Two of these stanzas are identifiable in the first Tiruvandādi ascribed to Poygai Āḻvār in the Prabandha collection of 4,000. It therefore seems to leave no doubt that the Poygaiyār referred to is the same as the Poygai Āḻvār. Poygai Āḻvār's poems so far known to us are all of them in the *Veṇbā* metre, and he is quoted along with a number of others who excelled in composing poems in this metre. Poygai Āḻvār is said to have come to Veḥkā at Kānchi in the course of his pilgrimage along with his two companions Bhūtattu Āḻvār and Pēy Āḻvār, in the course of which they are said to have met Āḻvār Tirumaḻiśai. This last Āḻvār is closely associated with Veḥkā, where he is said to have resided habitually. In the course of his long residence there, he came into contact with a more or less secular disciple by name Kaṇikaṇṇan through whom he came into contact with the ruler of Kānchi, a Tiraiyan himself, probably Iḷam Tiraiyan. The story is merely this. That Kaṇikaṇṇan was serving the Āḻvār with devotion, and, in connection with his service, he brought in a woman to assist him. She earned, by faithful service, the favour of the Āḻvār so much that she was granted by the Grace of God perpetual youth and unfading beauty, with which she was able soon to attract the attention of the ruler of the locality to become ultimately his sweetheart. In the course of his long dalliance he was able to learn from her how she came by the unfading youth and beauty which proved to be such an attraction to him, and, having heard that it was due to the favour of Kaṇikaṇṇan, who served alike the Āḻvār and the God at Veḥkā, he sent for Kaṇikaṇṇan to see him. Finding out from him that he had not so much part in the matter as the Āḻvār, the king commanded the presence of the Āḻvār through Kaṇikaṇṇan. Kaṇikaṇṇan protested that the Āḻvār was not likely to go to see him even at the summons of the king. Wild with rage at what he thought was impertinent disobedience, he asked Kaṇikaṇṇan to take himself away from Kānchi. Kaṇikaṇṇan in due course went and reported the matter to his master the Āḻvār, and, through him, wanted to obtain the leave of the God at Veḥkā to go away from Kānchi. Sooner than let him go, the Āḻvār told him that he would himself follow, and that, if he followed, the God himself was not likely to stay in the place. Saying so, he addressed God in a verse which has come down to us and begged him to follow him as he had decided to leave the place and go along with Kaṇikaṇṇan who had been exiled by royal command. The God complied and hence the name for the God *Yadōktakāri*, the God who did as he was directed (by his devotee). The miracle in the story apart, the story itself is evidence of some kind of the contemporaneity which may be accepted as evidence of the contemporary character of Tirumaḻiśi Āḻvār with Iḷam Tiraiyan on the one side, and of his contemporaneity with Poygai Āḻvār and his reference to Tiraiyan on the other. Iḷam Tiraiyan is therefore thus brought into connection with the first Āḻvārs, namely, the three who are known as such and the fourth, Tirumaḻiśai. That marks the starting point of the history of Tirupati. We shall have to examine the other side of the tradition namely, what the Purāṇas have to say about the Toṇḍamān chieftains who were responsible for the unearthing of the God at Tirupati, the building of a temple for him and the organisation of worship and festivals in connection with it.

THE PURANIC ORIGIN OF TIRUPATI. The Purāṇa tradition concerning the origin of the temple at Tirupati is varied in character and voluminous. As many as eleven different Purāṇas refer to this subject, and give the account in circumstantial detail which would strike the ordinary reader as quite legendary in character. Having regard to the character of the subject, and the purpose of edification for which these are severally written, the legendary colour certainly would dominate. It would be surprising if it were otherwise. But, through all this legend, one can still find certain facts standing clear, which may be regarded as not belonging to the realm of pure legend, and may perhaps be regarded historical, though perhaps in a legendary garb owing to association. The basal fact is that God Vishṇu had, by his choice, come to live in Tirupati for which an occasion and a stimulating cause alike seem called for. These makers of legend provide both by taking the story of the great Rishi Bhrigu's investigation to find the Supreme in actual fact. Once upon a time there was a discussion among the Rishis, the most devoted to God and nearest in service to him, as to which of the three manifestations of the Supreme, Brahma, Vishṇu, Śiva, was really the Supreme. It must be remembered that the Supreme is One, but manifests himself in three forms, with one of the three qualities, *Sattva*, *Rajas* and *Tamas*, dominating in each case, and discharging functions suitable in consequence, which must and necessarily be discharged by the Supreme by his very nature, the three essential functions of creation, protection and destruction. Each one of these functions is allotted to one of the three: Brahma, having charge of all creation, as a result of his dominating quality *Rajas*, energy or activity. Vishṇu is given the function of looking after all creation with the dominating quality of *Sattva*, serene strength. Similarly Rudra or Śiva is allotted the function of destruction, his dominating quality being *Tamas*, generally regarded as involving unthinking irascibility. But at the back of all this division, there certainly is the notion which makes all the three but manifestations of the One, and, as such, each one of the three being regarded as the Supreme itself. In this notion of unity, there is the possibility of two classes, those who make Rudra the Supreme, and those who make Vishṇu the Supreme, Brahma often not coming in for that claim to the same extent. It is this unity in variety that formed the topic of discussion of these wise ones; but they found good reasons for regarding each one of these as the Supreme, and undecided, they induced Bhrigu, the most favoured among the Rishis and the wisest among them, to make a pilgrimage to the various abodes of the trinity and find out by himself and directly by experiment. Naturally he went first to the palace of Brahma in *Satyalōka*—heaven. He found Brahma seated in full durbar, and treated the guest who entered the durbar after due salutation, somewhat familiarly, and, without the due forms of welcome to which the great sage was entitled, in the belief that Bhrigu was after all Brahma's own son. Bhrigu noted the dominence of self in the mind of Brahma in thus regarding himself as the progenitor of Bhrigu, notwithstanding the height to which that progeny had risen by penance. Having noted that, he passed on next to Kailāsa, the abode of Śiva, and found the Lord God disporting himself with Umā, his consort. Resenting the freedom with which Bhrigu entered so familiarly, even into the secret conclave of his own sportive dalliance, and, taking to heart particularly that the Goddess felt very delicate about the matter, he chased Bhrigu out of the palace in anger. Bhrigu noted this incident, and passed on the purpose of his mission to the palace of Vaikunṭha, where the other member of the trinity, Vishṇu-Nārāyaṇa was in his Yoga sleep, Lakshmi in his chest, the other attendants, ladies and other, each in the appointed place. Affecting disappointment that the God, whose function was protection, should have thus gone to sleep, consulting his own comfort to the neglect of his duties, the Rishi went up to the sleeping God and kicked him on the chest to wake him up. Vishṇu woke up from his wakeful sleep, and apologised to the Rishi for having shown himself so careless and wished to know whether his foot suffered by coming in contact with His own hardened chest. So naturally, Bhrigu reported what took place in the three places to the assembled wise people, and they all voted in favour of Vishṇu as the really Supreme One, the other two being more or less slaves of their dominating qualities or passions. But for the purpose of the Tirupati story, this gave the occasion for Lakshmi to pick a quarrel with her husband. Bhrigu's kick on the chest of Vishṇu fell on her. She therefore was naturally wild that he should have been allowed the freedom to do such a thing, which did her the double insult, of the personal insulting treatment to her, and of the disregard of proprieties which the Rishi should have showed to her Lord. Vishṇu pleaded that the sage was justifiably beside himself with anger at Vishṇu's apparent neglect of duties, and that it would not do to deal with such people, as otherwise than he did. In a fit of rage Lakshmi declined any more to remain on his chest, which had ceased to give her the protection that it should have, and that she thought she was entitled to have. Lakshmi having gone away from heaven, Vishṇu could not go on for long thus bereft of his consort, and wanted to go away somewhere else to spend his time pleasantly and get on alone. After making due enquiries, he discovered that the hill Śēshāchalam provided a spot which would be quite an ideal place for his residence, pleasant to live in with surroundings which supplied everything that he would want for diverting himself in his serious and light-hearted moods, and so he arranged to come and live there. Knowing this the Rishis went there to perform penance The Gods and Goddesses each one contributed what he or she could to make the place pleasant, and thus fitted out, God Vishṇu came into residence there abandoning Vaikunṭha itself. He had been there aeons of time, and when we come to the particular *Manvantara* (Cycle of Manu) with which we are concerned, he showed himself there in the form of the primeval boar carrying the Goddess of the Earth, redeemed from the deep. This is indicated as the Varāha shrine on the west of bank of the tank on the hill at Tirupati called Vishṇu Tīrtha now, and after a considerable length of time, and, for the purpose of showing himself to a devotee who had long been performing penance to him, he assumed the form of Śrīnivāsa, God bearing Lakshmi on his chest, for his benefit, and thereafter lay buried in the earth. Ultimately some cowherds discovered the cows that they brought to graze over the hills, going up an ant-hill and milking of their own motion, and returning home dry. The king of the locality whose cows they happened to be, got informed of this phenomenon, and went down to investigate. Digging up the ant-hill, he discovered the God in a small shrine, well within the bowels of the earth. He got the spot dug up, and, unearthing the simple shrine, built a brick temple round it, and provided it with all that would make a temple of it. That is the famous Śrīnivāsa shrine at Tirupati, and with this temple we emerge from legend perhaps into history.

THE TONDAMAN RAJA OF THE PURANAS. The first question that would arise is, who is this Toṇḍamān who laid the foundations of Vishṇu worship in Tirupati, in proper form, with the temple and all its appurtenances. We shall have to go a little further into the Purāṇic story itself to gain the clue to an identification, if an identification for him is at all possible. A Toṇḍamān who was a great devotee of Vishṇu-Vishṇu at Tirupati and one in whom the God was deeply interested, interested to the extent of lending him his own characteristic weapons of the disc and the conch to bring him success in war, was given by him solemnly the highest teaching that a Vaishṇava could desire, directly. We come upon references to a Toṇḍamān who had earned the favour of the Supreme deity so far, as to have had these acts of grace in his favour directly from God himself, in the Prabandha literature. These therefore must have been based upon well accredited tradition, if they do not have a really historical basis. The Purāṇa stories however, continue that, after the foundation of the temple in the manner described above, and providing for worship therein, the God, having been deprived of the company of Lakshmi in the manner previously described, and, having elected to come down and live in Tirupati in consequence, was accustomed to diverting himself by hunting and such other engagements, habitual to him. In the course of one of these hunting expeditions, he happened to come upon a beautiful damsel in one of the deep glades of the forests round Tirupati. He discovered on enquiry, that the beautiful damsel was no other than the princess, the only daughter, and that, one not born to him, but bestowed on him by divine favour having been discovered by him in the forests. The ruler is known to Purāṇic tradition as Ākāśa Rāja, otherwise described by the synonyms of the word Ākāśa, whose queen bore a name synonymous with the earth, as if to give away the secret that the young lady concerned was the daughter, even as the foster-daughter, of the earth and sky, as if to take her away altogether from the human category. We may infer that this Rāja belonged to the family of the Toṇḍamān chiefs, as he is said to have had a younger brother who went by the name

Toṇḍamān who assisted the elder brother in sundry acts of administration and seems to have been more or less directly entrusted with the government of the region round about Tirupati itself. The Purāṇas certainly display all their resources in describing the marriage that was brought about between this foster-daughter of the "sky-king" and the God himself, accounting for this strange alliance by the story that when Sīta threw herself into the fire to prove her innocence, at the end of the Rāmāyaṇa, she prayed to be restored to her husband the great God Vishṇu himself, and the restoration was brought about in the human fashion in the marriage of Padmāvatī to God Venkaṭēśa at Tirupati. This is what is generally described as the marriage of Venkaṭēśa or the marriage of Śrīnivāsa, a story much affected by the professional story-tellers who perform *Harikathas* for purposes of edification. We may pass over these details as of no particular importance to the unravelling of the history of the temple. After the marriage was over and Padmāvatī returned to her original place, Ākāśa Rāja ruled for a short while and passed away, along with his queen, leaving only a young son who was born some time after the discovery of the baby Padmāvatī herself. Since Ākāśa Rāja associated with himself in his administration his younger brother, Toṇḍamān, the uncle and the nephew who was a young prince, went to war to decide who was to succeed Ākāśa Rāja as ruler. Both of them being, each in his own way, a superman, the war proved undecisive; but, in the course of it, the uncle Toṇḍamān felt his physical resources ebbing away and prayed to God for help. It was on that occasion that Venkaṭēśa is said to have parted, with his disc and conch for the use of this ruler. The war terminated however, without being clearly and decisively in favour of either. So ultimately they came to a compromise, and arranged to rule the vast territories of Ākāśa Rāja in two parts, the parts nearer Tirupati being given to the uncle, and the rest of it farther away to the nephew. The prince built for himself a capital lower down the river and ruled his kingdom in great prosperity, while the Toṇḍamān ruled from the original capital Nārāyaṇavaram, and did far more service to the temple, and in fact laid the foundations of the organisation and worship that obtain in Tirupati even down to modern times. It is in connection with this Toṇḍamān in the course of his service to the temple that we find mention of a secret passage through the hill leading from his capital up to the temple itself, to which the king could go from his capital unseen of others and quite unmolested. It was he that organised from time to time the various annual festivals, the first of which is the *Brahmōtśava* in the months of September—October of the year. The principal festival known is the *Brahmōtśava*, and probably this festival is what is referred to by Tirumaḻiśai Āḻvār as the *Ōṇa-Viḻavu* (the Śravaṇa-festival).

WHETHER TONDAMAN RAJA WAS A HISTORICAL CHARACTER. This Toṇḍamān ruler seems to be more or less a historical person, although, as we find in the tale recorded in the Purāṇas, there is much that is said of him which may be legendary, as certainly all that is said of his more illustrious brother, the Ākāśa Rāja, on the face of it appears to be legendary, even including his own name and that of the queen. It is just possible, notwithstanding the legendary details connected with him, to regard this Toṇḍamān as a historical character from the fact of his building the temple, and his organisation of worship there. Notwithstanding this probability, one might well ask the question whether we have any evidence on which to base a definite statement like that. The legends and the Purāṇas themselves appear to give a clue to this. One of the versions tries to define the time when all this organisation took place at

Tirupati, and states specifically that it took place in the *Kaliyuga* when the *Yuga* had advanced sufficiently to have given occasion to the institution of the era which now-a-days goes by the name *Vikramāditya*, and say definitely that the other era known to the Hindus, that of the *Śaka* had not yet come into existence. This would mean a period of time between 57 or 58 B. C. and 78 A. D. the period of time to which we have arrived by our previous line of enquiry, entirely independent of this Purāṇic tradition. We found that the region dependent upon Vēngaḍam or Tirupati changing hands from the Kaḷvar chieftain Pulli, and passing into the possession of the Toṇḍamān chieftains before the time of the great Pāṇḍyan victor at Talaiyālangānam, from references in the Śangam literature. That very literature gives us a Toṇḍamān, ruling from his northern capital at Pavattiri, Reḍḍipāḷem in the Gudur Taluk, and held rule over the northern Toṇḍamaṇḍalam. We have referred rather more elaborately to another Toṇḍamān that literature knows of, namely, the Toṇḍamān Iḷam Tiraiyan. So we seem to have now three Toṇḍamāns before us, the Toṇḍamān or Toṇḍamān Chakravarti referred to in the Purāṇas, the Tiraiyan of Pavattiri or northern Toṇḍamaṇḍalam and Toṇḍamān Iḷam Tiraiyan of Kānchi. Whether all these three were the same, or how they are to be connected one with the other is a problem which has to be considered now.

IS TONDAMAN RAJA TONDAMAN ILAM TIRAIYAN?

We have already seen that some of the literary references seem to leave the question open whether the Tiraiyan of Pavattiri and Iḷam Tiraiyan are one and the same. It seems on the whole the best course to take it that the two Tiraiyans are different from each other; at least those that were contemporaries of Iḷam Tiraiyan and those who wrote of him either as contemporaries or later seem to be under the impression that he was different as they call him distinctly *Iḷam* Tiraiyan which would presume an *Elder* Tiraiyan. If we should therefore take the two to be different, we shall have two rulers coming one after the other—perhaps with an interval of time—it may be a generation or perhaps even a little more. The title Tiraiyan would indicate the family to which they belonged. The name Toṇḍamān would really mean "the chief man among the people Toṇḍaiyar", at any rate, the person who was ruler of the people called Toṇḍaiyar, the inhabitants of Toṇḍamaṇḍalam, in fact, the people who gave the name Toṇḍamaṇḍalam to the locality. Even some of the Purāṇas seem to refer to these Toṇḍamān rulers as of the Chōḷa family. The Toṇḍamān who built the temple at Tirupati and organised worship there is the son of a Chōḷa ruler through a Toṇḍamān princess whom he used to meet in a love adventure, through a secret passage leading through considerable distance. The association therefore between the Toṇḍamāns and the Chōḷas is thus made clear even in the Purāṇas. This connection is specifically stated in the poem Perumbān-āṟṟuppaḍai, mainly to celebrate the liberality of the patron Toṇḍamān Iḷam Tiraiyan. Whether this would really warrant our identifying the Toṇḍamān Iḷam Tiraiyan, with the Toṇḍamān associated with the Tirupati temple, is a question which requires careful consideration.

TONDAMAN RAJA OF TIRUPATI DISTINCT FROM TONDAMAN ILAM TIRAIYAN. We have already noticed that the region round Tirupati passed from the hands of the Kaḷvar chieftain Pulli to chieftains known as Toṇḍamān, and that at least one Toṇḍamān is referred to as having ruled from Pavattiri over northern Toṇḍamaṇḍalam, the country dependent upon Tirupati. We do know of another Toṇḍamān, the famous Toṇḍamān Iḷam Tiraiyan of whom we have some details of information in the same Tamil classical collections, particularly one poem exclusively devoted to him by a poet Kaḍiyalūr Rudran Kaṇṇan, who has also a similar poem on the great ruler Karikāla. A Toṇḍamān is actually referred to in the Purāṇas as being specially attached to the God at Tirupati, and rendering great service to the temple there by constructing it for the first time and organising the worship. Of course, we shall have to take it, on the basis of these Purāṇic accounts themselves, that this was in all probability the Toṇḍamān to whom the God at Tirupati showed particular favour, by lending him his warlike weapons, and by giving him instruction in the secret of the eight letters (*Ashṭākshara*). Apart from the personalities named, all the three sources of information collated go to show that there was a dynasty of rulers in northern Toṇḍamaṇḍalam dominated by Vēngaḍam who went by the general name Toṇḍamāns. But there is one aspect of history in regard to these which deserves particular consideration. Speaking of the Toṇḍamān who rendered devoted service to the temple at Tirupati, the Purāṇas refer to his having been the son of a Chōḷa ruler, as the result of his love to a princess of the country, whom he was in the habit of meeting by going through a secret passage which may, in modern language, be described as perhaps a tunnel or a natural cave through the hills. Of course, the Purāṇas describe it as a *bhilam*, a hollow underground going into the depths of the earth. The Toṇḍamān devotee of the God at Tirupati was thus of the Chōḷa lineage through, of course, a princess of the locality, who might have been a princess of the family of the Toṇḍamān rulers. The Toṇḍamān Iḷam Tiraiyan is described in terms in the Perumbāṇ-āṟṟuppaḍai as having been born of a Chōḷa as well, but by a Nāga princess, whom the Chōḷa king met in the city of the Nāgas, Nāgapaṭṭinam, and with whom he carried on secret love by going to her through an underground passage which would be the equivalent of *bhilam* of the Purāṇas. But this story of a Nāga connection for a Chōḷa ruler and an offspring like this is referred to, in a Buddhist setting, in the Maṇimēkhalai, and all details concerned being taken together would seem to indicate the Toṇḍamān Iḷam Tiraiyan, the offspring of a Chōḷa ruler, successor either immediate, or one degree remote, of the great Chōḷa Karikāla. But the story here differs in this particular. She was a Nāga princess undoubtedly, but met the Chōḷa ruler in the outskirts of his capital at Kaverippūmpaṭṭinam at the mouth of the river Kaveri, not Nāgapaṭṭinam, the city of the Nāgas, as Nacchinārkkiniyār explains the passage in the Perumbāṇ-āṟṟuppaḍai which is actually worded much more generally and without specific details which would lead to an identification. The question naturally would arise whether we should identify the Toṇḍamān attached to the God in the temple at Tirupati, with Toṇḍamān Iḷam Tiraiyan. While there is nothing in the story specifically to lead us to an identification, the circumstantial details given seem to make it possible that the two personages were perhaps the same; but that is hardly enough for a positive identification. The Perumbāṇ-āṟṟuppaḍai which gives specific details regarding the Toṇḍamān Iḷam Tiraiyan and mentions the Vishṇu temple at Veḥkā at Kānchi, makes no mention whatever of Tirupati, nor of Iḷam Tiraiyan's association with Tirupati. This omission on the part of a poet who had laid himself out elaborately to sing the praise of Iḷam Tiraiyan is significant, and stands against an identification between the two. We have therefore to take it that the family of the Toṇḍamāns that ruled over northern Toṇḍamaṇḍalam had established itself and achieved a certain amount of distinction before Iḷam Tiraiyan came into existence and attained to fame, while it may not debar the connection between the family of Iḷam Tiraiyan on the mother's side with the Toṇḍamān chieftains of the region round Tirupati. We may therefore have to take the Toṇḍamān devotee of Śrīnivāsa referred to in the Purāṇas as one who came before Toṇḍamān Iḷam Tiraiyan, though the possibility of Iḷam Tiraiyan's mother being connected with the Toṇḍamān ruler is still made possible. Therefore the Toṇḍamān of Tirupati probably came in the generation previous to Toṇḍamān Iḷam Tiraiyan with whose family the Chōḻa king could have been brought into contact by the conquest of Toṇḍamaṇḍalam by the Chōḻa ruler Karikāla. Iḷam Tiraiyan therefore must have been a ruler of Kānchi who came somewhat later than the Toṇḍamān of Tirupati. We shall now proceed to consider how far other evidence supports this position.

CHAPTER III.

TIRUPATI AND THE EARLY ALVARS.

TIRUPATI IN THE PRABANDHA FOUR THOUSAND: MUDAL ALVARS, THE FOUR THOUSAND, ITS AUTHORS AND THEIR AGE. The most prominent piece of literature which throws a considerable amount of light upon the early history of Tirupati is "the Prabandha Four Thousand", which is a collection of 4,000 stanzas of Tamil poetry, celebrating the 108 places of worship sacred to Vishṇu by a certain number of devotees, generally counted twelve, who, because of their single-minded devotion and the consequent nearness to God, are called Āḻvārs. The general period to which the whole body of this literature is referable happens to be the five centuries 300 to 800 A. D. These did not all of them live at one and the same time, and, if the age of each one of them is not as yet precisely fixed, a broad classification of these into early, middle and later, can well be adopted as a recognised method of classification, and the probable period of time in which each one of these groups flourished seems also ascertainable. Without going into the whole of that question here, we may take it that three among them are known as the first Āḻvārs, described as the singers in classical Tamil (Śeṅ Tamil) by Tirumangai Āḻvār, namely, Poygai, Bhūtam and Pēy, and one other that follows, namely Tirumaḻiśai. These four constitute the early Āḻvārs. Of these comparatively little is known in the matter of life details, and in consequence we are left without much material by way of data for fixing their actual period of life. From the internal evidence of their works, however, it seems possible to come to some fairly definite conclusions in regard to their period of activity, and this, in itself, would throw a flood of light upon the history of a shrine like Tirupati, not to mention other general questions, such as the rise of the cult of Bhakti, and of the school of Vaishṇava worship generally known as the Pāncharātra, or Āgamāic worship more generally. This latter class of literature lays down the norms of the life of a devotee, and prescribes the various forms in which worship should be conducted by differing classes of people, with a view to achieving the ends of existence here, and attaining to a permanent one hereafter. It is this form of religion which postulates the existence of a personal god with attributes, capable of being pleased by service and of accepting devotion with a view to secure His grace ultimately and attain to salvation thereby.

These Āḻvārs are devotees of Vishṇu in that sense, and their works contain in them how exactly they devoted themselves to the service of God and attained ultimately to His grace, thereby providing, at one and the same time, not only an account of their edifying achievement, but also lays down a course of conduct which a devotee might follow with advantage to achieve the same supreme purpose.

THE FIRST THREE OF THESE AND THEIR LIFE AND WORTH. Coming down to their earthly history, we know almost nothing historically of the first three except that they were men who were born in different places and on different dates not much removed from each other either in point of place or in point of time. They led a single wandering life going from place to place, and visiting Vaishṇava holy places. The detail bringing the three together happens to be that they all met on a rainy night in the narrow vestibule of a small house in Tirukkōvilūr with a view to protection from the inclemencies of the weather. The first one who came there went in, and finding the platform that is generally found in village houses between the front door and the interior door leading into the house to one side of the passage, vacant, lay down there for the night. The second one came there seeking refuge similarly from the inclemencies of the weather, and he knocked at the front door. The one that was already there answered that all the room that there was, was enough for one to lie down. Finding that the second one was a Vaishṇava in distress, he added that, if there was room for one to lie down, certainly it would be room enough for two to sit on, and opened the door; and the two determined to sit out the night on the narrow *payal.* A short time after the third one came and knocked at the door similarly, and the two replied, as the one in the former case, that the place had just room for two men to sit on, and that, if two men could sit, it would be possible for three men to stand, and so the third one got admitted; and all the three resolved to stand out the whole night, and save themselves from the violence of the weather. It is said that God Vishṇu, installed in the temple in the locality, was pleased with their devoted service to him, and, wishing to show himself to them, came with his consort Lakshmi, without whom he does not usually proceed, particularly where acts of grace are intended, and, seeking admission as the others did before, almost squeezed the three out of their place by extending his body gradually and pressing them out. In the course of this process it dawned upon them that they were being tested by no less than God himself, and they broke out into song in praise of God, each one of them his own way. Each one of these is the author of one centum or a hundred of the *Prabandha* referred to above, and these, along with certain other pieces of literature of this school, constitute one main division named *Iyarpā* in the *Prabandha*.

THE GENERAL CHARACTER OF THEIR WORKS. Of these the first, and by far the most interesting, is Poygai Āḻvār. Poygai is the author of the first centum of the last thousand of the Four Thousand in the *Prabandha*. The first part of the word Poygai means a tank, a bathing tank, attached to the temple at Veḷkā in Conjeevaram. Āḻvār is the sacerdotal honorific given to this class of Vaishṇava devotees, holy ones in near association with God himself. He seems to be the person referred to by commentators, particularly by one commentator on the Alankāra *grantha* named Yāpparungalam belonging to the 11th or 12th century A. D., to which a commentary was written by a disciple of the author himself. This commentator quotes two stanzas from this centum, namely 40 and 51, as extracted from the author Poygaiyār. The latter part of the word in Tamil is a respectful honorific meaning a person belonging to or born in Poygai. So the difference of this designation from that of the previous one consists merely in this that the person so referred to is not given the Vaishṇava sacerdotal name, but still the quoting author feels that he ought to be referred to, or quoted with, due respect as the esteemed one coming of Poygai, the place. He is referred to by others as one who composed principally in the *Veṇbā* metre, and is counted as a model in that kind of composition along with other ancient Tamil classics famous for that. So this Āḻvār was not only a Vaishṇava devotee, but one who occupied a high place among the celebrities in Tamil literature. The question whether he is the same as the one who composed the Kaḷavaḻi Forty, celebrating the victory of the Chōḻa king Śeṁkaṇ over a contemporary Chēra ruler, Kaṇaikkāl Irumpoṛai, is more open to doubt. The first centum ascribed to him was sung by him when the idea dawned upon him that it was God Vishṇu himself that was practically elbowing them out of the narrow *payal* where he and his two companions had found shelter from the inclement weather. This idea is said traditionally to have risen in the three simultaneously, and each broke out, in his own characteristic way, into praising Vishṇu in a hundred verses. The first Poygai made the whole universe, the lamp vessel, the oceans, the ghee for feeding the lamp, the sun himself, the burning wick, and, lighting such a lamp, he placed, at the lotus feet of the One with the blazing disc, his garland of verse in order that the great ocean of evil besetting him may leave him. The second in his own way made his own loving devotion (*anbu*) the lamp vessel, his ardour (*dravam*) for service the ghee for feeding the lamp, and his mind melting with goodness, the lamp wick. He lighted the lamp of true knowledge (*gñāna*) and dedicated it to God Nārāyaṇa, as one capable of incorporating his divine knowledge in Tamil verse. The third on the contrary broke out "Lo, I see the Goddess Śrī. I see the golden body, I see the colour of the rising sun. I see the glorious disc. I see the dextral conch. I see all this in Him of the colour of the ocean, dear to me." The upshot of all the three is that the unlooked for and the ununderstood incommoding of these people by a pressure for which they could not divine a cause, put them in mind of the Supreme, and this community of thought runs through and through the three centums, though of three separate authors.

REFERENCES TO TIRUPATI IN THE FIRST CENTUM. Our concern in regard to these three centa of verse is not so much their import or philosophy, but merely their bearing upon the history of the shrine at Tirupati. The first of these Poygai has as many as 12 to 15 direct references to Tirupati in the centum ascribed to him. He refers to the place incidentally as one of the places in which Vishṇu in his grace has shown himself to mortal eyes for purposes of devotion and worship, so that people in this sin-promoting world might find it possible to realise the Supreme, and, by that means, shake off the shackles of the results of their deeds and attain to ultimate salvation. These references are of the utmost importance as they give us an insight into some of the characteristic features of the shrine, and have also been in a way responsible for certain false theories as to the actual character of the temple itself. The first point, a point perhaps of the greatest importance, is certain peculiar features in the image of the God at Tirupati which made it possible for raising a doubt whether the image enshrined in the temple is actually an image of Vishṇu or Śiva or some other manifestation. Without going into the claims set up and adjudicating as between rival claims, we shall have to consider what exactly these authors have said about the temple. Stanzas 5 and 74 *

---

* அரன் நாரணன் நாமம் ஆன்விடை புள்ளூர்தி
உரை நூல் மறை யுறையும் கோயில்—வரை நீர்
கருமம் அழிப்பு அளிப்புக் கையது வேல் நேமி
உருவம் எரிகார் மேனியொன்று. (5)

ஏற்றான் புள்ளூர்ந்தான் எயிலெரித்தான் மார்விடந்தான்
நீற்றான் நிழல் மணி வண்ணத்தான்—கூற்றொருபால்
மங்கையான் பூமகளான் வார்சடையான் நீள்முடியான்
கங்கையான் நீள் கழலான் காப்பு— (74)

of the first centum run like this. "His name, *Aran* (Hara) and *Nāraṇan* (Nārāyaṇa), His vehicle, the bull and the bird; His word, the book (Tam. *Nūl* equiv. Sans: *Tantra*, the *Āgamas*), and Maṛai (Veda); the house of residence, the hill (Kailāsa) and the waters (the ocean); His function, destruction and protection; the weapon in hand, the trident-spear and the disc; His form, though one, is fire and dark cloud." This is almost repeated in a somewhat different form in stanza 74 where it is said "He rides the bull and the bird. He burnt the castle (the three castles in the air) and broke open the heart (tore up Hiraṇya's chest with his claws as man-lion (Narasimha); He is smeared over with ash (Vibhūti); He is of the saphire blue colour. Part of His body is a lady (Pārvati), and in one part is the lady born of the lotus, Śrī or Lakshmi. His coiffure, the long matted locks; His head covered by a tall crown; He wears the Gangā (Ganges) on His head (Śiva), and on His lengthening foot (Vishṇu Trivikrama)". Here it will be clear that God is described as though he were possessed of a twin form, each with its own characteristic set of features and weapons; and, superficially interpreted, it might be held to mean that the form of the image is, to say the least, Hari and Hara in one, Vishṇu-Śiva; and so it has been seriously held on this evidence, and the contention raised that the temple was actually a Śiva temple. These two stanzas of which a translation is given above have certainly no reference to Vēngaḍam or Tirupati in either of them. But it may not be so baseless to regard it as applying to Tirupati, because Tirupati is under reference in this author in a number of places, and, on the whole, some of the less usual and more recondite features of the image at Tirupati seem to lend colour to this interpretation. Before proceeding to draw the important conclusion whether it is a Śiva shrine or a Vishṇu shrine on the statement of this author, we are bound in simple fairness to interpret the author of the centum as a whole, first of all to ascertain whether the deity having the greatest appeal to him is really Śiva or Vishṇu, doubtful details notwithstanding. The Vaishṇava holy places are 108, and the Śiva holy places are supposed to be 1,008. In all the works of these it would be difficult to trace a reference to any one of the Śaiva holy places as such, while all the holy places referred to by their specific names happen to be Vaishṇava holy places. The first is Srīrangam in stanza 6, Vēngaḍam itself in a number of others, Viṇṇagar, Veḥkā, Tirukkōvilūr (in 77). Of these places mentioned by him, it is doubtful if Viṇṇagar has reference to a place on earth, as in this place God Vishṇu is said, in that stanza, to be seated which is taken to be only in heaven (Vaikunṭha). There are places called Viṇṇagar, one very prominently near Kumbhakoṇam, where the posture of the image representing God is not that. The other places are within comparatively easy reach of Kānchi, which is the birthplace of this Āḻvār. Veḥkā is in Kānchi itself. Tirukkōvilūr is not at any great distance from it, and so Vēngaḍam. Śrīrangam may be counted a little farther, but perhaps the great reputation of the shrine may have brought it within his reach. These three Āḻvārs are said to have been moving from place to place on pilgrimage bound, although we do not find them mentioning the more distant places as the other Āḻvārs do. But what is really more useful for our purpose is that Poygai was associated with the town of Kānchi directly, the more so than even Tirukkōvilūr, and the details that he gives of Tirupati would perhaps warrant an equally intimate acquaintance. The reference to Śrīrangam is however only a single reference, and that says actually nothing more about the place than that he saw and worshipped God enshrined there. The most therefore that we could say about it is that he visited Śrīrangam. In regard to Tirupati, however, stanza 26 refers to Tirupati, the saving grace of which is enjoyed by the Gods themselves. In stanza 37 there is a more explicit reference. It refers to Vēngaḍam again as "a place acceptable to the God who blew the beautiful white conch, which receives constant worship from people of great learning who offered daily worship with incense, lamp, holy water, and proceeded to offer the worship from all directions." There is a similar reference to Vēngaḍam in stanza 39 where the God "who lies on the deep blue sea, who lifted the earth, and who killed Kamsa by striking fear into him, is in a standing posture." Stanza 40 refers to Vēngaḍam as well, but gives only a secular feature of the place where elephants are referred to as if threatened by the falling stars in the belief that they were torches held by the *Kuṛavars* of the place. There is another reference in stanza 68. This reference again is rather more general, that "the God Vishṇu is in the heaven on earth" in Vēngaḍam, and in the four Vedas. Stanza 76 refers to Tiruvēngaḍam describing the God there as the one who measured the earth (Vishṇu-Tṛivikrama). Stanza 77 similarly refers to Vēngaḍam where the image of God stands along with the other three places, Viṇṇagar, Veḥkā, and Kovalūr in which respectively He sat, He lay in bed and He walked. In stanza 82 there is a reference to Vēngaḍam, but the description of the place given here is worth noting for more reasons than one. Vēngaḍam is here described as the hill of him who on a former day shot effectively the deer (Rama killing the deer Mārīcha). But the description of the hill is interesting. It says that on *Dvādaśis* (the 12th lunar day) ladies were accustomed to offer worship with garlands and incense, which latter sent up so much smoke which made the sky itself clouded and the stars indistinct. * It must be noticed here that ladies were accustomed to offering worship, naturally with incense and flowers. It happened to be particularly on the 12th day of the fortnight. This *Dvādaśi* festival is counted the holiest among the large number of annual festivals organized in connection with the shrine at Tirupati, and the 12th day is described in the Purāṇas as peculiarly holy in respect of Vishṇu and that in Tirupati. Stanza 86 does not refer to Tirupati but refers to Tirukkōvilūr, and to the incident of the meeting of the three Āḻvārs that took place at the vestibule of the house there. The last reference to Tirupati is in stanza 99 where Vishṇu is spoken of as Eternal, and being

---

* படையாரும் வாட்கண்ணார் பாரசிநாள் பைம்பூந்
தொடையலோ டேந்தியதூபம்—இடையிடையில்
மீன் மாயமாக்கும் வேங்கடமே மேலொருநாள்
மான்மாய வெய்தான்வரை. (82)

in the heart of everyone who is capable of thinking of Him, as He is habitually in residence on the waters, and in the hill of Vēngaḍam. In all these stanzas where there is a reference to Vēngaḍam, while some references are general, a number, however, make specific reference to Vishṇu as the presiding deity, either in general terms, or in one of his innumerable manifestations, thus leaving very little doubt that the Āḻvār regarded the shrine in Tirupati as a Vishṇu shrine. This could be reinforced by the statement in stanzas 58, 64 and 65 which give evidence that the Āḻvār is devoted only to Vishṇu and to nobody else, thereby raising the presumption that he worshipped Tirupati, only as a place holy to Vishṇu. But as if to put the matter beyond a doubt, he refers in two stanzas * to his conviction that the God in Tirupati is Vishṇu beyond a doubt. He states in stanza 98 that "the golden coloured holy One with the matted locks (Śiva), and the

---

* பொன் திகழுமேனிப் புரிசடையம் புண்ணியனும்
நின்றுலகம் தாய நெடுமாலும்—என்றும்
இருவரங்கத்தால் திரிவரேலும் ஒருவன்
ஒருவனங்கத்தென்று முளன். (98)

கைய வலம்புரியும் நேமியும் கார்வண்ணத்து
ஐய மலர்மகள் நின்னாகத்தாள்—செய்ய
மறையான் நின் உந்தியான் மாமதிள் மூன்றெய்த
இறையான் நின்னாகத்திறை. (28)

One who stood and stretched out to measure the universe (Vishṇu-Tṛivikrama), though these two may move about and have their being in two bodies, the one of them (the former of them) is in the body of the other one (the latter); this would explain, and perhaps is meant to explain, the conviction of the author that Vishṇu could be represented as bearing Śiva in his body. This is made the more clear in stanza 28 where Vishṇu is addressed directly; "Oh, Dark One! In your hands are the dextral conch, and the disc. In your chest rests the flower born (Lakshmi). In your navel is the young author of the Veda. In one part of the body—generally described as on the right side—is the Iṛai (king) who destroyed the three fortresses (Śiva)". So far therefore as Poygai Āḻvār is considered, he may be regarded as a strict worshipper, whose devotion was paid only to Vishṇu, who could regard the worship of other deities particularly Śiva and Brahma as not altogether unobjectionable, as in the last resort they form but a part, in orthodox Vaishṇava notion, of the body of Vishṇu himself. On this basis therefore if we find the image in Tirupati sometimes described as exhibiting features of Śiva which is really the material point here, it is only in this aspect of Śiva forming a part of Vishṇu's body, Vishṇu being the soul, all else in existence being His body. It is only another way of stating the principle of immanence of Vishṇu. It would not therefore do to fasten upon stray references, and one or two expressions, such as *Iḷam Kumaṛan tan Viṇṇagar* as implying that the presiding deity at Tirupati is *Iḷam Kumaṛan* (the youthful young man, and therefore Subrahmaṇya). It cannot be so interpreted as the youthfulness of the deity is under reference in dozens of other places where the frolicsome youth is unmistakably described as the youthful Krishṇa, Bālakrishṇa, and as such, the equation with Subrahmaṇya, Skanda-Subrahmaṇya cannot hold. We may very well point out here that the idea is not peculiar to this Āḻvār, and is rather one of those general ideas constituting the Vaishṇava conviction. The sentiment runs through the works of all the Āḻvārs, and we might refer here prominently to stanza 481 of the Tiruvāymoḻi where Śiva of the bull-vehicle, Brahma of the four faces and Lakshmi alike claim parts of his body for their habitual residence. It therefore becomes clear that the conception of the three in one is neither strange nor peculiar, but is more or less an integral part of the concept of Vishṇu as the Supreme. It is possible to pick out a certain number of stanzas from this centum which would throw a distinct light upon the Vaishṇava character of the worship prescribed.

One more point in regard to Poygai Āḷvār may be worth mentioning here as bearing upon this particular question, namely, stanza 53, where the close association of the serpent Śēsha or Ananta with Vishṇu * is stated with a view, according to the Vaishṇava commentators, to declare to the world the intimate connection between Śēsha and Vishṇu as almost body and soul, which is the relation in which the Supreme is held in connection with all else. The statement here is that the great snake is to Vishṇu (Tirumāl) an umbrella when he walks, a throne when he sits, the wooden platform or sandal when he stands, the eternal bed when he sleeps on the sea. He also serves as the jewel lamp, or fine soft silk vestment, and the pillow beside him in bed. The notion that the Śēsha serpent constitutes a soft white silk which forms the upper garment of Vishṇu, would explain the symbolism of the snake that is said to be seen in parts of his body of the image of Vēnkaṭēśa at Tirupati. We may have to refer to this detail later.

* சென்றால் குடையாம் இருந்தால் சிங்காசனமாம்
நின்றால் மரவடியாம் நீள் கடலுள்—என்றும்
புணையாம் மணிவிளக்காம் பூம்பட்டாம் புல்கும்
அணையாம் திருமாற்கரவு. (53)

SRI VENKATESA-SESHAVAHANA (SERPENT VEHICLE) (*To face page 68*)

Passing on now to the second of this group of Aḻvārs, Āḻvār Bhūtan as he is called, this Āḻvār likewise refers to Vēngaḍam in eight places or stanzas directly. The first reference is in stanza 25 where Vishṇu is described as standing on the hill at Tirupati, and is referred to as the one who marched on Lanka and killed, in anger, Rāvaṇa. Stanza 33 merely expresses devotion to Vishṇu as he manifests himself in Vēngaḍam. In stanza 45 he makes a similar general reference, and in stanza 46 Vēngaḍam figures among a number of places such as Śrīrangam, Tirukkōṭṭiyūr, and Tirunīr-malai. In stanza 48 there is a reference to Iṛum-Śōlai, which is interpreted by the commentators as indicating Tirupati; but the reference seems none the less to Tirumāl Iṛum Śōlai, which is referred to as Iḷam-giri, and in stanza 54 as Iḷam-Kōvil. The reason for the use of the attribute is not quite clear unless it be in reference to the inhabitants of the locality who were of the hunter class, often referred to as Iḷaiyar, or the association of the place with young Krishṇa in which sense the name is used for Tirucchānūr apparently. In stanza 70 the Āḻvār refers to a number of Vishṇu shrines: Tanjai (Tānjore), Arangam, Taṇ-kāl, as in the minds of those devoted to Him; as also the cool hill and the ocean where they place Him. Māmallai

(Mahābalipuram), Kōval (Tirukkōvalūr) and Kuḍandai (Kumbhakoṇam) are similarly places cherished by them. In stanza 72 there is a general reference again to Vēngaḍam, where the very monkeys offer fully blossomed lotus flowers in worship. Stanza 75 contains a similar secular reference in which Tirupati is said to be the residence of the God of the blue colour where the male elephant is described as pulling out the tender shoot of the bamboo and giving it to its mate after carefully dipping it in honey. In addition to the usual Vaishṇava holy places, this Āḻvār makes reference to a place Pāḍaham in Kānchi in stanza 94; as also to Attiyūr (Vishṇukānchi of now-a-days,) in 95, and Kuḍamūkkil (Kumbhakoṇam) in 97. Stanza 28 * equates the ḍeity presiding in Vēngaḍam as the same as that in Śrīrangam, and both of them alike are described as the young one who tore up the animal by the mouth, *Krishṇa*, and the general reference in 46 to a number of Vishṇu shrines would give the same impression. Stanza 54 is a little more specific where it states that Tirumāl Iṛum Śōlai near Madura and Vēngaḍam are the two places where the God was pleased to stand

* மனத்துள்ளான் வேங்கடத்தான் மாகடலான் மற்றும்
நினைப்பரிய நீளாகத்துள்ளான்—எனைப்பலரும்
தேவாதி தேவனெனப்படுவான் முன்னொரு நாள்
மாவாய் பிளந்த மகன். (28)

and present himself to his devotees. Stanza 60 of this centum calls for attention where the Supreme is regarded as of two forms. One of these two however is subordinated to the other, which is the first, much as Poygai and Nammāḻvār make Śiva and Brahma as forming part of Vishṇu's body. This stanza is however interpreted in a more general way by commentators. So it comes out clearly that Bhūtat Āḻvār, no less than Poygai Āḻvār, was devoted to Tirupati as a Vishṇu shrine to which he was extremely devoted, notwithstanding the features which may seem Śaiva at first sight. There are stanzas in this centum which could be picked out detailing the ordinary norms of worship of all the Vaishṇavas. One feature in particular has to be noted in respect of this Āḻvār, which is also a common feature in the others, that the best form of worship is the orthodox Vaidic way; but it is recognised simultaneously that it is not actually possible for all. It certainly is the best for those that can do it; but, for those who cannot, other forms of worship are prescribed equally efficient in saving power; and, among these, the most efficient is the mere recital of the name of Mādhava as equally capable of saving. As a typical instance we might give the substance of stanzas 38 and 39. In the first he admonishes people against deluding themselves in the possession of the wealth that they may have, but exhorts them to devote themselves to that which is the mainstay for one's permanent good. The recital of His name, with a mind devoted to Mādhava, is our eternal saviour. It is stated in the next stanza that even the significance of the Veda is this alone, and therefore "Poor mortals, learn how to offer your devotion to God by reciting His name in the proper form. If you are learned in the Veda, well and good. If you are not, keep repeating His name with devotion; for the recital of His name is the abbreviation of the reciting of the Vedas themselves." * We can quote stanzas of this import from Poygai Aḻvār and the others as well.

---

* எமக்கென்று இருநிதியம் ஏமாந்திராதே
தமக்கென்றும் சார்வமறிந்து—நமக்கென்றும்
மாதவனே யென்னும் மனம் படைத்து மற்றவன்பேர்
ஓதுவதே நாவினாலோத்து. (38)

ஒத்தின் பொருள் முடிவும் இத்தனையே உத்தமன்பேர்
ஏத்தும் திறமறிமின் ஏழைகாள்—ஒத்ததனை
வல்லீரேல் நன்று அதனை மாட்டீரேல் மாதவன் பேர்
சொல்லுவதே ஒத்தின் சுருக்கு. (39)

சுருக்காக வாங்கிச் சுலாவி நின்று ஐயார்
நெருக்காமுன் நீர் நினைமின் கண்டீர்—திருப்பொலிந்த
ஆகத்தான் பாதமறிந்தும் அறியாத
மோகத்தாலில்லை பொருள். (40)

This idea of a single-minded devotion shown in the form of a simple prayer addressed to him by the mere repetition of his name, is enforced in several other stanzas. Stanza 64 expresses the hope that it might be given to the Āḻvār to realise Him who is described in the *Itihāsas* (Kathā) and the Vedas, the very names incorporating what is said of Him in these. He begins with 62 where he professes that he did not know His name before, nor has he had the chance since of acquiring it in proper form; but that he bowed down in worship with the recitation of His names as they came to him, though different in form. In 65 he speaks of his bowing in reverence at sight of His form, his offering lotus flowers at His feet with his own hands, and he came down to the conviction to devote himself to His service, so that when the opportunity came he could attain to the nearness where he can for ever remain in perpetual prayer. In 66 he declares his faith that all this life is nothing more than the repetition of the name of Nāraṇa (Sans. Nārāyaṇa), and by so doing, remove the causes that take one near to hell. In 67 he comes to a confession which is reinforced in stanza 81. He speaks of his having seen the form of God in a dream. Even in that dream he saw in His hand the golden disc. He was able to realise the strength of Him even then, which puts an end to the good and bad in him and prevents other such befalling him hereafter. In 81 he speaks of his having seen Him by day, and that none other than Nārāyaṇa. He dreamt of Him again the more. Then he realised Him in truth, and arrived at the settled conviction of the form of Him of the golden disc, His light-emitting feet, and His form, the very emanation of heavenly light. Then in 86 he asks what it was that great poets who offer worship, with fresh flowers along with their verses, gained; that which they were not able to realise by their true penance, "how am I going to realise; by what form of penance am I to realise it now? It is not by my penance now, that I am going to realise His great feet which measured the great earth itself. I realise, in all His greatness, Him, my father of Tirukkōṭṭiyūr, because I worshipped Him when I was still suffering in the womb from which I was brought into existence". Then he comes to his satisfaction in 90 when he declares roundly what it was that he could do. "Shall I not hold rule over this earth; will I not mount up to heaven by becoming the great one among the great in heaven itself; once I have approached and offered my sincere worship to Him, Lord Vishṇu". It would be easy in this connection to select about a dozen verses from this collection which would put in a nutshell the teachings of the Bhakti school of Vaishṇavism in all its orthodox aspects, withal simple, and designed, not for serving the purpose of worship by the elite, but to subserve similar ends for the quite ordinary folk.

PEY ALVAR. We come to the last of the triad, Pēy Āḻvār, of whom we know nothing in regard to the details of his life except that he was born in a well next adjoining the shrine of Kēśava Perumāḷ, which well is now pointed out as the one in Arundal Street, Mylapore. We know nothing of his birth or his parents, and the date that is given for him in the Guru Paramparas is of the same kind as the dates for the other two. While the other two who each of them lighted the lamp of divine knowledge in his own way with a view to the realisation of God, this Āḻvār on the contrary, breaks out "Lo, I see Śrī. I see His golden form. I see the glorious effulgence of the rising sun. I see the golden disc exuberant for war. I see the conch of the dextral curl. All these I see in my dear One of the blue colour of the sea." And immediately follows the confession that, having seen His feet, he destroyed all the seven of his births then and there, and then he proceeds to describe all that he knows of Vishṇu and his saving qualities. In stanza 11 he declares roundly "He is there in the four Vedas well cultivated, He of the colour of the flowing water fresh and fragrant. He is in the ocean of milk, on the bed of the great serpent, the wise one who is churned out of the sea of sciences (Tam. *Nūl*; Sans. Tantra) by the learned ones, and comprehensible only to those of the most acute intelligence; shutting out the passions by the bolt of wisdom, and cultivating the secret wisdom of the Vedas, the wise ones will realise easily the nature of Him who is of the colour of the sea." The first reference to Vēngaḍam occurs in stanza 14 where He is said to be "the One in Vēngaḍam whom the heavenly ones worship with their high crowned heads, and Who is said to preside in the Veda of the four divisions." In stanza 16 there is a reference to Triplicane (Tiruvallikkēṇi) and the God is described as one bearing the lotus born (Lakshmi) in his chest. In stanza 26 he declares that the God is either resident in his own heart, on the body of the red-eyed serpent, in the full and prosperous Kacchi (Kānchi); in Vēngaḍam, Veṇkā and Vēḷukkaippāḍi (a part of Kānchi) which he never quits. A similar sentiment is expressed in stanza 30 where the place that Vishṇu liked to reside in is the ocean, Kuḍandai (Kumbhakoṇam), Vēngaḍam, the properly intuned mind, the vast expanse of heaven, then Pāḍaham, full of people learned in the Veda, Ananta-Śēsha, the great Śēsha-serpent and the garland of sweet basil. Stanza 31 similarly speaks of "these are the temples of Him who tore up the heart of Hiraṇya by the assumed form of a lion, or a serpent with unseen ears, the four Vedas and the ocean of milk. But the statement is here thrown in that the great Śiva carrying the Gangā on his head of the bull vehicle, forms a part of his body. In 32 comes a similar recital of his abode as the ocean of milk, Vēngaḍam, Śēsha-serpent, the heaven, the ocean of sciences, the lotus figure prescribed by the Āgama Śāstras (Nuṇ-ṇūl), the mind of those devoted to Him. "That One is no other than the shepherd boy who broke the twin *Kurunda* tree." * Vēngaḍam is here described

---

* பாற்கடலும் வேங்கடமும் பாம்பும் பனிவிசும்பும்
நூற் கடலும் நுண்ணூல் தாமரைமேல்—பாற்பட்
டிருந்தார் மனமும் இடமாகக் கொண்டான்
குருந்தொசித்த கோபாலகன் — (32)

இறையாய் நிலனாகி எண்திசையும் தானாய்
மறையாய் மறைப் பொருளாய் வானாய்—பிறைவாய்ந்த
வெள்ளத் தருவி விளங்கொலி நீர் வேங்கடத்தான்
உள்ளத்தி னுள்ளே யுளன். (39)

உளன் கண்டாய் நன்னெஞ்சே உத்தமனென் றும்
உளன் கண்டா யுள்ளுவாருள்ளத்து—உளன் கண்டாய்
விண்ணெடுங்கக்கோடுயரும் வீங்கருவி வேங்கடத்தான்
மண்ணொடுங்கத் தானளந்தமண் — (40)

as the place sacred to Gōpālaka. In stanzas 39 and 40, Vēngaḍam is referred to as the holy place of Vishṇu, and the latter gives the detail that He measured the earth by bringing it all under His one foot. Stanza 45 gives the important detail that Vēngaḍam was full of elephants and was "the hill of Him who carried the earth at the point of his tusk." Stanzas 45 to 57 seem to be a continuation of the sentiment actually expressed in the latter part of the stanza 45, and refer to the various achievements of Vishṇu in his manifestations as Rāma, Krishṇa, etc., following up, as it were, the reference to Varāha Avatāra in the last line of stanza 45. He takes up the reference to Vēngaḍam in 58 again, and comes up in the last line to the same references that the God in Vēngaḍam is, "He who recovered the earth by the use of his acute intelligence", referring to his having outwitted Mahābali and got him to grant the three feet of earth. In stanza 59, the Āḻvār gives expression to his satisfaction that he had attained to the correct way of gaining salvation, since he attaches himself in devotion to Vishṇu. In the next three stanzas he makes reference to various of the playful activities of Vishṇu, and the places which have become his habitual residence.

* Among these figure Vēngaḍam, the ocean of milk, and Vaikunṭham as his ancient residence. These are described to be the seat of the youth (Iḷam-Kumaran). In the following stanza similarly are mentioned a number of places, Viṇṇagaram, Veḥkā, Vēngaḍam, Vēḷukkaippāḍi, Kuḍandai (Kumbhakoṇam), Tiru-Arangam (Śrīrangam), Kōṭṭi (Tirukkōṭṭiyūr). The last line specifies that these are places where "the One who received in the half-closed palm of His hand the water in token of gift", referring obviously to His accepting the grant of three feet of earth from the emperor Bali, given to Him with pouring of water. Stanza 63 is important as it says clearly that "To Him, my father who is on the hill (Tirumalai), both the forms have combined into one (the forms

---

* பண்டெல்லாம் வேங்கடம் பாற்கடல் வைகுந்தம்
கொண்டங் குறைவார்க்குக் கோவில் போல்—வண்டு
வளங்கிளரும் நீள் சோலை வண்பூங்கடிகை
இளங்குமரன் றன் விண்ணகர். (61)

விண்ணகரம் வெஃகாவிரிதிரை நீ வேங்கடம்
மண்ணகரம் மாமாட வேளுக்கை—மண்ணகத்த
தென்குடந்தை தேனார் திருவரங்கம் தென்கோட்டி
தண்குடங்கை நீரேற்றான் தாழ்வு (62)

தாழ் சடையும் நீள்முடியும் ஒண்மழுவும் சக்கரமும்
சூழரவும் பொன்னாணுந் தோன்றுமால்—சூழும்
திரண்டருவி பாயும் திருமலைமே லெந்தைக்கு
இரண்டுருவு மொன்றா யிசைந்து. (63)

of Śiva and Vishṇu)". The previous lines mention that, in His form, appear the flowing matted locks of hair and the high peaked crown, the shining dagger and the golden disc, the snake around the hip and the zone of gold alike. The next stanza makes a reference merely to Vishṇu in the lying posture at Veḥkā in Kānchi. The next three stanzas refer to incidents generally ascribed to Vishṇu; but the following stanza must be noted, as, in the last two lines, it states clearly that the "hill of Vēngaḍam is the hill of Him who whilom threw the calf at the wood-apple tree for bringing the fruits down", thus putting it beyond a doubt that he regarded the hill as belonging to Vishṇu-Krishṇa. The next five stanzas each one makes a reference to Vēngaḍam; while 69 and 70 only refer to some general features, 71 repeats the statement almost in the same terms to the incidents referred to in stanza 68. In 72 there is the specific statement that Vēngaḍam is the residence of "the prince among the youth" (Iḷam-Kumarar-Kōmān). Stanza 73 has a reference to Vēngaḍam but in general terms; 75 has similarly a general reference to Tirumalai as the hill of Vishṇu-Krishṇa (Āyan, shepherd). Stanza 76 states definitely that, if one should offer flowers and fold his hands in worship before the God at Veḥkā, no consequences of evil deeds would come to him, and that one need not stand amidst hills, or dip into water, or otherwise perform penance by standing amidst the five fires. Stanzas 77 to 88 recommend single-minded devotion to Vishṇu as the sole efficient way of getting rid of evil and attaining to salvation. 89 refers to Vēngaḍam and states clearly " it is the hill of the One who applied his lips to the flute emitting sweet music " (meaning young Krishṇa). * Stanzas 90 to 93 are general as usual, and 94 states that the Āḻvār succeeded in recapturing Him, who stands, sits or lies down (in various holy places) and in his own heart by the process of lighting the lamp of contemplation. Stanza 97 makes Vishṇu impossible even for contemplation by Brahma and Śiva. Stanzas 99 to 100 are again confessions of faith; but in 99 there is a reference to the eight weapons of Vishṇu wielded in eight hands, placing him specifically in Aṭṭapuyakaram (Sans. Ashṭa Bhuja Karam), a suburb of Kānchi. This brings us to the end of the third centum which is the work of Pēy Āḻvār.

---

*முடிந்த பொழுதில் குறவாணர் ஏனம்
படிந்துழுசால் பைந்தினைகள் வித்த—தடிந்தெழுந்த
வேய்ங்கழை போய் விண்திறக்கும் வேங்கடமே மேலொரு நாள்
தீங்குழல் வாய் வைத்தான் சிலம்பு. (89)

11

THEIR COMMUNITY OF RELIGIOUS FEELING. These three Āḻvārs are together called the first Āḻvārs because they were considered to have been contemporary, and the earliest among those known in Vaishṇava parlance as Āḻvārs. We shall see later that the next following one was probably also their contemporary and the four together will have to be assigned to the same age. The three centums which constitute the work of these three have such close similarity of features that it may be held on this ground alone that they were contemporaries, and probably flourished at the same time and in the same religious atmosphere. Each one of those may be regarded more or less in three parts for our purposes. The first is general. In almost every stanza of the hundred there is a reference, direct or indirect to Vishṇu ; some one or other of his beneficent manifestations is alluded to and it is made to serve to enforce the same conclusion, namely that Vishṇu is the Supreme Saviour of all, and there is no saviour other than He. It is sometimes recognised that benefits falling short of the eternal could be obtained of others, but it is carefully pointed out that ultimately these others are no more than other beings of the creation, and constitute as much and as really the body of the Supreme which is immanent in all; that Supreme is, according to these, no other than Vishṇu. Among the allusions which are scattered about through their works, the most striking ones are those relating to Krishṇa, while there are incidents relating to the other *Avatāras* of Vishṇu which also find frequent reference. There is a certain amount of commonness in the references even to these particular incidents among the three, which would make them products of the same religious surroundings more or less. Being entirely devotees of Vishṇu they refer naturally to Vaishṇava holy places which are traditionally counted 108 in number, but it cannot be said that all the 108 are referred to in the writings of these. These refer to a certain number, each one particularly, and among them Tirupati figures perhaps more frequently than any other single place not even Śrīrangam excepted. Hence it is that these Āḻvārs are regarded as having devoted their poems exclusively to Vēngaḍam by the commentators.

THE NORM OF WORSHIP AMONG THESE. In regard to the norms of worship, these Āḻvārs recognise the efficacy of *vaidīc* ceremonies, and regard worship according to Vedic ritual as of the highest importance and efficacy. They recognise at the same time that it is a kind of worship which is possible only for the elite, and requires learning of a high order, and a training and discipline which is beyond the competence of ordinary folk. In fact they recognise frankly that this course of religious service is possible only for the very elect, even among the Brahmans. They are at pains therefore, not exactly perhaps to devise, but to emphasise the other norms capable of being more easily practised, being more simple in the performance. What is essential is the sincerity of the worship offered, not exactly the elaborateness of the ritual, so that it will be found that in places they do make broad references to these elaborate rituals and say plainly that they certainly are very good for those who can go through that course of worship of God who, to them, is Vishṇu and no other. But then it is not possible for all. They therefore prescribe other courses generally accepted as of efficacy at the time, and these, it will be found, are almost the same as the course of worship prescribed in the chapters on *Bhaktiyōga* of the Bhagavatgīta and in the Pāncharātra. In these again they recognise the value of knowledge (*gñāna*) and regard *gñānayōga* as of high efficacy. But falling short of that, comes the offer of worship with flowers and incense, and prayers of various kinds. That means worship offered in private houses of individuals and in shrines intended for the worship of the particular worshipping community. But where even this is found too elaborate for adoption, as it might well be for those who may not have the means, material as well as intellectual, they go one simpler, and merely prescribe repetition of the name of the saving God. The most popular of several of these saving names is what is generally described in Vaishṇava parlance the *ashṭākshara*, the name of eight letters, namely Nārāyaṇa with the *praṇava* before and the affix following. This simple form of worship it will be seen is capable of performance by all whatever their condition in life, and, by each one, by himself or herself alone, without the aid of a priest or anybody else. This transformation of the highly ritualistic religion described as Brāhmanism is what transformed Brāhmanism into Hinduism, and is the actual work of a school of thought which may for convenience be described as the *bhakti* school. It may be that we are able to trace back the history of the *bhakti* cult at least to the Upanishads very plainly, if not to the Veda itself. But that is not our concern for the present. That the school of *bhakti* it is that was responsible for the simplification of worship which transformed Brāhmanism into Hinduism is a matter that ought to be borne in mind in studying the history of the holy shrine at

Tirupati. The work of these early Āḻvārs shows this transformation as having been completely effected, and is in full swing of active practice. There is also a hint here and there in the work even of these Āḻvārs that the ideas of popular worship current at the time had perhaps other leanings, namely, towards the two rival religions of Buddhism and Jainism, in both of which the fundamental principle of religious worship is something essentially different. It is not real worship or service that brought about salvation. It is much rather knowledge of a particular kind which illumined the nature of life and the right conduct in life activity, without reference to a personal God and the attainment of salvation by worship and service to Him. In the first centum Poygai Āḻvār states "who will hereafter enter the gates of hell (*Naraka*)? Bolt its door without any compunction, because this land surrounded by the *Jambu* tree has now learned very well that the feet of Him who threw the calf to bring down the fruit of the wood-apple is the sole saviour". This seems intended to indicate the successful vogue this new teaching had attained to. That may give us an idea also of the actual age of its popularity, and the circumstances under which this movement attained to the popularity that it actually did.

SIVA-VISHNU COMBINATION A FEATURE OF VISHNU AT TIRUPATI. It was pointed out above that these are essentially Vaishṇavas. But they actually describe Vishṇu in a number of places as being compounded of the features of Śiva and Vishṇu. They go the whole length of describing circumstantially the various weapons which form the characteristic features of these deities as being seen in one and the same image at certain places, among them primarily Tirupati. On the face of it one is likely to get the impression that the image so described ought at least to be regarded as the image of God in the twin *Hari-Hara* form. We shall not now go into the controversy as to the nature of the image at Tirupati. We shall return to that later. But from the description by these Āḻvārs one is likely to get the general impression that the image described is the image of *Harihara*. It is important to note it here, as that is not merely a feature of the description of Vishṇu by these Āḻvārs, but other Āḻvārs also indulge in this, particularly Nammāḻvār, so that it is to be regarded more or less as a feature of the times to describe the supreme deity Vishṇu in these terms. While therefore a number of stanzas could be selected from the writings of these three Āḻvārs which imply Śiva alone in some, Śiva and Brahma in others, forming part of the body of the deity, it is clear that in so describing they had no more idea than to point out what is plainly pointed out in one of the poems of Nammāḻvār that these deities were as much his creatures and constituted his body as other created beings, and that their appeal lay to the Supreme One who is above these. Stanza 98 of the first centum says in so many words that while the holy One of the colour of molten gold and of the matted locks, and the One who stood with one foot on earth and measured out the universe by the other, though these two live and move about in two different bodies, the one (the first one) is in the body of the other. That sentiment is expressed somewhat differently in stanza 28 of the same Āḻvār. "You carry in Your hand the dextral conch and the disc, O, My Lord of the blue colour. On Your chest is the daughter of the flower (lotus). The young author of the Veda is in Your naval, and the lordly One who destroyed the three fortresses is on one side of Your body". Stanzas of the same import could be quoted from the other two authors as well. So then the description which apparently conveys the impression that the image of Vishṇu is part Śiva and part Vishṇu is not to be interpreted as involving the conception of the form of God being that of Harihara, and should be interpreted as that of Hari himself normally and necessarily carrying the other deities as his body.

THE PRESIDING DEITY IN VENGADAM IS VISHNU ACCORDING TO THESE. Coming down to the specific references to Vēngaḍam in these Āḻvārs and their description of the deity there, we find that, while no doubt in a few places, about half a dozen all told, the description may be regarded as of Śiva-Vishṇu combination in form, yet on closer examination, it will be found that they do not leave it in any doubt that the deity that they offer worship to in Vēngaḍam is Vishṇu and none other; and such description as give the indication of Śiva forming a part of Vishṇu is nothing peculiar to Śiva alone, as Brahma, Lakshmi and the very weapons characteristic of Vishṇu are in terms so described as part of Vishṇu's body, almost in the same terms as Śiva. There are about 35 references to Vēngaḍam in these 300 stanzas which have been referred to in detail in the pages immediately preceding. Some of these references are either very general, or make a poetical reference to some feature or other of Tirupati. But there are some which give one unmistakably to understand that the God worshipped in the shrine there is distinctly Vishṇu and no other. Stanzas 33 to 40 of

Poygai Āḻvār make reference to Tirupati in each case definitely. In the first it is said that Vēngaḍam to which the learned in the Veda come and offer worship from all points of the compass, is the shrine of Him who blew the white conch; without a doubt Vishṇu. The next one speaks of Vēngaḍam as the town of *Māl* at the mention of whose name the *Asuras* felt frightened. In 39, Vēngaḍam is described as a place where the God is said to be in a standing posture, the God who lies on the sea, who killed Kamsa, who held aloft the hill and who dug up the earth, all attributes which cannot be interpreted as belonging to any other than Vishṇu. In 40, Vēngaḍam is said to be the hill of Him who was delighted with the fall of the king of the *Asuras*. In stanza 68 the God in Vēngaḍam is addressed as one who is in the sky, who is on the earth, who is in the verses of the Veda along with being in Vēngaḍam, again referring specifically to Vishṇu alone by these attributes. Stanza 76 is even more specific. It mentions Tiruvēngaḍam as the place of the one who measured the earth. In 77, Vēngaḍam, Viṇṇagar, Veḥkā and Tirukkōvalūr are mentioned as places where the God stood, sat, lay or walked, necessarily meaning that the four manifestations are one and the same. In 82 there is a more definite reference to the festival on the 12th day of the fortnight (*Dvādaśi*), when, on account of the large quantity of smoke from the burning of the incense by ladies, the very sky itself got so clouded that the stars became invisible. While the mention of this festival may be interesting in itself for the history of Tirupati, it does not make it in terms, quite clear that the deity is Vishṇu. The mention of *Dvādaśi* makes it certain as that day is peculiarly holy to Vishṇu according to the Āgamas. Stanza 99, the last of the first centum speaks of the deity in Vēngaḍam as the one who is in the floods, undoubtedly referring to Vishṇu.

Stanza 25 of the second centum refers to the deity in Vēngaḍam as one who marched upon Lanka and killed Rāvaṇa. Stanza 33 contains a general reference. The reference in 45 may also perhaps be regarded as quite general. But 46 is definite, inasmuch as the deity in Vēngaḍam is said to be the deity in Śrīrangam, in Tirukkōṭṭiyūr, and in Tirunīrmalai. The reference in 48 is indirect inasmuch as it says the hill surrounded by deep dense groves, which the commentators interpret as Tirupati; but the actual terms of reference would indicate Tirumālirumśōlai near Madura. The deity is of course specifically referred to by clear allusions as being Vishṇu. In stanzas 53 and 54 we come upon references to Vēngaḍam. In the first it is referred to as Iḷam-giri, and is equated with Vēngaḍam in the 4th line. In the next stanza the Āḻvār refers to Tirumālirumśōlai and Vēngaḍam as the two places where the God was pleased to stand, naturally therefore meaning that the deity in the two places ought to be regarded as the same, and ends the verse with the exhortation "Do not therefore give up Iḷam-kōil (temple of the youth)." This Iḷam-giri and Iḷam-kōil were taken to refer to Subrahmaṇya, who undoubtedly is referred to as a youth; and, if we could take these terms out of their context and interpret them independently, it may be capable of that interpretation. But in the context that interpretation could hardly be held to be admissible. Stanza 72 contains a mere general reference to Vēngaḍam, and so stanza 75.

Coming to the third centum we note that there are a far larger number of references to the shrine, and this Āḻvār gives more specific details which would put this question as to the nature of the deity in Tirupati altogether beyond all doubt. Stanza 14 makes the first reference and starts with the attraction of the feet of Vishṇu to his mind, and refers to the God in Vēngaḍam as the one in the Veda of the four sections, whose feet are marked by the crowns of the Gods themselves. The next reference in stanza 26 where Vēngaḍam is mentioned amidst a number of other places including his own heart, where God is resident, in all other cases Vishṇu, and therefore also in Vēngaḍam. So in stanza 30 where Vēngaḍam figures along with the sea, the sky, Kuḍandai, Pāḍaham, Ananta, the great serpent, and the garland of basil. Similarly in stanza 32 some of these very places happen to be mentioned, and in addition the ocean of sciences (Nūl-Kaḍal), and the lotus of very fine thread, and the hearts of those devoted to him, as if to clear the doubt definitely that the person so present in these places including Vēngaḍam, is said to be the young shepherd boy who broke the twin *Kurunda* tree (the young shepherd boy, Bālakrishṇa). In stanzas 39 and 40 Vēngaḍam is referred to, and the deity there is described to be the one who measured the earth. In stanza 45 similarly Vēngaḍam is said to be the place of Him who, on one occasion previously, carried the earth on his tusk. The same idea is expressed in stanza 58, but here the God is referred to as one who acquired the earth by desiring to get it from Bali. In stanzas 61 and 62, the heavenly city of Iḷam-Kumaran surrounded by flower gardens is said to be his residence, Vēngaḍam, and the ocean of milk, etc. So in stanza 62 a number of holy places of the Vaishṇavas is mentioned, some of them in heaven, and some on earth, among them Vēngaḍam; but they are said to be places sacred to Him who received the water in the outstretched hand, referring to the Vāmanāvatāra of Vishṇu. Stanzas 68, 69, 70, 72 and 73, all make references to Vēngaḍam. In the first it is said to be the place of the one who threw the calf to bring down the wood-apple. The reference in 69 is quite general, as also in the following stanza 70. 71 makes a similar reference to the throwing of the calf. 72 speaks of Vēngaḍam as a place of residence of the prince among the youth (Iḷam-Kumarar-Kōmān). In stanza 73 *Vaḍa mukha Vēngaḍam* (northern Vēngaḍam) is the place of the one who danced with the water-pot (one of the frolics characteristic of young Krishṇa). In 75 Tirumalai (Tiruvēngaḍam) is said to be the hill of the shepherd (Āyan). 89 clinches the whole matter where Vēngaḍam is described in general terms as remarkable for its tall bushes of bamboo reaching up to the skies as the place of the one who whilom applied his lips to the flute emitting sweet music.

VENGADAM AN UNDOUBTED VAISHNAVA CENTRE OF WORSHIP. This elaborate series of references to Vēngaḍam in all the 300 stanzas of these

Āḻvārs establishes beyond a doubt that Vēngaḍam was a place of great importance as a Vaishṇava centre of worship. The Āḻvārs knew the place sufficiently familiarly even to be acquainted with some of the small details of worship there. That while some stray verses may perhaps be interpreted as referring to Śiva rather than Vishṇu, even these specific references ought properly speaking to be explained with reference to the context, as referring to Vishṇu. But what is really more important, the proper interpretation of these verses that could thus be picked out ought certainly to be in their proper context, and no particular verse, or even particular stanza, could be understood in full significance unless each is taken in full association with the whole work. Thus interpreted, it is clear beyond a doubt that, to these Āḻvārs, Tirupati was pre-eminently the shrine of Vishṇu, and they tendered their worship at that shrine as an important shrine of Vishṇu and none other than Vishṇu.

CHAPTER IV.

TIRUPATI IN SILAPPADHIKARAM.

CONFIRMATION FROM THE SILAPPADHIKARAM. This position of the Āḷvārs finds unlooked for confirmation which puts it altogether beyond any doubt. The Tamil classic Śilappadhikāram, the author of which is not a Brahmanical Hindu, whether he be a Jain or Buddhist, was still enough of an Indian man of learning to make impartially respectful statements in regard to faiths even other than his own; nay, even those to which he may by conviction be expected to be opposed. References in his work to Tirupati as a Vishṇu shrine puts the whole position beyond any doubt, all cavilling to the contrary by modern scholars notwithstanding. These seem after all to follow in the footsteps of their predecessors of old who set up a similar claim during the period of influence of Rāmānuja's mission. We shall revert to this subject later and will have to deal with it rather elaborately. Suffice it here to say that Iḷangō-Aḍigaḷ, the author of the Śilappadhikāram has no doubt whatever that the deity which stands on the hill of Tirupati is no other than Vishṇu. He describes Venkaṭēśa on the hill in the following terms in Book XI, lines 41 to 51 *:—

High on Vēngaḍam's towering crest, with flowing streams in flood,

Betwixt the effulgent glory, of shining Sun and Moon,

Like unto a blue cloud in lightning dresst

In all the brilliance of rainbow dight,

The Red-eyed great One, majestic stands

In dress of flowery brilliance with garland bright,

One lotus hand with fearsome disc adorned, and milk white conch (the other held.)

The passage occurs in a context which leaves little doubt as to the knowledge of the author of what he thus describes. This description is put into the mouth of a Brahman pilgrim, a native-resident of the village of

---

* வீங்கு நீரருவி வேங்கடமென்னு
மோங்குயர் மலயத்துச்சிமீ மிசை
விரிகதிர் ஞாயிறுந் திங்களும் விளங்கி
யிருமருங்கோங்கிய விடை நிலைத்தானத்து
மின்னுக் கோடியுடுத்து விளங்கு விற்பூண்டு
நன்னிற மேக நின்றது போலப்
பகையணங்காழியும் பால் வெண் சங்கமும்
தகைபெறு தாமரைக் கையினேந்தி
நலங்கிளராரமார் விற் பூண்டு
பொலம் பூவாடையிற் பொலிந்து தோன்றிய
செங்கணெடியோ னின்ற வண்ணமும்.

Māngāḍu in Malaināḍu (Malayālam or Malabar). Prompted by a feeling to pay worship at the great Vishṇu shrines of Śrīrangam and Tirupati, he was on his journey coming across the Pāṇḍya country, and staying for the night in the outer groves of the Chōḻa capital at the time, Uṛaiyūr. To that self-same grove also went the hero of the epic, Kōvalan with his wife, and the Jain ascetic Kaundi Aḍigaḷ, whom he picked up near Māyavaram on his way from Kaverippūmpaṭṭinam. He was going forward to Madura to set up as a merchant there, and recover his lost fortune, which he squandered away in a life of youthful dalliance with the bewitchingly beautiful courtesan Mādhavi in the Chōḻa capital, his own native city, all the accumulated wealth which was given to him by his father, who was a great merchant (Mā-Śāttu-vāṇigan; Sans: Mahā-Sārtha Vāha) of the place, for setting him up in life. Disgusted with this mismanagement, and, feeling guilty of having neglected his own good wife who would not stay behind when he wanted to launch out into the world as a merchant to gain back his wealth, he travelled on to Madura and came as far as Uṛaiyūr in his journey without incident. There were more than one route between Uṛaiyūr and Madura, and these roads were in those days, no less in these, by no means particularly safe for pilgrims travelling by the ordinary roadway. When he was naturally looking out for some one who could enlighten him as to the particular road to take, he heard a Brahman who was resting for the night, not far from him, get up early in the morning and launch out into a eulogy of the Pāṇḍyan ruler for the time being across whose territory he travelled before reaching Uṛaiyūr, and came to the end of the first stage of his journey and into the outskirts of the actual Chōḻa capital of the time. Naturally, in gratitude for the safe journey that he had through a danger-infested road between Madura and Trichinopoly, due to the efficient administration of the Pāṇḍya ruler, he felt called upon to sing his praise. To Kōvalan's enquiry as to who he was and why he was belauding the ruling Pāṇḍya in those strains, the Brahman answered that he had just passed through the Pāṇḍyan territory unscathed; a pilgrim that he was, to visit the famous Vishṇu shrines, at Śrīrangam and Vēngaḍam, he was able to travel in perfect safety. Since he found the most dangerous routes in that part of his journey, he thought that it was due to the ruler of the locality and that his praise should be loudly sung. Kōvalan naturally took advantage of the occasion to ask him what he wanted, and, at the end of his enquiries, determined upon the road that he should take for his journey to Madura. This, however, is not of interest for the moment. The terms in which the Vishṇu shrine both at Śrīrangam and Tirupati, and the one at Tirumāl Iṛumśōlai, are referred to, give clear evidence that the shrine at Tirupati had the reputation of being a Vishṇu shrine and nothing else, and that reputation had reached so far out as the West Coast and people there were in the habit of going on a pilgrimage to Tirupati as they do now as one of the holy Vaishṇava centres. A statement like that from an author who was not himself a Vaishṇava, and who makes the statement no doubt in poetry, and in the course of a romantic epic, does not invalidate the general position that the temple at Tirupati was by common repute a temple dedicated to Vishṇu. This confirms the conclusion to which we have arrived by a detailed study of the three centa of the early Āḻvārs, Poygai, Bhūtam and Pēy, from which efforts have been made, from time to time, to draw the contrary inference by some who took occasion to refer to this topic in the course of their investigations. We shall next proceed to examine what another early Āḻvār, Āḻvār Tirumaḻiśai (Bhaktisāra, as he is called in Sanskrit) who, for very good reasons, could be regarded as contemporary with these early Āḻvārs has to say of Tirupati.

CHAPTER V.

TIRUPATI IN TIRUMALISAI ALVAR'S WORKS.

TIRUMALISAI ALVAR, HIS LIFE AND TIME. Āḻvār Tirumaḻiśai is said to have been a foundling child taken up and brought up as his own by a cane-worker by profession, and as such belonging to a class in the Hindu social order below the recognised four. The tradition recorded however is that he was actually the son of Rishi Bhārgava and his wife, born as a result of a great sacrifice (Yāga) that they performed, and, having been born too early and in an unformed condition, the foetus was left in a cane bush and discovered by the cane-cutter. Possibly this was invented to give him a higher birth. We can say this, with some little assurance as he himself states in the course of one of his works, that he had not the good fortune to be born in one of the four recognised castes (kulam) of Hindu society. Whatever it is, the truth seems to be that he was a person of unknown birth like the other three Āḻvārs, possibly belonging to one of the classes outside the recognised four. But somehow he had gained intuition, perhaps from birth, to know the truth better, and, like the three others that we have already spoken of, lived not merely to discover, but even to expound the truth to the world. The same tradition associates his name with the village Tirumaḻiśai near Poonamallee, a few miles to the west of Madras from which he takes his name, Tirumaḻiśai Āḻvār. Of course, what is known of him is, as tradition records it, miraculous and superhuman, possibly because of ignorance of his life, or, it may be, that he exhibited some extraordinary features as a man. We get from his works however, a few details of a biographical character, such as the one mentioned above in respect of his caste, which give us perhaps all the historical information regarding him that we can really depend upon. Leaving aside therefore the legendary, we might take it that he was apparently one very greatly devoted to Vishṇu, and had attained to that extraordinary devotion, not altogether by mere instinct alone, but really by an elaborate study and search which ultimately led him to reject all contemporary persuasions and pin his faith to Vishṇu as the sole saviour. He says, in the course of one of his works *, that the "Śramaṇas are ignorant men, while the Bauddhas are under a delusion; while those that have fallen into

* அறியார் சமணர் அயர்த்தார் பவுத்தர்
சிறியார் சிவப்பட்டார் செப்பில்—வெறியாய
மாயவனை மாலவனை மாதவனை யேத்தாதார்
ஈனவரேயாதலாலின்று.

Nānmukhan Tiruvandādi, 6.

devotion to Śiva are of comparatively inferior intellect. Those who will not worship the fragrant feet of Vishṇu are indeed inferior people." This is put in another form in the traditional account in a fugitive verse, where the Āḻvār himself is made to say "We learnt the Sānkhya, we learnt the teaching of the Jina; we learnt the Āgamas taught by Śankara; but as good luck would have it, we have resolved to devote ourselves to Vishṇu of the dark colour and the red eye, and thus put ourselves beyond harm's reach. There is nothing therefore that is impossible for us *". That apart, he is said to have spent a considerable part of his time in the village of his birth where he met the first three Āḻvārs on their usual round of pilgrimage. Coming near to this place, they are said to have discovered a column of light and approaching to where it emanated from, they enquired, almost by intuition, whether the holy one in contemplation was well, without seeing him. He is said to have replied in turn, similarly without seeing the others, whether the three, mentioning them by name, were keeping well and going round their pious work of life

* சாத்திரங் கற்றோம் சமண் கற்றோம் மற்றச்
சங்கரனாராக்கிய வாகமநூலாராய்ந்தோம்-பாக்கியத்தால்
செங்கட்கரியானைச் சேர்ந்தியாந் தீதிலோம்.
எங்கட்கரிய தொன்றில் —

quite happily. When this casual meeting struck up a friendship between them, it lasted on to the end of their time. Some time after they left, this Āḻvār himself left on a pilgrimage and went to Veḥkā in Kānchi, the birthplace of Poygai Āḻvār and there he remained for a long time devoting himself to the God of the locality and residing on the banks of the holy tank in which was born the Āḻvār of that name, the first of the Āḻvārs. Here he came into contact with a Śūdra by name Kaṇikaṇṇan, who is said, in the traditional account, to have been born of parents who fed the Āḻvār with milk when he was still a baby. He was in the service of a Pallava King of Kānchi, but was offering devoted service to the Āḻvār nevertheless. A woman servant of the palace, old and poor, used to be rendering some menial service to this Āḻvār, such as cleaning up his place of residence, etc., and, in response to her request, the Āḻvār blessed her with perpetual youth and beauty. She became thenceforward an object of attraction to the monarch. In answer to his enquiry as to how she obtained that unfading beauty, she replied that she was indebted to it to the grace of the Āḻvār, and offered the information that through his servant, Kaṇikaṇṇan who was a favourite of the Āḻvār, he could get at him if he so desired. The Pallava

King, as became his position, asked Kaṇikaṇṇan to bring the Āḻvār to his court, and got the surprisingly decisive reply that the Āḻvār would not vouchsafe to go down to see him, and he could not take the responsibility of persuading him to do so. In a fit of anger, the monarch ordered Kaṇikaṇṇan out of his territory if he would not do the behests of his sovereign. Naturally Kaṇikaṇṇan went and told the Āḻvār that he had to leave the place under orders, and the Āḻvār determined forthwith to follow his friend; not only that, but he told the God to follow him, and they all left. This strange phenomenon brought the Pallava King to a humbler frame of mind, and, as a result of his earnest entreaty, the whole party returned after remaining one night at a particular place some distance away, which thereafter got the name the "placo of one night's stay". Thenceforward the King treated the Āḻvār with the greatest respect, and the place where he lived, and the deity there, became cherished objects of worship for the monarch. After remaining there for a considerably long time, the Āḻvār went on a tour of pilgrimage to the south passing through Chidambaram on his way to Kumbhakoṇam. In Chidambaram there occurred an incident of some importance As he was going through a Brahman quarter of the place on a particular morning, the Brahmans who were engaged in reciting the Veda in the course of celebrating a sacrifice, stopped the chant and fell into silence, as soon as he entered the hall of sacrifice in the belief that he was of a caste within whose hearing the Veda should not be chanted. Unfortunately however, when they had come to know that he was a great devotee of Vishṇu, they wanted to resume their Vedic chant, but forgot where exactly they left. The Āḻvār understood their difficulty; but without giving the passage by word of mouth, which one of his birth should not do, showed by sign, by splitting with his finger-nail the husk on a grain of paddy, the particular passage last recited. The Brahmans were able to resume their chanting and proceed. Some time later some of the people in the assembly did not show themselves to be quite inclined to accept him for the great devotee of Vishṇu that he was. To demonstrate to them that he was one who had realised Vishṇu actually, he asked the God to whom he was devoted exclusively, to show himself, to the unbelieving antagonists of his, just as he was always housed in his own heart. On seeing this they regretted the error of their ways and accepted him as one very near indeed to God. Then he passed on to Kumbhakoṇam and to various other holy places, and passed away at the end of a fabulously long life.

This recital of the details of his life perhaps is of some little value as the one detail regarding his contemporary monarch of Kānchi may possibly lead us to locate him in point of time. The details given of this ruler are nothing very specific, and all that is said is, that, under this ruler, the Vishṇu shrine at Veḥkā, now-a-days called generally *Yadōkta-kāri* (he who did as he was told) was in existence. In the poem, obviously composed to celebrate the Toṇḍamān Iḷam Tiraiyan, ruler of Kānchi, Kānchi is found to be described in general terms as a place where people of all persuasions found objects of worship which to them were holy, refers only to the shrine at Veḥkā * specifically in some little detail without the possibility of being mistaken. This would raise the presumption whether this Āḻvār was not contemporary with Iḷam Tiraiyan of Kānchi. According to another version of the tradition of his life, he is said to have been one who had studied the various systems of religion current, and, in the course of his study he was at one stage of his life an

---

* மலர் தலையுலகத்துள்ளும் பலர்தொழ
விழவு மேம்பட்ட பழவிறல் மூதூர்—

Perumbāṇ-āṟṟuppaḍai, ll. 410-11.

ardent Śaiva (worshipper of Śiva) and a man of great ability. Pēy Āḻvār is supposed to have met him in controversy, weaned him out of that faith and led him ultimately to become a Vaishṇava. There is no specific reference that we know of for the present to confirm this tradition from his works; but the general trend of these may go some way to make the change possible. Neglecting the details of the tradition, the general drift of it seems to be that this Āḻvār was contemporary with the other three, belonged to a locality not far from Kānchi, and was contemporary with the Pallava monarch who may be identical with the Pallava Iḷam Tiraiyan of Kānchi. Of his works included in the Prabandham there are just two, the one a centum like that of each of the three earlier Āḻvārs named *Nānmukhan Tiruvandādi*, and another a little over a hundred (actually 120 stanzas) called *Tiruchanda-viruttam* These are the only two works of the Āḻvār which we shall have to discuss.

THE ALVAR'S CONVICTION. Like the other three Āḻvārs we have already dealt with, this one is also similarly devoted to worship of Vishṇu as the sole saviour. It may also be stated that this Āḻvār is not only of this conviction like the other three, but quite fanatically so. The three early

Āḻvārs would show a tolerance of the worship of others, such as Brahma, Śiva, Indra prominently mentioned. This one went the length of saying positively that he would not, as stanza 66 shows clearly*. He states categorically "Now my heart is the permanent abode of Him who, for a long time before, had for his place of residence the serpent couch. I affirm that I would not place, along with him, Śiva who wears the crescent moon on his head, nor Brahma (Ayan); nor would I offer them service and go round them rightwise as a worshipper." This is a clear and unmistakable statement of his sole and exclusive faith in the saving grace of Vishṇu and of none other. Numbers of other stanzas from this centum itself could be pointed out indicating this conviction, but in a much less aggressive form. He is as thoroughly convinced as the others, in fact as the Āḻvārs generally are, that the power to save in others is comparatively less efficient and is always governed by the consideration that the supreme Saviour really is Vishṇu. He states this idea equally clearly in stanza 26 where he states it

---

* இடமாவது என்னெஞ்சம் இன்றெல்லாம் பண்டு
படநாகணை நெடியமாற்கு—திடமாக
வையேன் மதிசூடி தன்னோடு அயனை நான்
வையே னாட்செய்யேன் வலம்.

Nānmukhan Tiruvandādi, 66.

broadly that "for my not having anybody else to worship than Vishṇu, Śiva of matted locks is witness. * " We have already referred above to stanza 6 where he speaks of the people of other persuasions as pursuing faiths of inferior efficacy, and mentions among them Jains, Buddhists and Śaivas particularly. In stanzas 14 and 15 he states his faith with equal emphasis "Nārāyaṇa is my Lord. Nārāyaṇa is He that guards against my going to hell. It is strange that there should be people who, without reciting His name, are deluded in believing the false teachings of others" (stanza 14). "Those who are able to worship Vishṇu by placing flowers at his feet worshipped by the very Gods themselves, would have the same saving benefit that Mārkanḍēya has had by worshipping the blue-throated Śiva," referring to Mārkanḍēya's escaping death without gaining the eternal life. In stanza 17 he states unmistakably that Śiva himself, as Dakshiṇāmūrti, taught the four Rishis his pupils that he offered his worship to Him who measured the earth and slept on the baniyan leaf floating on the primeval waters,

---

* மற்றுத்தொழுவா ரொருவரையும் யானின்மை
கற்றைச்சடையான் கரிக் கண்டாய்—எற்றைக்கும்
கண்டுகொள் கண்டாய் கடல்வண்ணா யானுன்னைக்
கண்டு கொள்கிற்குமாறு.

Nānmukhan Tiruvandādi, 26.

that is, Vishṇu. A number more of stanzas of similar sentiment could be quoted with various illustrations taken from Indian religious literature. He completes the centum with the following statement in stanza 96. * "I have learnt, for all time hereafter. You are my Lord, You are the God of Śiva and the four-faced Brahma. I have learnt, for all time, that You are the cause of everything. You are the ultimate object of all learning, past and present. You are the good deed. You are Nārāyaṇa. I have learnt this very well indeed," as summing up his own conviction.

In what we have stated above already, we see the clear conviction of the Āḻvār that the two out of the three constituting the Hindu Trinity form a part of the supreme One Nārāyaṇa. He starts the centum therefore with a series of statements that Nārāyaṇa created the four-faced Brahma; that the four-faced one created Śankara with the same number of faces as himself. This profound truth he let the world know by means of this *Andādi* (series of verses linked up by taking one word of the last line to begin the following

* இனியறிந்தேன் ஈசற்கும் நான்முகற்குந் தெய்வம்
இனியறிந்தேன் எம்பெருமான் உன்னை—இனியறிந்தேன்
காரணன் நீ கற்றவை நீ கற்பவை நீ நற்கிரிசை
நாரணன் நீ நன்கறிந்தேன் நான்—

Nānmukhan Tiruvandādi, 96.

verse). He follows this statement by more clearly stating the supremacy of Vishṇu as the Saviour.* "On consideration, they (wise ones) say that there is but one God; that no one knows the extent of his greatness; that that is the ultimate end of all thought; that the saving grace for all who devote themselves to doing penance; is to be found only in Him who bears the disc (Vishṇu)". In stanza 4 he clearly states that Śiva who hides in his matted locks Gangā (Ganges) and the king of the Gods alike form part of his body.† In stanzas 42 and 43 he states in clear terms that both Brahma and Śiva were among the worshippers of Vēngaḍam. In 54 comes in the general statement ‡ that He shows himself as Gods, and, among them, the

---

* தேருங்கால் தேவன் ஒருவனே யென்றுரைப்பர்
ஆருமறியார் அவன் பெருமை—ஓரும்
பொருள் முடிவும் இத்தனையே எத்தவத் தார்க்கும்
அருள்முடிவ தாழியான் பால்.

Nānmukhan Tiruvandādi, 21.

† ஆறுசடைக்கரந்தான் அண்டர்கோன் தன்னோடும்
கூறுடையனென்பதுவும் கொள்கைத்தே—வேறொருவர்
இல்லாமை நின்றானை எம்மானை எப்பொருட்கும்
சொல்லானைச் சொன்னேன் தொகுத்து.

Nānmukhan Tiruvandādi, 4.

‡ தேவராய் நிற்கும் அத்தேவும் அத்தேவரில்
மூவராய் நிற்கும் முதுபுணர்ப்பும்—யாவராய்
நிற்கின்றதெல்லாம் நெடுமாலென்றோராதார்
கற்கின்ற தெல்லாம் கடை.

ibid, 54.

three prominent ones ; and all the others who exist are the great Vishṇu himself. Those who do not hold this conviction make all their learning useless. In 73 again is a clear statement "Who can understand the greatness of Him, who swallowed the whole earth and threw it up again, of the great disc. That supreme body of His, neither the blue-throated Śiva nor the eight-eyed Brahma have seen". In 75 he states clearly, although the occasion is not altogether obvious, that Śiva of matted locks worshipped him with flowers to the best of his ability, and did not attain to Vishṇu's grace nevertheless. This should be enough to convince one that his devotion to Vishṇu was such that he considered it that Vishṇu alone was the Supreme Being and the fountain source of all grace and nobody else, and that other Gods worshipped by votaries of other persuasions were but following worship of beings inferior to Him.

Coming next to this Āḻvār's references to Vēngaḍam, there are certainly a number of references in this centum. The first reference is in stanza 31. It is a bare reference to Vēngaḍam along with the other Vaishṇava place Kōṭṭiyūr. There is a simple reference in stanza 39. There is a specific reference in 40 where it says that he was devoted to the God at

Vēngaḍam, who was constantly in his thought; * "He is the beloved of Her who is described and quite extolled in the sciences, and I am inextricably caught in the net which is His feet". There is a very interesting reference in 41 where he refers again to the holy One at Vēngaḍam having entered his mind by being in residence at Vēngaḍam. † In describing this hill at Vēngaḍam there are two points that are brought out. The first is the mountain streams running down scattering pearls. By implication there is also the rattle of the running stream. Another kind of sound that is referred to as the normal feature of Vēngaḍam is the sound that arises from the celebration of the festivals on Ōṇam (Sans. Śravaṇa) days. This asterism is of course sacred to Vishṇu, and is, in some form, attached to Vishṇu as almost the asterism of his birth (one that has no birth). But the festival on this

---

* வெற்பென்று வேங்கடம் பாடினேன் வீடாக்கி
நிற்கின்றேன் நின்று நினைக்கின்றேன்—கற்கின்ற
நூல்வலையில் பட்டிருந்த நூலாட்டி கேள்வனார்
கால்வலையிற் பட்டிருந்தேன் காண்.

Nānmukhan Tiruvandādi, 40.

† காணலுறுகின்றேன் கல்லருவி முத்துதிர
ஓண விழவிலொலியதிர—பேணி
வருவேங்கடவா என்னுள்ளம் புகுந்தாய்
திரு வேங்கடமதனைச் சென்று.

ibid, 41.

THE SRI VENKATESA SHRINE

(To face page 114)

asterism is, in some respects, peculiar to Tirupati, and is also usual in shrines where the ḍeity installed is Śrīnivāsa, the abode of the Goddess Lakshmi, which is the ordinary familiar name of the God at Tirupati. The most sacred day in the year at Tirupati is this Śravaṇa in the month of Pūrvā-Bhādra. The next stanza * has reference to Vēngaḍam also where the Āḷvār exhorts people to go and offer worship at Vēngaḍam as it permanently destroys the evils of *Karma*, and offers as inducement that the lotus-born Brahma and the three-eyed Śiva alike placed lotus flowers at the feet of the God at Tirupati and worshipped Him. The next following stanza has a similar reference to the worship offered by the same two Gods. Stanza 44 is particularly interesting, as, in making a reference to Vēngaḍam, he exhorts younger people particularly to go and offer worship at Vēngaḍam. "Where stands the young one (prince, Kumāra), who of old counted up the heads of the Rākshasa, being a child in the lap of Brahma, whose beneficence the Rākshasa sought (by penance)." This is an

* சென்று வணங்குமினோ சேணுயர் வேங்கடத்தை
நின்று வினைகெடுக்கும் நீர்மையால்—என்றும்
கடிக்கமல நான்முகனும் கண்மூன்றத்தானும்
அடிக்கமல மிட்டேத்து மங்கு.

ibid, 42.

allusion to Vishṇu who assumed the form of a baby and placed himself in the lap of Brahma just on the eve of his granting the boon prayed for by Rāvaṇa after he had performed the severest penance. There is a similar reference to this incident in stanza 45 of the centum of Poygai Āḻvār and in stanza 77 of Pēy Āḻvār. I have not been able to discover the Purāṇic authority for this incident which is likely to be found in some one or other of the various sources of that kind of information. But the point that should be specially noted in regard to this incident is that the God standing in Tirupati is described by the term *Kumaran* (Sans. Kumāra), which was taken to mean Bālasubrahmaṇya exclusively, and to support the theory that the Tirupati shrine was a Subrahmaṇya shrine. This reference puts that out quite unmistakably, as also several others we have quoted from Pēy Āḻvār. The next following stanza 45 has a reference to Vēngaḍam also of the ordinary kind. The next three stanzas 46, 47 and 48 refer to Vēngaḍam. The special feature of the reference in the first is that the *Kuṛavar* of the locality were accustomed to surrounding the elephants for the purpose of capturing them, a sort of an ancient kheddah. In the next one Vēngaḍam is described as peculiarly famous for its trees, for its monkeys and the class of people called *Vēḍar* (Vēṭṭuvar or the hunter class). The next one is a little more interesting which states broadly that Vēngaḍam is the place worshipped by those of heaven. Vēngaḍam is really the place which destroys the results of *karma*. Vēngaḍam is the place of Him who, by the use of his disc, destroyed the *Dānavas*, and thus protected the heavenly hosts, making a clear equation of the God in Vēngaḍam with Vishṇu. The next reference to Vēngaḍam is in stanza 90, although the reference is general. That is so far as this particular centum of this Āḻvār is concerned. It comes out again and again in the course of this work of the Āḻvār that Tirupati was a place sacred to Vishṇu, and the God installed in the temple there is Vishṇu and nobody else. Mention is made of the presence of other Gods particularly the two Śiva and Brahma as forming part of his body, but none the less it is clearly stated that the object of worship is Vishṇu and not the others, even to the extent of declining to offer worship to this God if these two happened to be really any integral part of the Supreme.

There are a few other interesting general references which may be noted before we close this section. We have already referred to the

Āḻvār's acquaintance with, or his knowledge of, other religions. There are two very specific references—a few more general ones can be quoted also—to the Gīta. Stanza 50 says specifically that "the words of Kaṇṇan who is lying on the bank of a river" and "Māyan who is lying asleep on the sea" "lie embedded in my heart". A similar sentiment is expressed in 71 where the God is referred to as Māyan who was the shepherd king (Āyan) of Dvāraka, and states it roundly that all that people in the world know is not knowledge if they do not know "the words that this Māyan spoke on that day", referring undoubtedly to the Gīta. In stanza 54 he gives expression to the same sentiment in much more general terms asserting the supremacy of Vishṇu. In stanza 60 is a reference, where Vishṇu is addressed as the God resident in Śrīrangam, and is stated to be the rare good substance to those of great hearing (learning which is only heard, *Śruti*; compare 69.) In stanza 75 there is a definite statement that he "would not use the tongue to sing the glory of man" but would "sing only of Him, who was not pleased to accept the prayer of even Śiva who went and offered the highest worship to him with flowers in the prescribed form". Stanza 76 is much more interesting in this line as it refers definitely to Manu as a *Śruti* work (*Kēṭṭa Manu*), and then follows the term Śruti which commentators interpret as a specific reference to a part of the Taittirīya Samhita of the Yajur Veda, a part of the Veda peculiarly sacred to the *Bhakti* school of Pāncharātra. And then follows the four Vedas in the ordinary way of reference to Vedas generally. All these are said to be "the truths which in his Māya, Vishṇu taught to people." * There is an interesting reference in stanza 88 that those alone live that live in constant contemplation of him who is ever sedulous in the removal of all that gives pain to his devotees, while the life of those who follow the instructions of other persuasions is life wasted. In the final stanza of the centum, † he declares emphatically his faith in Vishṇu as if he made that discovery just then "I have now learnt that Thou art the God of Śiva (Īśa) and

---

* பாட்டும் முறையும் படுகதையும் பல்பொருளும்
ஈட்டியதீயுமிருவிசும்பும்—கேட்ட
மனுவும் சுருதி மறை நான்கும் மாயன்
தன்மாயையிற் பட்ட தற்பு.

Nānmukhan Tiruvandādi, 76.

† இனியறிந்தேன் ஈசற்கும் நான்முகற்குந்தெய்வம்
இனியறிந்தேன் எம்பெருமானுன்னை—இனியறிந்தேன்
காரணன் நீ கற்றவை நீ கற்பவை நீ நற்கிரிசை
நாரணன் நீ நன்கறிந்தேன் நான்.

ibid, 96.

Brahma (Nān-mukha.) I have learnt as well that You are my Lord. I have now learnt further that You are the cause of all. You are the end of all learning. You are certainly the object of all learning and of all good deeds. You are Nārāyaṇa. All this I have learnt very well indeed."

We next pass on to the other of his works called Tirucchanda Viruttam, a work of 120 stanzas cast in a peculiar alliterative metre which gives it the name. In this work the Āḷvār shows himself to be thoroughly acquainted with the whole of the Vaishṇava teaching for a complete exposition of which one has to be thoroughly acquainted with what is generally known as Śruti literature, the Vedas, Upanishads, and accessory literature necessary for their understanding. Then come the Purāṇas and the Itihāsas which are illustrative of what Śruti literature is supposed to expound. Lastly the teaching of the *Bhāgavatas* called *Pāncharātra* which it is that gives a clear exposition of the supremacy of Vishṇu, the way of service to Him to earn His grace, and ultimately that, for all that one might do, His grace and nothing else is the means to the attainment of salvation. While his Nānmukhan Tiruvandādi, the centum we have already discussed states in general terms, like the three centa of the other three Āḻvārs, this teaching, this work of Tirumaḻiśai seems to lay down more thoroughly his conviction in regard to this particular matter, and may, more or less, be regarded as a declaration of faith by the Āḻvār, and how he came to it, forming as such a sort of hand-book to his Vaishṇavism. Apart from the Vaishṇava teaching in this work, it has also some references to Vēngaḍam and we shall deal with these as we have done with the others.

In the first half of this work he describes clearly the fundamental teaching of the Vaishṇavas which makes Vishṇu the supreme deity. This, of course, he could establish only by reference to authorities such as are recognised by believers in the teaching of the Veda, direct and indirect. This Āḻvār brings into this part of the work, as though it were the really orthodox teaching, the *Pāncharātrāic* notions, the really peculiar ones, of the *Vyūhas*, *Vibhava*, etc., as is clear in stanza 17;* "Thou art of one form. Thou art of three forms. Thou art likewise of four forms. Thou art again of

* ஏகமூர்த்தி மூன்றுமூர்த்தி நாலுமூர்த்தி நன்மைசேர்
போகமூர்த்தி புண்ணியத்தின் மூர்த்தி எண்ணில் மூர்த்தியாய்
நாகமூர்த்தி சயனமாய் நலங்கடல் கிடந்து மேல்
ஆகமூர்த்தியாய வண்ணம் என்சொல்லாதி தேவனே. (17)

various forms for the enjoyment (by worship) of people; Thou art of forms suitable to the good that people may have done (in this or in previous births). Thou art thus of forms innumerable. Oh, the First one (God), how is it that Thou hast become the First one of different forms according to the wishes of your worshippers, having been abed on the great serpent in the great ocean?". The doctrines of the *Pāncharātra* are so inextricably mixed up in the works of these Āḷvārs that it would be a matter of very considerable difficulty to separate these as distinctive of the *Pāncharātrāic* teaching. None the less, they are very clear to those who have primed themselves with the necessary introductory preparation. Further he shows, in the course of the work, that he is acquainted with the teaching of the Śaiva Āgamas, and is well posted in the details of the Paurāṇic teaching of Hinduism. It is really this kind of a synthesis that perhaps transformed the Vedic Brāhmanism of old into the Hinduism, as we sometimes distinguish the one from the other. This is not the place nor the occasion to deal with that general question. It should be enough here to state it broadly that the so-called *Pāncharātrāic* teaching is not quite so recent as is often times asserted—nay it would be more justifiable to regard it as a teaching running concurrently with the Brahmanical teaching of sacrifices as the means to ultimate salvation. Much that is actually taught in the Gīta is scattered through the works of this Āḷvār, who mentions the work in unmistakable terms, as also in those of the other Āḷvārs, recognising the threefold path to salvation by *Karma* (deeds or works), *Gñāna* (true knowledge) and *Bhakti* (devotion and service). This Āḷvār comes to the conclusion that these recognised means, in the last resort, have to depend entirely upon His grace for receiving their fulfilment. In other words one can never attain to salvation whatever his position in regard to works, knowledge or service, unless he had served to gain the grace of the Supreme. Again and again the Āḷvār repeats in the work that he was not entitled to adopt the recognised method of Vaiḍīc practices for the attainment of salvation; but that he could hope to achieve salvation only by earning His grace efficaciously. There are services of various kinds laid down as part of Āgamāic teaching and expounded in the *charya* (service) chapters of these works, offering devoted service and worship to God, imaged in various forms and placed in particular localities with a view to worship and service offered therein in various ways. The orthodox way of worship involves knowledge of the Veda and performance of certain Vaidīc ceremonies for which every one is not competent. To those who cannot attain to salvation by that means, other kinds of service are indicated as equally efficacious, namely, services rendered to bring about this worship by building temples, providing the means and making the necessary arrangements for conducting this worship properly, both for the benefit of those that worship and for the much larger body of people who are not able to conduct that worship for themselves. Such as could really render service of various kinds, even of a manual character, and such services rendered with sincere devotion, entitle one to salvation almost in the same way as the service rendered by those who are learned in the Veda and could render service in the recognised orthodox fashion.

Having arrived at this conviction, the Āḷvār proceeds to expound it through this work of 120 stanzas, in a systematic form. He expounds the general principles of the faith in which is comprised the whole of the *Pāncharātrāic* teaching in the first section which may go down to almost the first third of the work. The actual *Pāncharātrāic* doctrines plainly come in stanza 17 already referred to in detail above, and that is enforced in stanza 29, not altogether in the same detail, but none the less unmistakably. This is repeated in stanzas 31 and 34 as well. After having expounded clearly the conception of the Supreme, in accordance with the teaching of the orthodox Vaidīc literature as well as the Āgamāic, he proceeds to consider in the next part of the work as to what actually should be done by those who had not the means by birth, capacity and qualifications to understand His inscrutable nature by the methods open to the enlightened. He lays down clearly that the orthodox and complicated way of propitiation by the highly enlightened is impossible for others; but there are ways of offering worship open to them which would be quite as efficacious to attain the ultimate object. This is the path of service, service rendered in various ways. In this section the worship of God in the various forms in which he is installed for worship in temples is next indicated as easily as possible, provided one is determined to pursue the path with sincerity and devotion. Having laid down this general principle, he describes in a number of stanzas his devotion to the image in the temples at Śrīrangam, at Kumbhakoṇam and in Conjeevaram, all dedicated to Vishṇu, pointing out, *inter alia* here and there, that that is a kind of service that even Gods like Brahma and Śiva have had to render to the Supreme in order to obtain the very power for the discharge of their respective functions even. Then he points out that, so long as one pursues this with complete sincerity and single-minded devotion, it would not matter who he is, he may be sure of God's grace. Then he proceeds to point out that, notwithstanding this devoted service, and the title that one gains in consequence to His grace, grace cannot be compelled and demanded as a matter of right. It must come as the outcome of the graciousness of the Supreme. So he lays down in the last part of the work that it is absolutely necessary for one, however sincere and devoted he be in his service to God, that he resign himself in His hands for the final attainment of grace. It is here that he takes occasion to point out that he had not had the good fortune to be born in the four castes *(kula)* nor to have had the opportunity to have studied the Veda and accessory literature, nor had he practised the control of the five senses and their activities. Thus having been driven to the only course open to him, he confesses that there is no means to gain salvation except by single-minded worship at His sacred feet. He makes this great confession in stanza 90 *

---

* குலங்களாய ஈரிரண்டிலொன்றிலும் பிறந்திலேன்
நலங்களாய நற்கலைகள் நாவிலும் நவின்றிலேன்
புலன்களைந்தும் வென்றிலேன் பொறியிலேன் புனித நின்
இலங்குபாதமன்றி மற்றோர் பற்றிலேனெம்மீசனே
நாவிலும். (90)

of the work, and, having said that, he lays down in the following thirty verses the greatness of God's grace, and resignation to His will as the natural means to salvation to all alike, stating, in so many terms, that the safest vessel by means of which to carry oneself across the ocean of *saṃsāra* is the sacred feet of God. In stanzas 100 and 101 he makes the point clearer by saying that he makes efforts to do his best to be perpetually contemplating on His lotus feet; but prays that He would so regard it; and follows it up in 103 by a further prayer to God, whom he describes as One who carries on His chest the Goddess Lakshmi, as the conduct prescribed in the Rig Veda, as the one of the colour of a heavily laden cloud, that He might enable him to recite His name without intermission. He comes to the conclusion at the end of the work that "having made me wander through various births, He has at last come to save me by making my mind devote itself to Him (without any delusion) as the sole Saviour".

Other points worthy of note in this work are where the Aḻvār speaks almost contemptuously of other Gods of repulsive appearance and of reputation hard to reconcile with godhead, and exhorts people to devote themselves to Vishṇu and destroy birth. In 72 there is a specific reference to Lakshmi and Bhūmi being His consorts; he also states that the lotus-born Brahma was his son, and his son is the one the half of whose body is Umā and whose vehicle is the bull, and states clearly that this relationship found described in Vedic works is certainly not without truth. In 87 he makes a declaration that his devotion goes to the feet of Him exhibited in the Veda as the Supreme, who is worshipped with conviction, arising out of learning, by him with an eye in the face (Śiva), the king of heaven (Indra) and the Lord of the flower (Brahma), alike. In stanza 90, he comes to the definite statement:— "I was not born in any one of the divisions which goes by the name *kulam* (class or caste). I am not learned in the good things which the four Vedas teach. I have not succeeded in gaining control over the five senses. I am still labouring in the meshes of the passions. Notwithstanding all this, I have no attachment but to Your holy feet". This autobiographical detail expressed with so much emphasis gives indication of at least an unknown, if not an inferior birth, and therefore his incapacity to follow the orthodox teaching and the prescribed methods for the pursuit of salvation. He is therefore driven to adopt other methods, to gain the same end, open to those of his condition. He ultimately expounds in the course of the work what those are, and indicates by his own example the efficaciousness of simple prayer by the recital of His name, provided only one exhibits, in the performance of this simple form of worship, unalloyed sincerity and absolutely exclusive devotion to the Supreme God. He is convinced, not without investigation of the prevalent alternatives, that throwing himself upon God's mercy is the surest way to the attainment of His grace provided the path is pursued with whole-hearted devotion.

This elaborate study of these early Āḻvārs gives us an insight into the condition of religion at the time that these flourished. We see from the works of these alone that the religion of worship and service to God, in some one form or another with a view to the attainment of His grace, is regarded as the most efficacious method of gaining the most cherished of human ends, the destruction of birth, growth, decay and death; all that is included in *samsāra*. As far as these Āḻvārs are concerned however, the only deity capable of showing this saving grace is Vishṇu, and the other deities who had perhaps a certain amount of following at the time, were of inferior capacity for this particular purpose. Coming down to the actual exercise of this devotion, we find that the methods prescribed as validly efficacious are those of service essentially, service by means of Vedic learning and Vedic rites, we might almost say primarily. Where this is found to be impossible, as in the case of the great majority of people, except in the case of the very *elite*, service of a simpler kind is recommended, and even this service may take a large variety of forms according to capacity and means. The best in the last resort, and well within the capacity of all, is the mere recital of the name of the deity; but the essence of the service of worship thus rendered is in the sincerity and single-mindedness of the devotion shown in the performance of the service. It would not matter what form of service devotion takes, salvation is certain; but not as the inevitable return for the service, but as a matter of grace by the deity, pleased with the devoted service rendered to him. This is what in Vaishṇava parlance is called *prapatti* resignation or surrender into the hands of the deity, placing oneself in the position of being deserving of His grace. If the details of this norm of worship found scattered through the works of these Aḻvārs could be collected together and examined as a whole, it will be found that that is almost in every detail the teaching of the Vaishṇava Āgamas, called *Pāncharātra*, which, in times much before this, was known as the teaching of the Bhāgavatas. These Bhāgavatas were a set of people who regarded Bhagavān Vāsudēva (Krishṇa) as the sole Supreme being capable of exercising His grace and giving salvation to people. They did not consider it necessary to sacrifice animals in the performance of *Yagñas* (the great sacrifices), and would preach the doctrine of *Ahimsa* in consequence. That teaching runs through and through the works of these Āḻvārs, so that what was merely the persuasion of a section of the people had become gradually transformed into one of general efficacy for all alike, though the prescribed method might vary in detail according to capacity.

The teaching of the Gīta is constantly there in addition to this, as well as what is sometimes described as Paurāṇic Hinduism, a distinction which it would be rather difficult to justify and almost impossible to make. So then with these Āḻvārs, we seem to be living in an age when modern Hinduism, as distinct from the Vedic Brahmanism which alone is generally taken to be described in the Vedas and Vedic literature, had gained great vogue. It would be much better to regard these two not in contra-distinction, but more or less as two phases or aspects of the same teaching, the only difference being a difference of emphasis.

The norms of worship being thus laid down, it follows, as night follows day, that the most popular feature of worship is the worship of forms of God visible to the eye, and understandable to the average intelligence of uncultured humanity. Abstract conceptions are brought down to definite forms perceivable by the senses and appealing even to the physical eyes, although in origin subjective. Worship of images, originally conceived in the mind and actually translated into material forms for congregational worship, comes to be the essence of general religious service. Worship of images or forms of Gods of various kinds, in temples, the undertaking of pilgrimages to these, devotional service of various kinds, material and personal in respect of these, all became part and parcel of this form of religion. We see this in full swing in the works of these Āḻvārs. It is not only Tirupati or Vēngaḍam that figures in the works of these Āḻvārs specifically; but a fairly large number of other places of repute as places of pilgrimage sacred to Vishṇu, are also mentioned. The references to Tirupati go sometimes into circumstantial detail to indicate, if not to describe to us in so many words, that the course of worship prescribed and conducted throughout the year had already attained to some considerable vogue. A specific feature like the worship on *dvādaśi* days, the festivals of *śravaṇa* and things like that, lets us know that the annual arrangements had already come into practice. These, taken along with the general statement made by a classical Tamil author like Māmūlanār, and the practice of worship of various deities in an important place like Conjeevaram referred to by Rudran Kaṇṇan would give us clear indication that the age of temple worship and worship conducted in the manner prescribed by the Bhakti school, had already come to prevail in full form. The teaching of the Vaishṇavism of Rāmānuja seems to be already found in full growth, if not perhaps in all its detail, and the three different bases of that teaching, the Vedic literature, the teaching of the Gīta and the Āgamāic teaching of the Pāncharātra are all of them found in these works as they are found in the works of Rāmānuja and his predecessors. We shall now pass on to Nammāḻvār, the central figure among these Āḻvārs.

CHAPTER VI.

NAMMALVAR.

NAMMALVAR AND HIS POSITION AMONG ALVARS.

We have already noted that the three Āḻvārs, called Mudal Āḻvārs by way of distinction, and Tirumaḻiśai Āḻvār who followed can be regarded as contemporaries on the basis of the tradition that they met with one another at Tiru Veḥkā in Kānchi, and even that Pēy Āḻvār was responsible for reclaiming him to Vaishṇavism from Śaivism. Whatever be the value of the tradition as such, there is enough evidence, internal evidence in their works, for us to take it that they cannot be regarded as far removed from each other in point of time, the closeness of the works going far enough to justify the position, apart from other extraneous evidence. It would therefore be in keeping with our present knowledge of the state of affairs to take it that these four may be regarded as of one age, and in a class by themselves, among the Āḻvārs. Next after them comes Nammāḻvār generally regarded by Vaishṇava tradition as the best and the greatest of them all, and his works have come to be regarded as quite a faithful rendering of all that is of value in the teaching of the

Veda, so that the *Tiruvāymoḻi* of Nammāḻvār is regarded generally as being a rendering of the Veda in Tamil. Not only that, the very name *Tiruvāymoḻi* (Sans. *Śruti*) seems intended to convey that meaning. We have high authority, the authority of the Śangam literature for *vāymoḻi* being just the rendering, and quite a correct rendering, of what the Sanskritists call *Śruti* as distinct from perhaps the Upanishads, although *Śruti* in a general popular sense includes not only the Veda proper, but all the literature dependent upon the Veda and cultivated in the world as accessory studies essential to the understanding of the Vedic texts. The earliest Tamils seem to have made the distinction between the Veda proper, and the Upanishads, by calling the first *vāymoḻi* and the second *maṛai*, which latter has now become more or less the popular name for all that is included in what might be called Vedic literature. That distinction between *vāymoḻi and maṛai* seems to have been real enough down to the time of Tirumangai Āḻvār in the middle of the 8th century, as some references in his work could be quoted to justify the position. The term *Tiruvāymoḻi* therefore would be an exact Tamil rendering of an expression like *Śrī Śruti*, *Śruti* of course, with the complimentary attribute *Śrī*. Speaking from the point of view of pure literature, Nammāḷvār may be regarded as a transition as it were between the first Āḷvārs, including in that designation the first four and the later ones down to Tirumangai Āḷvār. The first three Āḷvārs have cast their poems in the *veṇbā* metre in Tamil, and where the classical commentators on even the Tolkāppiyam quoted Poygai Āḷvar, all the stanzas quoted against that name happen to be in the *veṇbā* metre. Among them two are from the first Tiruvandādi of this Āḷvār. In respect of the fourth, however, there are 200 verses in the Prabhandha Four Thousand ascribed to him. The first 100 is in the *veṇbā* metre, like the works of the first three, and is as a matter of fact included in that section of the collection. In regard to the other centum which is really 120 stanzas, it is in the *vṛitta* metre, itself called Tirucchanda *Viruttam*, which would simply mean poem in *vṛitta* metre alliterative and adaptable to music. Therefore Tirumaḻiśai is in part with the Mudal Āḷvārs holding them by one hand and stretching out the other to come into connection with the rest of them from this point of view. Further, as a rule these early Āḷvārs, who are characterised as "*Singers of Classical Tamil*" by Tirumangai Āl̤vār, * are much more naturalistic and objective in their description, and do not indulge in the more or less well-developed imaginative emotionalism of Nammāl̤vār and the other later Al̤vārs. Nammāl̤vār's Tiruvāymol̤i carries this feature to perfection and has become the model, more or less, for all later literature of the school of Bhakti which have developed this side to a much greater extent even than these. While we would be justified in saying that the Mudal Āl̤vārs show fairly full acquaintance with Sanskrit literature, Paurāṇic and other, relating to the subject of Bhakti, Tirumal̤iśai Āl̤vār goes much farther afield in the exhibition of his knowledge of Sanskrit literature bearing upon Bhakti, even to the extent of exhibiting full acquaintance with the Āgamāic teaching of the Pāncharātra and of the Veda proper. Nammāl̤vār goes much farther and shows, in his extensive writings, a full grasp of the teachings of the Veda as a whole, or the Vaidic bases of Vishṇu Bhakti, that he may well be regarded an interpretor in Tamil of the Vedic lore on the particular subject.

---

* வெந்திறல் வீரரில் வீரரொப்பார்
வேதமுரைத்து இமையோர் வணங்கும்
செந்தமிழ் பாடுவோர் தாம் வணங்கும்
தேவரிவர் கொல் தெரிக்க மாட்டேன்

Periya Tirumol̤i, II, 8, 2.

Hence his principal works are regarded as each one expounding a particular Veda of the four Vedas and thus justifying the encomium bestowed on him by later writers, such as Kamban, "the learned one who had rendered the Veda in Tamil".

NAMMALVAR AND VENGADAM. Our purpose is not to expound the teaching of Nammāḻvār here, but to indicate his position in regard to the knowledge which he exhibits of Vēngaḍam. His works are, as they appear in the Prabandha collection in order (1) *Tiruviruttam* said to be an exposition of the Rig Veda; (2) *Tiruvāśiriyam* of the Yajur Veda; (3) the *Periya Tiruvandādi*, of the Atharva Veda, and the last but the best work of his the *Tiruvāymoḻi*, of the Sama Veda. Of these the third is in the *veṇbā* metre. The first is in the *vṛitta* metre. The second is in a metre which may be said to be rather characteristic of Tamil, and the last mostly *vṛitta* of different varieties. He may be regarded therefore purely from the literary point of view to have come in between these early Āḻvārs, and the later ones. What is really more to our point, the references to Vēngaḍam in the works of this Āḻvār are entirely of a different character as we shall notice. In the work Periya Tiruvandādi, which comes closest to the work of these early Āḻvārs, the references that he makes to Tirupati seem to be of a character similar to those of the others. As we pass on from them, we find him moving away more and more into the artificiality and high convention of Tamil literature.

We shall next proceed to the details regarding his references to the Vishṇu shrine at Tirupati. Unlike the Mudal Āḻvārs and even Tirumaḻiśai Āḻvār, it may be said of Nammāḻvār at the outset that such references as he makes to Tirupati are more or less of a character to meet the requirements of the literary artist. Like the later *kalambakam* writers who are often content with the mere mention of the name of the shrine they write about, so in the case of this Āḻvār the references are of a subordinate character and border quite on the mere mention of the name. He devotes one ten of the *Tiruvāymoḻi* to Tirupati itself, and there he says certain things which may be regarded as something much more specific than the mere references adverted to above. In this case, he makes explicit references to the great shrine at Tirupati. There are just one or two other tens where he does indeed refer to Tirupati, but the references are not of this explicit character, though they may be regarded as indubitable references to the particular shrine. He seems to be writing on the whole from what he had heard of the great reputation of the shrine for holiness, and has therefore to be regarded as writing of that shrine, as he does of very many others of holy reputation, without that intimate knowledge of the place that the other Āḻvārs exhibit in regard to Tirupati. There are actually seven references to Tirupati in the *Tiruviruttam.* They are more or less of the form of address where he apostrophizes some of the flower gardens as being of the country of Tirupati, or of Tirupati which has beautiful gems all round the hill glowing in daylight. The *Tiruvāśiriyam* has no direct references to Tirupati. The *Tiruvāśiriyam* and the Periya Tiruvandādi do not contain any direct reference to Tirupati as such, but stanza 7 of the latter contains a reference to Lakshmi being on the chest of Vishṇu, which is the exact meaning of the term Śrīnivāsa, the name of the God at Tirupati.

These three works taken together, however, form a methodical presentation of the Āḻvār's petition to the God to exhibit His saving grace. So he begins by saying that his object was to get rid of birth in this life of *samsāra*, and would appeal to Him who is ever on the look out for saving souls and who had put himself through a number of births to the same great purpose. The whole of the 100 stanzas are to the same purport, and the idea is presented in all the variety of literary form of which the Āḻvār shows himself to be a perfect master. In this centum the Āḻvār draws a comparison between those who have once had attained to eternal life and remained perpetually in the enjoyment of His immediate presence, and the great majority like himself still wallowing in the seemingly inextricable mire of worldly life, and naturally prays that he may be enabled to get rid of the entanglements of worldly life and be enabled to join the select company of those. Incidentally therefore he has to describe the great qualities of God, the praise of which and the resigning of oneself to His discretion, are the only means for the attainment of emancipation. This cannot be attained except by one's own effort, and the opportunity is offered for him to exert himself; and how he exercises himself to attain this end is what is expounded in the following works of his. In the *Tiruviruttam* he is made to expound as it were what is possible of achievement in this life, the realisation of the great qualities of the Supreme Being and the way of knowledge to attain to this experience. This is further expounded in the *Tiruviruttam* as, in the case of what relates to God, what has come into one's experience is something which is likely to be very small in comparison to the infinite character of His great qualities. It is those ideas that are expounded in the three works. The first may be regarded as a set of prayers offered to God with a view to gaining His sympathy for the attainment of salvation; the next one is devoted to a description of God, and how He works his purpose on earth; and then in the third, the means by which worldly life could be got rid of and the eternal life achieved by service, knowledge and devotion culminating in complete self-surrender are described. The Āḻvār comes to this conclusion in the third of these poems and this idea is carried forward in the main work of his, the *Tiruvāymoḻi*, that God has taken possession of him, and it is He, not the Āḻvār himself, who sings the verses, ascribed to him whether it be those of the Tiruvāymoḻi, or the other three works of this Āḻvār. The idea runs through and through these works, as in the case of the other Āḻvārs, that Vishṇu in any one of His forms is the Great Supreme, and that He works His purpose on earth in many forms. The other Gods who come in for worship by others are no more than certain forms or aspects of this One, and the worship that is offered to them is no more than worship offered to Him, only indirectly. That is the general basal idea which often times gets to be expressed in the course of these poems. * Stanzas 68, 71 and 72 of the Periya Tiruvandādi express these ideas, and states that idea, with which we are familiar in the first four Āḻvārs, that, in the body of Vishṇu, Śiva finds a place in His chest, and Brahma in His navel, and the other gods in other places so that all of them together constitute His body, Himself being the soul infusing life into them and making them do what they do.

The *Tiruvāymoḻi* has about 16 separate references to Tirupati of about the same character we referred to already in his other works. He devotes one ten completely to Tirupati itself, and, in one or two other tens further down in the

---

* கல்லும் கனைகடலும் வைகுந்தவானாடும்
புல்லென் றொழிந்தனகொல் ஏபாவம்—வெல்ல
நெடியான் நிறம் கரியான் உள்புகுந்து நீங்கான்
அடியேன துள்ளத் தகம். (68)

இனி நின்று நின்பெருமை யானுரைப்பதென்னே
தனி நின்ற சார்விலா மூர்த்தி—பனி நீர
அகத்துலவு செஞ்சடையான் ஆகத்தான் நான்கு
முகத்தான் நின்னுந்தி முதல் (71)

முதலாம் திருவுருவம் மூன்றென்பர் ஒன்றே
முதலாகும் மூன்றுக்குமென்பர்—முதல்வா
நிகரிலகுகாருருவா நின்னகத்ததன்றே
புகரிலகு தாமரையின் பூ. (72)

Periya Tiruvandādi.

course of the work, he is supposed to refer to Tirupati in particular, though Tirupati is not specifically referred to in these tens. The same general idea runs through and through. In this work he works out to the full the literary form that shows itself already in the *Tiruviruttam* which has become the characteristic of the later emotional forms of Vishṇu worship all over India, South as well as North. Love becomes the theme, and it is the pining away of a damsel for the company of her lover that is the form that is most affected, although often times maternal love, the love of the mother to the child in all its frolics, and the sympathetic suffering of the mother for a daughter pining away in a lovelorn condition in various aspects, constitute the other possible forms for this to take and find exposition in the *Tiruvāymoḻi* in as good and full a form as it could be found anywhere else. In the whole range of Tamil literature, this work forms the basis upon which is built the emotional worship; even such distant schools of thought as the Gujarat school of Vaishṇavism of Vallabhā-chārya and the Bengal school of Chaitanya drawing their inspiration therefrom. These schools differ only in mere detail, and sometimes in the local colour, but in essentials they are absolutely nothing more than what is found in the works of Nammāḻvār.

The *Tiruvāymoḻi* Thousand serves for the Āḻvār to depict the progress of a soul hankering for that association with God which is the lot of the emancipated elect *(Nityasūri)*. The work therefore begins with his giving the fullest expression to his devotion generally, and all the details of service by means of which that devotion can be made manifest. He struggles to find a way to describe Him and His qualities in a way acceptable to Him. This is service by prayer as it were, when rendered properly and adequately, to enable him to reach this goal of his ambition. Finding that it does not effectuate immediately in the much desired union, he tries to change his method, and see whether he could canvass it, not by the mere mechanical service, but by an effort at a correct exposition by way of knowledge, which implies the practice of *Yogic* concentration for acquiring that correct understanding. While this course gives him more satisfaction, it still falls short of enabling him to reach the goal, and he has recourse to the other course, the course of Bhakti, complete devotion, by means of love and self-surrender, as the fitting terminal of service to God. Then comes the feeling of realisation, and the Āḻvār expresses his gratification that he has ultimately achieved the end he strove so far to achieve.

In the course of the work therefore, all the thousand verses are divided into ten groups, each group containing ten stanzas, more often eleven than ten, and thus provides a Tamil literary classic, almost a model for this kind of expression of high emotion in all its glorious forms. Naturally therefore such a mode does not admit of much of objective description, and we fail to find, even in the references to Tirupati as such, the references to such details even of worship, or of festive celebration, as we occasionally do come upon in the earlier poets of this group. Even in the tens specially devoted to Tirupati the Āḻvār does not give us any definite knowledge of details which would warrant the inference of his direct acquaintance with the place, or the organisation of worship in the temple. Nevertheless he reminds us constantly that, for a true knowledge of God, one has to seek it in the Veda, "the flowering flame, that is the four Vedas, which contain sacred knowledge" in III, 1, 10.* The same idea recurs in another place where he refers to the same knowledge as "the nectar churned from

---

* சோதியாகி யெல்லா வுலகுந் தொழும்
ஆதிமூர்த்தி யென்றால் அளவாகுமோ
வேதியர் முழுவேதத் தமுதத்தை
தீதில் சீர் திருவேங்கடத்தானையே.

Tiruvāymoḻi, III, 3, 9.

out of the Veda cultivated by Brāhmaṇas", I, 3, 5. This section III is devoted entirely to Tirupati, and the details that he gives of Tirupati are more or less of a general character absolutely, a description of the natural features of the hill, In I, 3, 7, however, there is a reference to the offer of worship with flowers, water and the burning lamp, with which the heavenly ones offer worship. Anything more specific than this we do not get from him. In III, 7, 9., the Āḻvār counts himself as the devoted slave many times over of those devoted to Vishṇu, even if they should be born in a class below the four which go by the name of *kula* (caste) and lead the life of the *Chanḍāḷa.* * Such an idea often occurs not merely in the writings of this Āḻvār, but even among those of several others. While from this it is clear that it is possible for inferior mortals to attain to that correct understanding of God, and even of

---

* குலந்தாங்கு சாதிகள் நாலிலும் கீழிழிந்து எத்தனை
நலந்தானிலாத சண்டாள சண்டாளர்களாகிலும்
வலந்தாங்கு சக்கரத்தண்ணல் மணிவண்ணற்காளென்று உள்
கலந்தார் அடியார் தம்மடியார் எம்மடிகளே.

Tiruvāymoḻi, III, 7, 9.

வேதம் வல்லார்களைக்கொண்டு விண்ணோர் பெருமான் திருப்
பாதம்பணிந்து இவள் நோயிது தீர்த்துக்கொள்ளுது போய்
ஏதம் பறைந்து அல்ல செய்து கள்ளூடுகலாய்த்தூய்
கீதமுழவிட்டு நீரணங்காடுதல் கீழ்மையே.

ibid, IV, 7, 8.

nearness to his presence, it must be borne in mind that this should not be interpreted as any kind of an assertion of secular equality. We find a clear evidence of his condemnation of the habits of this class of people in IV, 6–8 in unmistakable terms. The actual kind of worship he prefers is referred to again in V, 2–9, which consists in the repetition of His name and the praise of His qualities, and the presentation to Him of worship in forms prescribed by the knowing, with flowers, incense, lamps, unguants, water and other such gifts. *

Coming down to the more general character of his devotion, we find him stating it clearly and unmistakably, in the ninth ten of the third section, † that what powers of poetry he

---

* மேவித்தொழுதுய்மினீர்கள் வேதப்புனிதனிருக்கை
நாவில் கொண்டச்சுதன் தன்னை ஞானவிதிபிழையாமே
பூவில் புகையும் விளக்கும் சாந்தமும் நீரும் மலிந்து
மேவித்தொழுமடியாரும் பகவரும் மிக்கதிவ்வுலகே.

ibid, V, 2, 9.

† சொன்னால் விரோதமிது ஆகிலும் சொல்லுவன் கேண்மினோ
என்னாவிலின் கவியானொருவர்க்குங் கொடுக்கிலேன்
தென்னா தெனாவென்று வண்டுமுரல் திருவேங்கடத்து
என்னானை என்னப்பன் எம்பொருமான் உளனாகவே.

ibid, III, 9, 1.

கொள்ளும் பயனில்லை குப்பைகிளர்த்தன்ன செல்வத்தை
வள்ளல் புகழ்ந்து நும்வாய்மை யிழக்கும் புலவீர்காள்
கொள்ளக்குறைவிலன் வேண்டிற்றெல்லாம் தரும்
கோதில் என்
வள்ளல் மணிவண்ணன் தன்னைக்கவிசொல்ல வம்மினோ.

ibid, III, 9, 5.

might have, he would devote only to Him of Tiruvēngaḍam and to none else. In the course of this very ten, he points out the uselessness of utilising this gift in praise of the rich ones among the world, and inveighs against such an improper use, giving one almost the idea that, in the age in which he lived, such was largely the prevalent practice. The definite reference to *Vaḷḷal* (patron) in the 5th verse of this ten, seems to be a clear and specific reference to this particular feature of the Tamil poets of this age, which may throw indirectly some light upon the time in which he flourished.

One other detail of a similar general character calls for notice. The Āḷvār expresses himself immensely gratified at the prevalence of devout service to Him as in the second ten of the fifth section. This idea recurs time and again, and he seems almost to repeat the idea so tersely expressed in stanza 87 of the first Tiruvandādi of Poygai Āḷvār. The similarity of notion is so great that the age was remarkable for the way of Bhakti coming into its own, as against other forms of religious service. A general review of these details taken together gives the impression that, at the time that these Āḷvārs flourished, Hindu society, if it should be so-called, was just returning from other forms of worship, or religious service, to this particular form and when the Āḻvār actually gloats in joy over the passing away of the *Kali Yuga* (age of sin) in stanza V, 2-3, and the coming of the *Kṛta Yuga* by the Gods themselves entering this way of service, and that the world had become actually full of those devoted to Vishṇu * who dance in joy and sing songs of devotion to Him, we seem to feel a sort of re-establishment of orthodox worship according to the school of Bhakti, the more so when he gets to exhort, in stanza 9 following of the same section, where he calls upon all to come and worship at the shrine of the holy One

---

* திரியும் கலியுகம் நீங்கித் தேவர்கள் தாமும் புகுந்து
பெரிய கிதயுகம் பற்றிப் பேரின்பவெள்ளம் பெருக
கரியமுகில் வண்ணனெம்மான் கடல்வண்ணன் பூதங்கள் மண்மேல்
இரியப்புகுந்திசை பாடி எங்குமிடங்கொண்டனவே.

ibid, V, 2, 3.

மேவித்தொழுதுய்மினீர்கள் வேதப்புனிதனிருக்கை
நாவில் கொண்டச்சுதன்தன்னை ஞானவிதி பிழையாமே
பூவில் புகையும் விளக்கும் சாந்தமும் நீரும் மலிந்து
மேவித்தொழுமடியாரும் பகவரும் மிக்கதிவ்வுலகே.

ibid, V, 2, 9.

மிக்க உலகுகள் தோறும் மேவிக்கண்ணன் திருமூர்த்தி
நக்கபிரானோடயனும் இந்திரனும் முதலாக
தொக்கவமரர் குழாங்கள் எங்கும் பரந்தன தொண்டீர்
ஒக்கத் தொழுகிற்றிராகில் கலியுகமொன்றுமில்லையே.

ibid, V, 2, 10.

of the Veda, and save themselves by singing the praise of Achyuta without deviating from the course of knowledge. When he makes a positive statement that the world had got to be full of those who worship Him with flowers, incense, lamps, unguants and water, those being both men in worldly life and those that have renounced it alike, he seems almost positively to affirm such a reversion to orthodoxy. This idea he elaborates somewhat in the following stanza where he states that the world is already full of not only the Supreme Vishṇu (Kaṇṇan as he is called here), but of the other Gods of the Hindu pantheon, and exhorts the devoted ones of the earth to offer similar worship to all, and get rid of the sinful *Kali Yuga*.

One other feature of some importance to us for the history of Tirupati is the notion that runs through and through, that God is really one, and that one is Vishṇu in any one of His innumerable aspects. Such a notion is scattered all through his works, and, in some places, they get to be mentioned specifically. The general notion is that all things existing of all kinds, merely constitute the body, the soul infusing all being His self. In expressing this general notion, the Āḻvār sometimes indulges in the specific statement that Brahma, Śiva, Indra, and other Gods of high rank constitute parts of His body. Śiva is generally allotted a place on the chest of Vishṇu, and Brahma in the navel. In this specific statement, he speaks almost in the same terms as the earlier Āḷvārs of Brahma, Śiva and Indra constituting each a part of His body, a mere part of His body, much as *Śrī* (Lakshmi) is supposed to be, although Nammāḷvār does not come down to the level of putting these on a footing with Vishṇu's weapons like the disc and the conch. * This firm conviction, and the description in terms alike, have their light to shed upon the controversy regarding Tirupati at one time, that the representation of the deity in the shrine was that of Śiva or Skanda-Subrahmaṇya, and it had to be proved that the deity represented there is Vishṇu and no other.

---

* ஏறாளும் இறையோனும் திசைமுகனும் திருமகளும்
கூறாளும் தனியுடம்பன் குலங்குலமாயசுரர்களை
நீறாகும்படியாக நிருமித்துப்படை தொட்ட
மாறாளன் கவராத மணிமாமை குறைவிலமே.

ibid, IV, 8, 1.

தாளதாமரையானுன்னுந்தியான்
வாள் கொள் நீள் மழுவாளியுன்னாகத்தான்
ஆளராய்த்தொழுவாருமமரர்கள்
நாளு மென் புகழ்கோ உன் சீலமே.

ibid, IX, 3, 10.

The fervour of the Āḻvār's devotion begins, as in ordinary cases, with prayer, intense and devoted though that prayer be. From that it gradually advances to contemplation, contemplation of the divine in various forms and in essence, and ultimately it rises to the pitch of being absorbed and attaining to the condition of complete similarity, to almost the sameness with the deity. When he works up to this condition, the Āḻvār makes it clear by telling us that the very poems in which he describes his experiences of devotion to God are poems sung not by him, but by the God himself within him, * as if in His infinite mercy to the struggling soul, He infuses his own spirit within the struggling individual, and takes it through even composing

---

* செஞ்சொற்கவிகாள் உயிர்காத்தாட்செய்மின்
திருமாலிருஞ்சோலை
வஞ்சக்கள்வன் மாமாயன் மாயக்கவியாய் வந்து என்
நெஞ்சும் உயிரும் உள்கலந்து நின்றார் அறியாவண்ணம் என்
நெஞ்சும் முயிருமவையுண்டு தானேயாகி நிறைந்தானே.

ibid, X, 7, 1.

நண்ணா அசுரர் நலிவெய்த நல்ல அமரர் பொலிவெய்த
எண்ணாதனகள் எண்ணும் நன்முனிவர் இன்பம் தலைசிறப்ப
பண்ணார் பாடலின் கவிகள் யானாய்த் தன்னைத்தான் பாடி
தென்னாவென்னும் என்னம்மான் திருமாலிருஞ்
சோலையானே.

ibid, 5.

[*Compare other stanzas in this Ten as well.*]

and singing His own praise. When this feeling settles down in him, he realises he had then reached the goal of his ambition, and had become one like God himself, always in His presence and enjoying His company for food, water and the very air for breathing. Coming to this mystic position, the Āḻvār feels he had reached the goal of his soul's journey.

In the course of this discipline, the Āḻvār gives expression to his devotion to God in all his innumerable forms, the *Vyūhas*, the *Vibhavas* and the *Archa*; that is, the emanations of God for various purposes, His coming down on earth in various forms, and the various material forms in which He is worshipped by those devoted to Him. Naturally therefore, Rama, Krishṇa, and all the well-known *Avatārs* on the one side, and the various images which are forms of God enshrined in temples alike, come in for their share of reference. * The more recondite references to the other forms for specific purposes are also found, if not with the same frequency. Not only these; but the Āḻvār does actually put himself in all kinds of attitudes

* மேயபுன் வேங்கடம், காயாமலர் வண்ணன்
பேயார் முலையுண்ட வாயான் மாதவனே.

ibid, X, 5, 6.

known to literature * for expressing high emotion. We may therefore conclude that Nammāḻvār exemplifies *par excellence* the methods of personal devotion to the deity with a view ultimately to the attainment of that realisation which is the goal of the mysticism of this school of *Bhakti*.

---

* திருமாலிருஞ்சோலை மலையே திருப்பாற்கடலே
யென்றலையே
திருமால் வைகுந்தமே தன்திருவேங்கடமே யெனதுடலே
அருமா மாயத்தெனதுயிரே மனமே வாக்கே கருமமே ...
ஒருமாநொடியும் பிரியானென் னூழிமுதல் வனொருவனே.
—*ibid*, X, 7, 8.

CHAPTER VII.

OTHER ALVARS.

THE OTHER ALVARS. Passing on from Nammāḻvār, we pass on to the rest of this group, seven in number. (1) Madhurakavi, whose work is included in the Prabandham, consists of ten verses expressing his indebtedness to Nammāḻvār as his *Guru* (teacher). His personality as such therefore gets merged in Nammāḻvār. Then follow the names of (2) Kulaśēkhara, (3) Periya Āḻvār, though his actual name is Vishṇuchitta, (4) his foster-daughter Āṇḍāḷ. The tenth is called in Tamil, Tonḍar Aḍi Poḍi Āḻvār, or in Sanskrit Bhaktāngrirēṇu. Then Tiruppāṇ Āḻvār, called Yōgivāha in Sanskrit, and lastly Tirumangai Āḻvār. Of these six, Nos. 10 and 11 may be disposed of at once. No. 10 is credited with a hundred and ten verses of the *Prabandha* all devoted to Ranganātha at Śrīrangam. He was born not far from the place, but lived all his life and was devoted entirely to the deity in that shrine, and no more. The next one Yōgivāha also belongs to a similar category and his devotion is to the temple at Śrīrangam, and none else. The other four have more poems to their credit, and make references to Tirupati. The general character of their devotion however, was as single-minded as that of Nammāḻvār ; but they have chosen somehow or other to exhibit their unalloyed affection to God, not by adopting the method of Nammāḻvār exclusively, of that intimate affection of the young woman in love pining away for the company of her lover. While we cannot say that he has altogether no other relationships giving rise to similar affection and the painfulness of the deprivation of that affection, this is the form which appealed most in his case. But in the case, at any rate of Periya Āḻvār, it is rather the affection of the parent for the frolics of the child; in the case of the daughter however, it was the unalloyed love to Ranganātha at Śrīrangam which terminated only in her marriage to Him. Periya Āḻvār, however has 473 verses to his credit in the first thousand. The first ten of this is in glorification and praise of Vishṇu in general terms. The rest are devoted to the *Krishṇāvatāra* of Vishṇu and describe, with touching affection and fulness of detail, the frolics of child Krishṇa, and Krishṇa as a young lad still engaged in the occupation of his temporary residence, the cowherd village where he was being brought up without his identity being known to his enemy uncle Kamsa.

THE CHARACTER OF THE TIRUMOLI OF PERIYA ALVAR. The next following tens are devoted to various purposes. Two or three of these give expression to the feeling of a love-lorn damsel pining away in her love for Krishṇa, and the sorrow of the mother for the daughter who had elected to follow the course of her affection and abandon herself in favour of the object of her love. The last ten of the third section and the following tens are in various ways intended to exhibit why one ought to devote himself to the worship of Vishṇu in various of His manifestations. This is generally done by choosing certain incidents in the life of one or other of the many manifestations of Vishṇu on earth. The tenth ten of the IIIrd section is a rendering of what Hanumān said to Rāma to convince him that he had actually seen Sīta, describing various incidents of his conversation with her to confirm the identity. The next following sections are devoted to a conversation between those that have realised God and others who wished to realise Him. The next three are devoted to Tirumālirumśōlai and Tirukkōṭṭiyūr to enforce the need of devotion to Him. The next following ten is instruction to those in worldly life to persuade them into devotion to

Him. The next ten enforces the necessity of naming children after Him, and calling them by such names, as one way of reminding themselves of His presence. The next three are devoted to the holy place of Dēvaprayāga and Śrīrangam Then follows in the tenth ten of section IV, his self-surrender to God while yet in active life, so that He may, in the last moments of the Āḻvār's life, receive him into His favour. In section V, the Āḻvār gives expression to his feeling that God is, already near him, and realises His immanence in Him. He discards all those ailments to which human beings are heir as having no more place in him, and ultimately gives expression, in the last two tens, to his feeling of the immanence of God in him and of the good that he derived from Him. While giving expression therefore to the progress of a believing soul's devotion to God till it realises God in him, the Āḻvār does make a number of references to various places sacred to Vishṇu in which he is particularly interested. Śrīrangam, Tirumālirumśōlai and Tirukkōṭṭiyūr, in addition to his own native place, Śrīvilliputtūr are his favourite places. But there are a few references, two or three of them, to Tirupati which he seems to have known, at least to have heard of. He has some references to places even in the distant north, as if to indicate they were places of holy reputation to Vishṇu, and therefore to be cherished by Vaishṇavas.

His section of the *Tiruvāymoḻi* specifically named Periya Āḻvār Tirumoḻi is a very good illustration of that section of devotional works in which the affection that is shown by the soulful devotee to God takes that form of affection which a mother exhibits to her child in all its various frolics of babyhood. In his case, it takes the form of the youthful love of Krishṇa which is so beautifully described in the Bhāgavata. He is certainly not oblivious of the other popular manifestations of Vishṇu in the form of Rāma, which also come in for treatment in a considerable part of his work. That is not all. There are incidental references to many other of the beneficent manifestations of Vishṇu in various forms. The references to Tirupati or Vēngaḍam are so far only two in the 473 stanzas of this Āḻvār's work. The only historical references that we find in his works are a reference in two places, Tirupallāndu II, and section IV, 4, 8 to the *Purōhita* (high priest) of the Pāṇḍya monarch contemporary with him by name Śelvan, who had done much for God manifesting Himself in Tirukkōṭṭiyūr, and had been instrumental in the bringing about of the Āḻvār's visit to the Pāṇḍya capital. In regard to the Pāṇḍyan himself, the Āḻvār has just two references. The first is in IV, 2, 7 to a Neḍumāran ruler of Ten-Kūḍal (the southern Kūḍal, another name for Madura) carrying a death-dealing spear, as being devoted to Tirumālirumśōlai. We have certainly also a specific reference in this Āḻvār's works to the belief * that Rudra, Brahma, and Indra, though worshipped as Gods are not capable of granting the best of all boons that of getting rid of births.

NACCHIYAR TIRUMOLI OF ANDAL. Next follow 143 stanzas ascribed to the lady devotee generally known by the name Āṇḍāḷ or Gōdā (Tam. Kōdai, also periphrastically described in Tamil, Śūḍikkoḍuttāḷ, one that gave the flowers that she herself wore.) She is generally described as a foundling child, and therefore regarded as an *Avatāra* of *Bhūmi (Goddess of Earth)* herself. Periya Āḻvār picked her up from his flower garden, and brought her up as his own dear child. He had devoted himself to the service of making garlands of flowers and presenting them for daily service to the God in the temple at Śrīvilliputtūr which was his native

* எருத்துக் கொடியுடையானும் பிரமனு மிந்திரனும் மற்றும்
ஒருத்தரும் இப்பிறவியென் னும் நோய்க்கு மருந்தறிவாரு மில்லை
மருத்துவனாய் நின்ற மாமணி வண்ணா மறுபிரவி தவிரத்
திருத்தி உன் கோயிற் கடைப்புகம் பெய்த் திருமாலிருஞ்
சோலை யெந்தாய்.

Periya Āḻvār Tirumoḻi, V, 3, 6.

place. This daughter of his who had attained to the age of discretion, when the father was away for his ablutions after making the garlands etc., ready, used to take them without being noticed, put them on, and look before a mirror just to see that they all fitted very well, and then place them again as before. This was discovered by the father one day, who, in great pain, his disgust struggling against the affection for his own child, refrained from presenting the flowers to the God and remained fasting. God is said to have appeared to him in a dream, and asked for those very garlands as being particularly acceptable to Him after being used by the daughter. She grew up a young woman, and would not marry anybody else except God himself, and had to be, with God's approval, taken over to Śrīrangam and left there in the temple. It is said that she was miraculously accepted by God and disappeared in His image. Miracles apart, her poems give expression to the feeling of a damsel grown to the age of discretion devoting herself to God Vishṇu, we might almost say exclusively in the form of Krishṇa, and enjoying herself in the contemplation of various of the activities of young Krishṇa and of the manifestations of Vishṇu generally.

THE SPECIAL FEATURES OF HER WORK. The first section of her poems consists of 30 stanzas and is devoted to the worship of the image of a goddess after early morning bath in the first month of the year, *Mārgaḻi* (November—December.) That is devoted to young Krishṇa. The next section of ten is devoted to the worship of *Kāma*, the God of Love, in the month of January, which young women of marriageable age generally perform. In that ten there are two references to the God at Tirupati. The next four sections are devoted to the mischievous frolics of Krishṇa destroying their houses built in sand, and interrupting the girls at play, and begging him to give back the garments that he had taken away from them while they were at bath and carried to the top of a tree, and features of that kind. There are two or three references to Tirupati in the conventional way in these sections. The next following section VI is devoted to the details of the ceremony of her marriage with Krishṇa that she herself dreamt of. The next ten is devoted to a description of the *Pānchajanya* conch that Vishṇu carries in His left hand as a special feature of His. Section VIII is devoted entirely to Tirupati, and each stanza in it does mention Tirupati. But the references are all of them conventional as already stated, and give us no details of a realistic character that we find in the *Mudal* Aḻvārs. This may be explained as being due perhaps to her not having visited the place, and referring to this as only a distant holy place dedicated to Vishṇu. The next section is devoted to Tirumālirumśōlai, and the next ten which contains two references to Vēngaḍam, devotes itself to the description of a love-lorn damsel describing her suffering to her companion

The next ten follows almost the same theme, but this time it is the mother's sorrow for the love-sickness of the daughter. The following section is an earnest entreaty by the love-lorn damsel to be taken to where Krishṇa was, and the next is a prayer that she might be allowed to console herself by contact with the dress, etc., worn by Krishṇa. The last section purports to describe her having seen the Supreme One in Brindāvanam. Here again we see the struggle of a loving soul, this time, a young lady, making its progress step by step to the ultimate realisation of the object of love. Some writers and commentators would describe it as superhuman (*ati-mānusha*). While the father pursues his course like a grown up man of mature learning and wisdom, the daughter pursues the same course in her own characteristic way by dedicating herself to Him in love and realising God by that means. The hagiologists who have laid themselves out to write the lives of these saints locate these two Āḻvārs, the father and daughter, by giving them a date not far remote from the date given to Nammālvār. While the style of the poems ascribed to these and the art of the poetry alike may support the contention that they could not be far removed from Nammālvār, the details that we referred to already to a contemporary Pāṇḍya monarch would seem to indicate that these should have lived some time in the seventh century. That may be taken to be more or less roughly the period during which they flourished. That they were father and daughter perhaps we can infer from stanza III, 8, 4 * where Periya Āḻvār almost seems to be autobiographical when he states it that "he was the father of an only daughter whom he brought up like Lakshmi herself and whom the red-eyed Vishṇu carried away from him as His own". While this is in keeping with the subject-matter and the mode of expression of the ten, which is that it is the wailing of the mother whose dear daughter had abandoned her and gone away with her lover, and comes in naturally there, it

---

* ஒரு மகள் தன்னையுடையேன் உலகம் நிறைந்த புகழால்
திருமகள் போலவளர்த்தேன் செங்கண்மால் தான்
கொண்டு போனான்
பெருமகளாய்க்குடிவாழ்ந்து பெரும்பிள்ளைபெற்றவசோதை
மருமகளைக்கண்டுகந்து மணாட்டுப்புறஞ்செய்யுங்கொலோ.

Periya Āḻvār Tirumoḻi, III, 8, 4.

would still bear the inference that the Āḻvār is here perhaps, not altogether unwittingly, giving expression to a fact of history; at any rate, this would confirm that Periya Āḻvār and Anḍāḷ were related in the manner generally described.

ALVAR KULASEKHARA. The next in point of time comes Āḻvār Kulaśēkhara, the ruler of the Chēra country (Cochin and Travancore), and to whom the hagiologists ascribe a date almost the same as that of Periya Āḻvār, making the two somewhat older than Nammāḻvār. But the details that we can gather regarding his position among South Indian rulers of his time would give clear indications of a later date some time in the 7th century probably. He has 105 stanzas to his credit included in the First Thousand of the Prabandha Four Thousand, and this group of ten tens goes by the specific name Perumāḷ Tirumoḻi as if to indicate the characteristic title of these rulers of the Chēra country of the Perumāḷs in Kulaśēkhara Perumāḷ. The collection goes by the name Perumāḷ Tirumoḻi to be in keeping more or less with the designations of the other sections of this group, namely Periya Āḻvār Tirumoḻi, and Nācchiyār Tirumoḻi of the first two. The first three sections of the Perumāḷ Tirumoḻi are devoted to the temple at Śrīrangam, to which Kulaśēkhara was particularly devoted, as in fact the other two go there for their emancipation. There is nothing in these three tens excepting an expression of his extreme devotion which finds vent in his longing to be there in the temple so that the dust of the feet of those who come to worship Ranganātha in the temple might fall on him. The first ten is a graphic description of the image enshrined in the temple. The second expresses the longing to be there and enjoy the holy dust from the feet of the other devotees, and in the third he describes himself as something very distinct from the rest of the world in his single-minded devotion to Ranganātha. In these three he gives himself titles indicative of his position among South Indian rulers. In the tenth stanza of the second ten, he calls himself ruler of Kolli (Quilon), Kūḍal (Madura) and Kōḻi (Uraiyūr), the Chōḻa capital near Trichinopoly, and in stanza 9 of the next section he calls himself the ruler of Kongu.*

---

* அல்லி மாமலர் மங்கைநாதன் அரங்கன் மெய்யடியார்கள் தம்
எல்லையிலடிமைத்திறத்தினில் என்றும் மேவுமனத்தனாம்
கொல்லி காவலன் கூடல் நாயகன் கோழிக்கோன்
குலசேகரன்
சொல்லினின் தமிழ்மாலை வல்லவர் தொண்டர் தொண்டர்க
ளாவரே.

Perumāl Tirumoḻi, II, 10.

அங்கை யாழி அரங்கனடியிணை
தங்கு சிந்தை தனிப்பெரும் பித்தனாய்
கொங்கர் கோன் குலசேகரன் சொன்ன சொல்
இங்கு வல்லவர்க்கேதமொன்றில்லையே.

ibid, III, 10.

Combined this would mean that he was some sort of an overlord of all South India, at any rate, of Tamil India. The next ten is devoted to Tirupati. As in the previous thirty, here again he longs to render devoted service at the holy shrine in Tirupati, and would rather be any one of the things or beings on the hill, the water-bird, or fish, or a menial servant in the temple, or the *Champaka* tree, the door-step, or in fact anything else, and concludes with the determination that he would not exchange the lordship of the heavenly world for being anything in fact on the hill of Tirupati. Although in all the eleven stanzas he refers to Tirupati by name, he does not give any specific detail, apart from natural features, in relation to the God and worship in the temple, thus being exactly in the position of Nammāḻvār and Periya Āḻvār and Āṇḍāḷ, and no more. The next ten, the fifth ten, is devoted to Vittuvakkōḍu in Travancore, to the God in which he expressed himself completely devoted; and the manner in which he gives expression to this single idea is so natural and moving. In the first stanza he describes himself in attachment to the God much as a baby beaten by the mother still returns to her. In the next following he likens himself to a good wife attaching herself to even a bad husband who spurns her, and then again he makes his attachment to God that of the loyal subject attached to, and dependent upon, the sovereign even negligent of his duty of protection. He goes on through the ten the same way. The last detail referred to above seems almost reminiscent of one of the verses in the Kuṛaḷ*. The next section is devoted to expressing his dissatisfaction at the want of response to his fervent prayers. This comes in the form of *Gōpikas* blaming Krishṇa for showing himself irresponsive to their appeals. The next ten again is one of disappointment where he puts himself in the position of Dēvaki, the mother of Krishṇa, who though she actually did give birth to Krishṇa, was deprived of the enjoyment, altogether of the frolics, of the baby. The third ten again expresses, as if in contrast to the one preceding, Kausalyā's enjoyment of tending baby Rāma. The next one gives expression to the bewailing brought about under tragic circumstances of Rāma's banishment, and Daśaratha bewailing the fate that brought this about. The last ten is devoted to the celebration of the deity in Chitrakūṭa (Chidambaram), and this ten recounts the story of the Rāmāyaṇa completely, but in an abridged form. Here again, we have the same progress in the realisation of the faithful devotee who, after many struggles and

* No. 542.

disappointments, reaches ultimately to the end desired of God-realisation, according to the ideals of Vaishṇava devotion. All that we learn from this Āḻvār is that Tirupati gets a very high place among the holy places of Vishṇu, and a royal personage such as the ruler of Travancore, would in fact aspire to be the very door-step of the holy shrine, thus giving indication of the high esteem in which the shrine was held as a holy place.

THE THREE OTHERS. Reverting for a moment to the three names, namely, Madhura Kavi, Toṇḍar Aḍippoḍi, and Tiruppāṇ Āḻvār, the first is one whose contribution to the Prabandham is only one ten describing his devotion to his *Guru* Śaṭakōpa to enforce the doctrine that once the really satisfactory teacher is secured, all else is secured for the attainment of the highest. Toṇḍar Aḍippoḍi, who has a large number of verses, is so entirely devoted to Śrīrangam that he has practically no room for any direct reference to other shrines, as it were. In regard to Tiruppāṇ Āḻvār, however, though he is also one who lived all his life not far from Śrī-rangam—in fact he is placed in Uṛaiyūr not far from Śrīrangam—he has only one ten—all that he wrote apparently. In that one ten which is given entirely to describe the image of Ranganātha in the holy shrine at Śrīrangam, he finds means to refer to Vēngaḍam or Tirupati in two places which would indicate the great importance attached to the shrine at the time. The references, however, are of a general kind, but in both cases, the reference is to the image enshrined in Vēngaḍam being that of God almost as much as the image enshrined in Śrīrangam.

TIRUMANGAI ALVAR: PERIYA TIRUMOLI. We shall now pass on to the Periya Tirumoḻi and other poems of Tirumangai Āḻvār. Of these latter, two are included in the group Periya Tirumoḻi, namely, Tirukkuṛum Tāṇḍakam, and Tiruneḍum Tāṇḍakam, and three others included in the *Iyarpā* thousand—which forms a separate section—namely, Tiruveḻukkūṛṛiṛukkai, Śiriya Tirumaḍal and Periya Tirumaḍal making a total of 1,134 stanzas in all of varying lengths. Judging by quantity, his is the largest contribution to the Prabandha, and this Prabandha includes more verses of his than of any other Āḻvār, and the character of the poetry itself is much more elaborate in particulars so that the orthodox regard his works as a whole, as more or less an exposition of that of Nammāḻvār. Tirumangai Āḻvār happens to have been born in the Tānjore District and came of the Kaḻḻar community. He was a military man essentially, and had, as usual in those days, a small civil government under the Chōḷas, his government lying in the modern Shiyāli Taluk. He happened to fall in love with a foundling daughter of a physician of the locality who had no children of his own. She stipulated, as a condition of her marriage with him, that he should feed 1,008 Brahmans a day for a year before she could consent to become his wife. He agreed to do that, and had begun to even waylay people and commit dacoity upon them for the purpose of securing the wherewithal for the purpose; it is said that, in order to exhibit His grace to the devotee and reclaim him, God Vishṇu himself came at the head of a bridal party in the garb of one recently married with all the wealth and ornaments suitable to the occasion. In stripping him of his jewels in the course of a dacoity, the Āḻvār was so thorough-going that he fell prostrate to pull off the tightly fitting rings on the toes of the God. He got the inspiration immediately and burst into song confessing access of devotion to Nārāyaṇa in complete self-surrender. This constitutes the first ten of the thousand ascribed to him. Thereafter he devoted himself entirely to benefactions to various Vaishṇava shrines known at the time both in the south and some few elsewhere in the north. His works contain more references which would lead to the fixing of his age than those of any other Āḻvār, and specifically Nammāḻvār whose work is about as much in quantity as that of this Āḻvār. From these references, it is possible to fix his date in the reign of the great Pallava ruler Nandivarman, whose period would be the whole of the 8th century. This is supported by a number of historical incidents alluded to in the course of this work. He sets about celebrating the shrines in the north, Dēvaprayāga on the Himalayas, and comes regularly down through Badrināth, for which he devotes two tens, then Sāḷagrāma, and then the forest of Naimiśa. He then comes down to Śingavēḷkunṟam, as it is called, the modern Ahōbalam, and then enters the Tamil country. The first shrine that he celebrates in this region is Tiruvēngaḍam, for which he gives four of his tens. Before proceeding to that, we may in passing note that, speaking of Ahōbalam, he refers to the place as almost inaccessible as it may be said to be to some extent, even now. In regard to the four tens they are professedly celebrating Vishṇu as He presents himself in Tirupati. But the references are more or less of a general and of the ordinary Vaishṇava religious character. There is one reference in stanza 2 of the first ten where the God there is referred to as of the white-blue and of the saphire blue colour. This is the ordinary description of Vishṇu as being of the white colour in the first *Yuga*, of golden red in the second, saphire blue in the third and dark blue in the fourth, thereby making it clear that it is a form of Vishṇu that is represented there. In stanza 5 of the same section, He is referred to, among other features, as possessed of eight arms, and of being on the Himalayas. These two might lead to the inference that perhaps it is Śiva. But that is negatived immediately by the next statement that He is the same deity that is on the hill at Tirumālirum-sōlai*. The other references are more or less of a general character such as that in stanza 9 of the fourth ten where the deity is spoken of as the one worshipped by Brahma, Śiva and Indra.†

---

* வண்கையான் அவுணர்க்கு நாயகன் வேள்வியில் சென்று மாணியாய்
மண்கையால் இரந்தான் மராமரம் ஏழும் எய்தவலத்தினான்
எண்கையான் இமயத்துள்ளான் இருஞ்சோலைமேவிய எம்பிரான்
திண்கைம்மா துயர்தீர்த்தவன் திருவேங்கடம் அடை நெஞ்சே.

Periya. Tiru. I, 8, 5.

† கூடியாடி யுரைத்ததே யுரைத்தாய் என்னெஞ்சமென்பாய் துணிந்துகேள்
பாடியாடிப் பலரும் பணிந்தேத்திக் காண்கிலா
ஆடுதாமரையோனு மீசனும் அமரர்கோனும் நின்றேத்தும் வேங்கடத்து
ஆடுகூத்தனுக்கின்றடிமைத்தொழில் பூண்டாயே.

ibid, II, 1, 9.

But, in stanza 5 and the next two following two stanzas of that section, the Āḻvār makes a reference that his own mind was attracted to the religion of the Jains and Buddhists at one time, and had then been drawn towards the deity at Vēngaḍam. There is nothing however that we know of that he was actually a Buddhist or a Jain. It may be a mere reference to the vacillation of mind amidst the prevalent wordliness. Such a reference would warrant the inference that Buddhism and Jainism were in his time religions which counted a considerable number of votaries in this part of the country. The reference which one finds in stanza 7 of the ten devoted to Tiru-evvuḷūr (modern Tiruvaḷḷūr) * that Śiva formed a part of His body, and had his position on the right side of His chest, is one among many such references scattered throughout the work, so that this only confirms what we find in the early Aḻvārs describing plainly the features of Śiva found on the image. The last stanza of the ten devoted to Tiruvallikkēṇi (Triplicane) has a historical reference of importance. The stanza states clearly that the southern Toṇḍamān (Toṇḍaiyar-Kōn) king constructed

---

* *திங்களப்புவானெரிகாலாகி திசைமுகனார்*
தங்களப்பன் சாமியப்பன் பாகத்திருந்தவண்டுண்
தொங்கலப்பு நீள்முடியான் சூழ்கடல் சூழநின்ற
எங்களப்பனெம்பெருமான் எவ்வுள் கிடந்தானே.

***ibid*, II, 2, 7.**

for the temple the gardens and the rampart walls surrounding the tall buildings about the temple, the pavilion with it, and so on. This would mean in fact that this particular Pallava sovereign laid out and constructed the town round the temple. Because of a few inscriptions in the temple by Vairamēgha Pallava one may be tempted to infer that this is a reference to that great Pallava who was the son of Nandivarman Pallava, who, we stated already, was a contemporary of this Āḻvār. It seems however to be a reference to that early Toṇḍamān Chakravarti, so much associated with Tirupati, as the author of the laying out of the town and the building of the shrine as the early Āḻvārs have a great deal to say about this temple. Coming down to the eighth ten of the second section the Āḻvār celebrates the Ashṭabujam shrine in Kānchi. The characteristic feature of the deity here is eight hands to which we already made reference in regard to Tiruvēngaḍam. Speaking of the deity there he makes a specific reference to the place as having been worshipped by those who sang in *Śen Tamiḻ* (classical Tamil)*. These

---

* வெந்திறல் வீரரில் வீரரொப்பார்
வேதமுரைத்திமையோர் வணங்கும்
செந்தமிழ்பாடுவார் தாம் வணங்கும்
தேவரிவர் கொல் தெரிக்கமாட்டேன்
வந்துகுறளுருவாய் நிமிர்ந்து
மாவலிவேள்வியில் மண்ணளந்த
அந்தணர் போன்றிவரார் கொலென்ன
அட்டபுயகரத்தேனென்றாரே.

ibid, II, 8, 2.

poets of Tamil are interpreted as the early Āḻvārs, *Mudal Āḻvārs* as they are called, namely, Poygai, Bhūtam and Pēy, as they are said to have worshipped here chanting their Tamil poems as the Gods themselves worship chanting the Veda. It is in the concluding stanza of this ten that there is a reference to a Vairamēgha who seems to be Dantidurga Vairamēgha the founder of the Rāshṭrakūṭa empire, who was in alliance with the reigning Pallava Nandivarman *. Passing down we come to Chidambaram, for which he devotes two tens. For our purposes there are only two references in the first ten. The shrine of Gōvindarāja is said in the first, stanza 3, to have been worshipped by the Pallava king which may refer either to Nandivarman or his father who was in government in the locality, according to the Vaikunṭhaperumāḷ inscription, wherefrom Nandivarman himself came to Kānchi as king by the nomination of the people. In the following stanza is the interesting reference that the deity which lay abed in the great dark sea was abed in this temple, on the couch formed by the great

---

* மன்னவன் தொண்டையர் கோன்வணங்கும்
நீள்முடிமாலை வயிரமேகன்
தன்வலி தன்புகழ் சூழ்ந்த கச்சி
அட்டபுயகரத்தாதிதன்னை
கன்னி நன் மாமதிள் மங்கைவேந்தன்
காமரு சீர்க்கலிகன்றி குன்றா
இன்னிசையாற் சொன்ன செஞ்சொல் மாலை
ஏத்தவல்லார்க் கிடம் வைகுந்தமே.

ibid, II, 8, 10.

snake with split tongue*. It is in identical terms that the Chōḻa Kulōttunga II is said to have referred to this deity when he ordered the removal of the shrine and the deity along with it. The ten devoted to Shiyāli, Śrī Rāma Viṇṇagar, according to the Vaishṇavas, there is an explicit reference to Śiva forming the right side of His body, Brahma being in the navel, Lakshmi on His chest almost exactly in the form in which they are described by the early Āḻvārs†.

---

* அருமாநிலமன்றளப்பான் குறளாய்
அவுணன் பெருவேள்வியிற் சென்றிரந்த
பெருமான்திரு நாமம் பிதற்றி நுந்தம்
பிறவித்துயர் நீக்குது மென்கிற்பீர்
கருமாகடலுட் கிடந்தானுவந்து
கவைநாவரவினணைப்பள்ளியின்மேல்
திருமால் திருமங்கையோடாடுதில்லைத்
திருச்சித்ரகூடஞ்சென்று சேர்மின்களே.

ibid, III, 2, 4.

கூத்தைக் களிகூரக் கும்பிட்டுப் போற்றினமேல்
தில்லைத்திருமன்றின் முன்றிற்சிறுதெய்வத்
தொல்லைக்குறும்பு தொடுத்தெடுத்து—

Kulōttunga Chōḻan Ulā.

பொன்னிற்குயிற்றிப்புறம் பிற்குறும் (பறுத்து)
முன்னர்க் (முன்னிற்) கடலில் மூழ்குவித்த—சென்னி.

Rājarājan Ulā.

† பிறைதங்கு சடையானை வலத்தே வைத்துப்
பிரமனைத்தன்னுந்தியிலே தோன்றுவித்து
கறைதங்கு வேற்றடங்கண் திருவை மார்பில்
கலந்தவன் தாளணைகிற்பீர் கழுநீர்கூடித்
துறை தங்கு கமலத்துத்துயின்றுகைதைத்
தோடாரும் பொதி சோற்றுச்சுண்ணம் நண்ணி
சிறைவண்டு களிபாடும் வயல் சூழ்காழிச்
சீராம விண்ணகரே சேர்மினீரே.

ibid, III, 4, 9.

The concluding stanza refers to Him in all his titles, as if he were roaring them out in victory, as against some opponents who called in question his claim to the titles, and there is an interesting reference to the work being in *Sangam* Tamil. It is in this place that he is traditionally said to have had a controversy with Tirugñānasambandar, although there are difficulties in the way of accepting it as a fact of history. In the fourth division, the first ten, the people of Nāngai (Tirunāngūr) are spoken of as those who defeated the king who attacked them in full force. We shall come to this again when we make a fuller reference to this particular. There is a reference in stanza 8 of section 3 of this part to Vēngaḍam where the God on the hill is spoken of as the very lamp of the Veda. In stanza 6 of the fifth ten, * the people of Nāngūr are said to have put to flight the Pāṇḍya (Tennan) and the northern king (Vaḍa Araśu) which could only mean the Pāṇḍya and the Pallava in alliance; and this alliance and the war had taken place just about the time or somewhat earlier, and took place in the Kāveri region between the Chāḷukyas

* கெண்டையுங் குறளும் புள்ளும் கேழலுமரியுமாவும்
அண்டமும் சுடரும் அல்லாவாற்றலுமாய வெந்தை
ஒண்டிறற்றென்னனோட வடவர சோட்டங்கண்ட
திண்டிறலாளர் நாங்கூர் திருமணிக்கூடத்தானே.

ibid, IV, 5, 6.

and the Pallavas. The first stanza of the seventh ten has a reference again to this feature of the people of Nāngūr in a more general way. Stanza 5 again makes a reference to God at Vēngaḍam as a lamp on the hill.

In section IV, the ninth ten, there is a reference in stanza 8, setting forth clearly the four colours that Vishṇu assumed in the four great periods of time. In section V, third ten there is a reference to the God at Tiruvēngaḍam as Krishṇa who assisted the Pāṇḍavas, and in the fifth ten of the same section, the very first stanza mentions Vēngaḍam, although the section itself is in celebration of Śrīrangam. In the next following section there is a reference to God as Vaḍamalai, which may be taken as referring to Vēngaḍam. In the same section relating to Śrīrangam, stanza 9 of the eighth ten has a reference to God teaching the secret *Mantra* of the worship of Vishṇu to the Toṇḍamān, apparently in reference to what took place between Toṇḍamān Chakravarti * and the God

* துளங்குநீண்முடி யரசர் தம் குரிசில்
தொண்டைமன்னவன் திண்டிறலொருவற்கு
உளங்கொளன்பினோ டின்னருள் சுரந்து
அங்கொரு நாழிகையேழுடனிருப்ப
வளங்கொள்மந்திரம் மற்றவற் கருளிச்
செய்தவாறு அடியேனறிந்து உலகம்
அளந்தபொன்னடியே யடைந்துய்ந்தேன்
அணிபொழில் திருவரங்கத்தம்மானே.

ibid, V, 8, 9.

in Vēngaḍam. In the tenth ten of the same section, stanza 7 there is a reference to Nandipura Viṇṇagaram (Nādankōvil), a short distance from Kumbhakoṇam, where the holy place is referred to as the one that received services in dedication to the temple of a certain Nandi. The historical reference is held to refer to the great Nandivarman II, the Pallava king. The sixth ten of the sixth section is in celebration of Tirunariyūr, and makes a reference in each stanza to a Chōḻa King Kō-Śengaṇ, and of his achievements including the construction of 70 temples to Śiva for worship. He is included among the Nāyanārs of the Śaivas, but the reference here is that, after having done so much to earn the grace of Śiva, he felt the need for an appeal to Vishṇu and rendered similar service to Vishṇu. It looks however as though he was a king, like many other Hindu kings, who had made his benefactions to both alike. There is an interesting reference in stanza 5 of the same section where the king is spoken of as of the Tamil land in the south, and also as the king of the north, whatever this latter might mean at the time, unless it be the Pallava country. There is another reference to Vēngaḍam in section VIII, stanza I, third ten, and in stanza 5, section VII. VII, 10, 4 contains an interesting reference to the deity at

Tirukkōvilūr, and his act of grace in connection with the first Āḻvārs. In VIII, 1 he addresses the Vishṇu at Kaṇṇapuram as one having eight arms. In the next section, stanza 3 has a simple reference to Vēngaḍam. IX, 2, 5 has a reference to Kōḻi and Kūḍal, the capitals respectively of the Chōḻa and Pāṇḍya in reference to the manifestation of Vishṇu in other places as Krishṇa. IX, 6, 1 has an expressive reference to Śiva forming part of Vishṇu. The same section, IX, 7, 4 has a simple reference to Vēngaḍam, and stanza 9 to the false teaching of the Jains and the Buddhists. IX, 8, 9 has a similar reference. IX, 9, 9 has a simple reference to Vēngaḍam. IX, 10, 4 states clearly that Vishṇu allotted a part of His body on the right side, to *Īśa* who rides a bull and holds *Maḻu* or *Śakti* *. In X, 1, 2 there is a clear reference to Vēngaḍam. In section X, 6, 1 celebrating Krishṇa *Avatāra*, there is a statement

---

* ஏறுமேறியிலங்கு மொண் மழுப்பற்றும் ஈசர்க்கிசைந்துடம்பிலோர்
கூறுதான் கொடுத்தான் குலமாமகட்கினியான்
காறு சண்பகம் மல்லிகை மலர்புல்கி இன்னிறவண்டு நல்நறும்
தேறல் வாய் மடுக்கும் திருக்கோட்டியூரானே.

ibid, IX, 10, 4.

மல்கிய தோளும் மானுரியதளும்
உடையவர் தமக்குமோர்பாகம்
நல்கிய நலமோ நரகனைத்தொலைத்த
கரதலத்தமைதியின் கருத்தோ.

ibid, X, 9, 4.

that Vishṇu gave to the world a treatise on *Dharma* assuming the form of Nara-Nārāyaṇa. This is obviously a reference to the gift of the Pāncharātra *. X, 9, 4 has a reference to Śiva forming part almost like the one above. XI, 5, 10 has a simple reference to Vēngaḍam. That takes us through the Periya Tirumoḻi proper.

OTHER WORKS OF TIRUMANGAI ALVAR. Coming to the miscellaneous poems Tiruneḍum Tāṇḍakam, section 2 contains a reference to the various colours assumed by Vishṇu. Stanza 9 refers to Śiva forming part of Vishṇu. Stanza 16 has a reference to Vēngaḍam, and there is one reference each to Vēngaḍam in the Śiriya Tirumaḍal and Periya Tirumaḍal. In the latter work, couplet 122 contains perhaps a more explicit reference to the part played by God in Tirukkōvilūr in connection with the Mudal Aḻvārs. In couplet 131 God himself is addressed

---

* எங்காணு மீதோப்பதோர் மாய முண்டோ
நரநாரணனாய் உலகத்து அறநூல்
சிங்காமை விரித்தவனெம்பெருமான்
அதுவன்றியுஞ் செஞ்சுடரும் நிலனும்
பொங்கார்கடலும் பொருப்பும் நெருப்பும் நெருக்கிப்
புகப்பொன்மிடறு அத்தனைபோது
அங்காந்தவன்காண்மின் இன்று ஆய்ச்சியரால்
அளைவெண்ணெயுண்டு ஆப்புண்டிருந்தவனே.

ibid, X, 6, 1.

as the Four Vedas, as the Tamil of the Southern Pāṇḍya, as the speech of the North. From these references considered in detail, we see Tirumangai Āḻvār following the tradition of the other Āḻvārs, and exhibiting himself as belonging intimately to the same school of thought. What is really to our purpose for the history of Tirupati is that he makes a dozen simple references to God at Vēngaḍam in his address to the representation of God in well-known Vaishṇava shrines of the South, having no doubt as it were that the shrine in Tirupati was to him a Vishṇu shrine and nothing else. He also brings out clearly the features that Śiva formed a part of His body, and, as such, the feature discussed so elaborately by the Mudal Āḻvārs of Vishṇu, was a thing well-known even in the days of Tirumangai Āḻvār. We may now therefore conclude that, to the Āḻvārs whose period of life may be held to extend from the Śangam period in the third century after Christ the latest to the eighth century when Tirumangai Āḻvār flourished, there has been a continuous tradition that the shrine in Vēngaḍam was a shrine dedicated to Vishṇu.

CHAPTER VIII.

BHAKTI, THE DOMINENT FEATURE OF THE AGE.

THE VAISHNAVA CHARACTER OF VENGADAM MAINTAINED IN LITERARY TRADITION. While therefore Vaishṇava tradition is consistent that, notwithstanding some features which may admit of a suspicion, the deity in Vēngaḍam was Vishṇu, we have other evidence of a secular character, which would support this. We made reference already to the early poet Māmūlanār of the Śangam age who refers to Tirupati as a place which had attained to fame "for its festive celebrations during the year". A reference similar to that we find in respect of Kānchi in the age of Toṇḍamān Iḷam Tiraiyan clearly establishing that temples or shrines of worship dedicated to Vishṇu were not only known, but that festive celebrations associated with such shrines as in modern times, were, at least some of them, already prevalent. We next indicated that the Buddhist work Śilappadhikāram, the author of which Iḷaṅgo Aḍigaḷ was probably a Buddhist, refers in unmistakable terms to the shrine in Tirupati as a shrine holy to Vishṇu. Four Vishṇu shrines find reference in the work

Śilappadhikāram and spoken of with respect almost bordering on devotion by this author, an alien to the faith of the Vaishṇavas. These are the holy shrines in Tiruvanantapuram, (Trivandrum), Tirumālirumśōlai, Śrīrangam and Tirupati. Of these the latter three are regarded as of peculiarly holy reputation to the individual pilgrim concerned, who was a native of the Malabar country belonging to a village Māngāḍu to whom the deity at Trivandrum would be more or less his own. He is made to say that he was on a pilgrimage to the famous shrines of South India, outside of his native country, and these three find mention in this connection. The poet takes occasion to describe the God in Vēngaḍam in graphic terms, which leaves no doubt whatsoever that the deity according to him was Vishṇu in full form. For another secular literary reference, we may come down to the reign of Nandivarman III, Nandivarman of Teḷḷāṟu as he is called, in whose reign the Bhāratavenbā was composed by its author Perundēvanār. This Perundēvanār has a reference to Vēngaḍam * as

---

* தேனோங்குசோலைத் திருவேங்கடமென்றும்
வானோங்கு சோலைமலை யென்றும்—தானோங்கு
தென்னரங்கமென்றுந் திருவத்தியூரென்றும்
சொன்னவர்க்குமுண்டோ துயர்.

Bhārata Veṇbā—Bhīshma Parva:
First Day's War, Stanza 1.

a Vaishṇava shrine coupling it with Attiyūr (Vishṇu-Kānchi), where perhaps the author actually lived. The earliest known inscription in Tirupati is that of a predecessor of this Nandivarman of Teḻḷāṟu, Danti Vikramavarman. Therefore then we have references throughout the centuries to the shrine in Vēngaḍam as a Vishṇu shrine before we come to the evidence of the inscriptions.

THE GENERAL CHARACTER OF THE PERIOD OF THE ALVARS. We have so far covered the history of the shrine at Tirupati ever since its foundation down to the beginning of the 10th century almost. We noticed that all the Purāṇas together uniformly make out that the temple is, in its origin, what is called a holy place self-create (*svaymbhū*), that is, it is not a human foundation to begin with. All of them agree similarly that the human founder of the temple, apart from an individual devotee, was a Toṇḍamān ruler of the locality who had his capital near Vēngaḍam and ruled over the tract of country surrounding it. They also furnish us the information that the period during which he flourished and thus rendered the pious service to Vishṇu, was the early centuries of the Christian era, in fact, specifically the period between the foundation of the Samvat era of Vikramāditya and that of the Śaka, that is, between the years

57 B. C., and 78 A. D. Whether we accept this precise dating or not, we may take it that the foundation of the temple as a human institution may be ascribed to the first century of the Christian era. From that period on we have come down eight clear centuries noting down what we can glean of the history of the temple from literary sources alone. The period actually covered relates historically to the period of the three kingdoms of the South, which may be held more or less roughly to correspond to the Śangam age so-called, followed by that of the early Pallava kings of the Prākrit charters. This is followed by a period of rule of Pallava kings of the early dynasty which issued the few charters that its members did, in Sanskrit. The period of rule of this dynasty may be counted as from the beginning of the 4th century down to the latter part of the 6th century A. D. With the middle of the 6th century we come to the historical period, ordinarily described as the age of the great Pallavas of Kānchi. This dynasty ruled from the latter half of the 6th century down to Aparājita Pallava who was overthrown and Pallava domination extinguished almost at the end of the 9th century. In regard to this period, inscriptional records are comparatively few, and therefore the historical material generally available to us

for later periods is not available to us for this period. Not that inscriptions were unknown, but it had not become the fashion to issue these inscriptions in the elaborate form and the large number in which they got to be issued in the periods of history following that with which we are at present concerned. But even so, there is reference to a Vishṇu shrine dedicated to Vishṇu-Nārāyaṇa in one of the Prākrit charters which refers to a donation to the temple by a very early Pallava Queen, Chārudēvi.* Similar references to donations to Vishṇu shrines we have even among the Pallavas of the early Sanskrit charters. But the founder of the later dynasty Simha Vishṇu is definitely spoken of, in the later inscriptions, as a Vaishṇava devoted to the worship of Vishṇu specifically, and, among the rulers of this dynasty that succeeded him, there were some undoubtedly who made donations to temples of Vishṇu and otherwise contributed largely to the promotion of Vishṇu worship, particularly the great Nandivarman II, Pallavamalla. There are inscriptions of his son Dantivarman in the Vishṇu temple at Triplicane.† But there is no record of any of the kings before this one, having had anything to do with the

---

* *Epigraphia Indica, Vol.* VIII, 143.

† *Epigraphia Indica,* VIII, 291 (No. 29.)

temple at Tirupati, notwithstanding the fact that the temple itself was known popularly and was regarded as a holy place of eminence from the other evidence that we have so far considered. It would ordinarily be considered strange that, being as it is within the territory of the Pallavas and given the name to what may be regarded as one of the main divisions of the Toṇḍa-maṇḍalam, the territory prominently of the Pallavas, it should find no mention. This is perhaps due to the fact that the habit of making donations to temples and recording them in grants had not been adopted as a general practice in those days. In fact, this seems to have been set in full form by the great Chōḻa Rājarāja, and before him, inscriptions are only occasional and have reference more or less to incidents which are referred to in a more or less unconnected form and not set in formal documents as in the periods following. There is also the additional circumstance that the shrine in Vēngaḍam was in a comparatively inaccessible locality very difficult of approach generally, and therefore not perhaps quite as popular as other places. From this silence it should not be argued that either temples to Vishṇu did not exist, or that temple worship was not the fashion.

VISHNU AMONG THE EARLY TAMIL GODS. The Tamil grammar Tolkāppiyam, the earliest grammar extant and an authoritative classic on the subject, has an interesting reference in *Sūtra* 5 of the section on *Ahattiṇai* in *Poruḷ Adhikāram*, which makes four Gods as the recognised deities of the Tamil land.* The matter has reference to the division of land composing the country generally. The section on *Poruḷ* as it is called, Sanskrit *Artha*, refers to the norms of life, dealing as it does, with one, perhaps in general point of view the most important one, on wordly life, and, in trying to lay down the norms, the work begins with a division of land which may be regarded as naturally divisible into four; forest land, presided over by Krishṇa-Vishṇu (*Māyōn*), hilly parts presided over by Kumāra or Subrahmaṇya, Tamil *Muruga* (*Śēyōn*), then well-watered agricultural land, presided over by the *king* (Indra); and lastly coast land of sand presided over by *Varuṇa* (God of the Sea). It will be noticed that the names given leave it in no doubt what Gods are intended. The

---

* மாயோன்மேய காடுறை யுலகமும்
சேயோன் மேய மைவரையுலகமும்
வேந்தன் மேயதீம் புன லுலகமும்
வருணன் மேயபெருமண லுலகமும்
முல்லை குறிஞ்சி மருதம் நெய்தலெனச்
சொல்லியமுறையாற் சொல்லவும் படுமே.

Tolkāppiyam Poruḷ, Aham 5.

ascription here of particular kinds of land as being presided over by particular deities seems to be analogous to the Yajur Veda, * which goes farther and gives a far larger list of all things making Vishṇu the presiding deity over hills generally. But the Tamils generally divided the land only into four classes as above, adding a fifth, desert land, which however was regarded not as a separate class of land, but merely as one or the other of the former ones transformed, owing to a change of climatic conditions. Therefore then it is clear that Vishṇu as a deity is as old as the Tamil Tolkāppiyam.

This reference so far is merely to the names of the Gods, and all that is said of them is that they are presiding deities over particular classes of land. No further information, however, is given about them. In poem 56 of *Puṛanānūṛu*, however, we seem to get information of a different character. This is a poem by Nakkīrar celebrating a Pāṇḍya who died in 'a garden pavilion' as he is described. He is likened here to the four principal Gods in the various qualities he was possessed of, and the four Gods under reference are Śiva, Balabhadra or Balarāma, as he is called, Krishṇa-Vishṇu and Kumāra

---

* *Krishna Yajur Samhita, Kāṇḍa*, III, *Praśna* 4.

Subrahmaṇya*. The dominent quality of each of these Gods who are said to be above time, the ruler is credited with being in possession of. He is likened to the first one, who is here described as Death (God of Destruction) in anger. He is said to resemble the second in strength, the third in fame and the fourth in successful accomplishment. Though this is merely a reference for a poetical purpose, the features given of these Gods exhibit a considerable agreement to references in classical Tamil literature thereby giving us to understand without doubt, that these were Gods recognised in the Tamil land as the supreme deities deserving of worship. The first one is described as having a bull for his vehicle and matted locks of hair, the irresistible trident and blue throat, unmistakably a reference to Śiva. The second one is described as of the colour of the conch coming out of the sea, carrying the warlike weapon, the plough, and having on his flag a palm tree for his ensign,

* ஏற்றுவலனுயரிய வெரிமருளவிர்சடை
மாற்றருங்கணிச்சி மணிமிடற்றோனுங்,
கடல்வளர் புரிவளை புரையுமேனி
யடல் வெந்நாஞ்சிற் படைக்கொடியோனு,
மண்ணுறு திருமணி புரையுமேனி
விண்ணுயர் புட்கொடி விறல் வெய்யோனு,
மணிமயி லுயரிய மாறா வென்றிப்
பிணிமிகவூர்தியொண் செய்யோனு, மென
ஞாலங் காக்குங் காலமுன்பிற்
றோலாநல்லிசை நால்வர்.

Puṛam, 56.

undoubtedly a reference to Baladēva, the elder brother of Krishṇa. The third one is similarly described as of the colour of the blue saphire well washed, whose flag carried the ensign of Garuḍa and possessed of great valour. The fourth is described as carrying on the flag the ensign of the peacock, as uniformly victorious, riding on the peacock for a vehicle and of a red colour. These are described in the next following lines as deities protecting the earth and as being above time. We see therefore that, in the particular period to which this has reference, Krishṇa-Vishṇu and his elder brother Baladēva were known as the ruling deities of the universe along with the two others. The reference to Krishṇa-Vishṇu and Baladēva as it occurs here is just exactly how it occurs elsewhere in Tamil literature as we shall notice, as well as in the inscriptional literature of the centuries immediately preceding the Christian era in the Deccan and Central India, and perhaps even elsewhere. These two are two among the four *vyūhas* of Vishṇu according to the school of Pāncharātra and form the basis of the Bhakti school of thought. Nakkīrar's reference however is again a reference merely to the Gods as such and some of their features, but does not give us any detail as to the Vishṇu temples or places of worship.

REFERENCE TO THESE GODS IN TEMPLES WITH FESTIVALS, ETC. The Śilappadhikāram however, provides us with two references which take us much further in regard to these Gods as being among those worshipped in temples. They are said to be the principal deities to whom temples were built along with a number of others regarded as of comparatively inferior standing both in the Chōḷa capital of Kāverippūmpaṭṭinam and in Madura, the Pāṇḍya capital. The first reference is in Book V, lines 169–172, in connection with the celebration of the great festival to Indra, and temples to these are mentioned as having their own festivals in connection therewith. * The first of course is a reference to a temple of the great one not having birth (Śiva). The next one is the temple to the red one with six faces (Kumāra-Subrahmaṇya). The next one is that to the white one, whose body is of the colour of the conch (Baladēva), and the next one is the temple of the great one of the colour of saphire-blue (Krishṇa-Vishṇu). These are stated in so

---

* *பிறவாயாக்கைப் பெரியோன் கோயிலு*
மறுமுகச்செவ்வேளணி திகழ் கோயிலும்
வால் வளைமேனி வாலியோன் கோயிலும்
நீலமேனி நெடியோன் கோயிலும்
மாலைவெண்குடை மன்னவன் கோயிலும்.

Śilappadhikāram, V, 179, 183.

many words to be housed in temples, and worshipped accordingly with periodical festivals as well. Similarly in Book XIV, lines 7 to 10; here again as day broke in Madura, the morning band announced the break of day in the following temples. The first is the great temple to the Great One "with an eye in the face." The next one is the temple to the Great One who had the *Garuḍa* bird for his flag. The next one was again the temple wherein was housed the white God carrying the plough in his right hand, and the last one was the temple sacred to the God with "the ensign of a cock.*" Here we see that these Gods were housed in temples with organised worship and festivals as they do obtain in these days. It would not seem therefore anything extraordinary if in that early period a ruler up-country like the Toṇḍamān had come upon the image of a God at Vēngaḍam, felt it necessary to enshrine the image in a temple and arrange for its worship.

PANCHARATRA AND THE BHAKTI SCHOOL OF VISHNU IN FULL VIEW IN THE SANGAM AGE. We have already noted the reference in the Śilappadhikāram to the temple at Tirupati itself, wherein

* *நுதல் விழி நாட்டத்திறையோன் கோயிலும்*
உவணச்சேவலுயர்த்தோனியமும்
மேழிவலனுயர்த்த வெள்ளை நகரமும்
கோழிச்சேவற்கொடியோன் கோட்டமும்.

ibid, XIV, 7, 10.

THE SANCTUM OF SRI VENKATESA

(*To face page 197*)

the author gives a graphic description of the Vishṇu image there. This reference to Vishṇu in Tirupati comes as the account of a pilgrim from the Malabar country going on a pilgrimage to the most holy Vishṇu shrines in South India, among which he mentions the shrines in Tirumālirumśōlai, Śrīrangam and Tirupati. He also states, in the course of this narration, that he came from a village, Māngāḍu, in the west country, and, being a devotee of Padmanābha there, he says, that his anxiety to visit the shrines of great reputation, such as the three mentioned before, drew him on, and that he undertook the pilgrimage in consequence thereof. This statement and the manner in which the reference is made by the author to it, would alike make it clear that temples dedicated to Vishṇu were already well-known, and in great repute as holy places justifying pilgrimages being undertaken, and pilgrims from even distant countries made it a point to visit these places as part of their pious duty in life. Notwithstanding doubts expressed in certain quarters, there is nothing seriously to call into question the early age of the work, and it must be held to belong, by its character, to the same class as the Śangam works, whatever be its actual precise date. This work certainly has a direct bearing upon the history of this Tirupati hill by its specific reference to the shrine there; but the sister work Maṇimēkhalai does contain several references to the worship of Krishṇa-Vishṇu and Baladēva in the course of it. These references read in the light of the poems devoted to Vishṇu in the *Paripāḍal*, of which there are just five, not only show that the worship of Krishṇa-Vishṇu and Baladēva were widely prevalent and popular, but also that the Tamils were familiar with the whole theory of the Pāncharātra Āgama, devoted to the worship of Vishṇu-Vāsudēva and his four *vyūhas* of which these two form the first pair, the other two being Pradhyumna and Aniruddha.* It is matter for satisfaction that in these poems we get a reference to the Vishṇu shrine in Tirumālirumśōlai specifically. We see therefore that, in the period broadly to be described as the Śangam age, namely, the first three centuries of the Christian era, Vishṇu worship had already attained to a wide popularity. Temples to Vishṇu were well-known, and a feature of the capital cities of the Tamil land. The most popular forms of Vishṇu worshipped in these temples were Krishṇa-Vishṇu and Baladēva, the Āgamāic names Vāsudēva and Sankarshaṇa, not being unknown. That is not

* செங்கட்காரி கருங்கண் வெள்ளை
பொன்கண்பச்சை பைங்கண்மால்.

Paripāḍal III, ll. 82—83.

[*This poem gives in summary the Pāncharātra.*]

all. On the evidence of the *Paripāḍal* it can also be safely asserted that all the essential features of the Pāncharātra were already known in the Tamil land, and, not merely known, but had also attained to considerable vogue in practice. We see therefore Bhakti—we are concerned here only with Vishṇu Bhakti—in the most developed form already prevalent in this part of the country.

We have already indicated rather more elaborately than otherwise, that, in the age of the Aḻvārs, which may be held to extend from the 3rd century A. D. to the 9th century almost, the Bhakti school of Vaishṇavism had attained to wide acceptance and even to considerable importance. At the end of this period, we could say definitely the worship of Vishṇu on the Pāncharātra system had become a well recognised form of Bhakti, and constituted, if not the one system of Bhakti worship, at least a prominent one. It is just about this age, that we come upon the beginning of inscriptional records relating to Vēngaḍam, although as we have pointed out already, inscriptions found in relation to temples were already centuries old. In this position, and with such a volume of evidence before us, it would be carrying scepticism too far to deny the existence of a temple in Vēngaḍam, notwithstanding the fact that we have not come upon any inscriptions relating to the temple.

CHAPTER IX.

HISTORY OF TONDAMANDALAM.

TONDAMANDALAM, ITS EARLY HISTORY. In the age of the inscriptions, Vēngaḍam is generally described as belonging to Tiruvēngaḍakkōṭṭam of the Toṇḍamaṇḍalam. Toṇḍamaṇḍalam has to be understood as either the country of the Toṇḍaiyar the people, or the territory under the rule of the Toṇḍamān ruler. On the analogy of Tamil names however, Toṇḍamān would be nothing more than the chief of the Toṇḍaiyar. We have therefore to take it that the territorial name is derived from the people who occupied the territory. In classical Tamil literature, however, the division called Toṇḍamaṇḍalam is described generally as *Aruvānāḍu* indicating Toṇḍamaṇḍalam proper; and the country beyond and still dependent upon Toṇḍamaṇḍalam and having intimate connection with it, is described as *Aruvāvaḍatalai*, that is, northern *Aruvā*. Taking the two together the whole territory would be territory occupied by the people known as *Aruvāḷar*, made up of *Aruvā* and *Āḷar*, people to whom belongs the *Aruvānāḍu*. Therefore the whole territory included in Toṇḍamaṇḍalam of which Vēngaḍakkōṭṭam is a part was occupied by a distinct class of people and took its name from them. Where therefore the *Paṭṭinappālai*, celebrating the great Chōḻa ruler Karikāla, speaks of him as a prince from whom the old *Aruvāḷar* people took commands, would mean that he had subjugated these people and brought them under his authority; that is, Toṇḍa-maṇḍalam had been brought under Chōḻa authority in the days of Karikāla. It was nevertheless territory far away from the head-quarters, and therefore likely to throw off the yoke of the central authority at the earliest opportunity. In the period of decline of the Chōḻa power two generations after Karikāla, Toṇḍamaṇḍalam broke away from the Chōḻa country and relapsed into its old condition in which it was a territory under tribal organisation and government. From the earliest times of which we have any information, this territory is said traditionally to have been divided into 24 divisions, called here *Kōṭṭams*, each one of which was dominated by a fortress from which the governors governed in a sort of military government, and to which the people retired on occasions of danger. Twenty-four such forts are mentioned as belonging to this division, and there were 24 divisions under separate tribal chieftains. Tiruvēngaḍakkōṭṭam forms one such division. Ordinarily these divisions were brought under a central authority of some kind, which dominated the whole region. Within historical times that central authority happened to be located in Kānchi, and hence we have come to regard more or less Kānchi as the headquarters of the Toṇḍamaṇḍalam. According to tradition, however, there seems to have been a period when it was not Kānchi, but a fortified town called *Puḻal* now a village on the borderland of the Red-Hills Tank, which itself is known among the people as *Puḻalēri*. Whether it was actually so or not, we have information of Kānchi as a town of very considerable importance even in the days of the grammarian Patānjali about the middle of the 2nd century B. C. Kānchi dominated the division under the Chōḻas, and probably continued ever since to dominate the region, so that now Toṇḍamaṇḍalam generally is understood to have been dominated by Kānchi, and Kānchi and Toṇḍamaṇḍalam are treated as more or less interchangeable terms politically.

TIRUVENGADAKKOTTAM, AN EARLY DIVISION UNDER A TONDAMAN CHIEF. This Tiruvēngaḍakkōṭṭam dominated by the hill Tiruvēngaḍam from which it takes its name was regarded as of four divisions named after Chittoor, Chandragiri, Tiruchānūr and Kāḻahasti. This gives us an idea of the extent of the division, and the territory included in it must have been one of the oldest divisions of the Toṇḍamaṇḍalam. Under the original organisation of the land, each of these *Kōṭṭams* must have been dominated by a fortress. The chieftain who governed the locality, or the tribal chieftain, would naturally go by the name Rāja, although Tamil literature later on does make a division of rulers into classes and calls these people smaller kings (*Kuṛu-nila-mannar*), in contradistinction to the crowned kings of the three vast kingdoms of the south, namely, Chōḻa, Pāṇḍya and Chēra. It would be nothing surprising if these chieftains were ruling over one part or other of the Toṇḍamaṇḍalam. We have already noticed that the image at Tirupati was actually dug out of the earth by the Toṇḍamān chieftain, ruler of Nārāyaṇavanam not far from the locality, and enshrined it in the temple. He is also said to have been the organiser of worship there. It seems not unlikely, and the Purāṇic story is probably based on a foundation of fact so far as this particular goes. But the Purāṇic datum in regard to date would make his time the first century, A. D. or B. C. Again that period does not seem unlikely either, as we know this was an ancient division of the land, and its ancient organisation continued in historical times. Therefore then the foundation of the temple on the hill must have been at the very beginning of the Christian era, and under the native ruling chief who went by the name Toṇḍamān.

EARLY HISTORY OF TONDAMANDALAM, TONDAMANS AND PALLAVAS. The political changes that came over this region seem to have been somewhat as follows. The petty chieftains of the illcultured regions dominated by particular forts seem gradually to have been brought under one central control, and that controlling authority seems to have held rule at Kānchi. In the Śangam literature we know of two *Tiraiyans*, the elder Tiraiyan holding rule in the north at Pavattiri, Reḍḍipāḷem in the Gūḍūr Taluq, and the younger, or Iḷam Tiraiyan, ruling over Kānchi. This reduction of the whole territory to subordination to Kānchi probably was the result—it may be of the Chōḻa conquest, or it might have come about even previously. We have good reasons for assuming a Chōḻa viceroyalty earlier, and that Toṇḍamān Iḷam Tiraiyan we have good reasons for assuming was likewise a Chōḻa viceroy. It is in connection with him that the story is told that he was the son of a Chōḻa ruler by a Nāga princess. Almost the same story is told of Toṇḍamān of Vēngaḍam that he was the son of a Chōḻa ruler by a Nāga princess. As this story of the birth of Iḷam Tiraiyan is recorded by Nacchinārkkiniyār, the commentator, the place where this liaison took place is supposed to be Nāgappaṭṭiṇam, hitherto taken to be the Negapatam in the Tanjore District. It might just as well be the town, or the capital city, of the Nāgas. Whatever that be, we have no satisfactory grounds for identifying this early Toṇḍamān, the founder of the temple at Tirupati, with Toṇḍamān Iḷam Tiraiyan, who seems to have come later in point of time. We see therefore already that the early Toṇḍamān who constructed the temple for Venkaṭēśa at Vēngaḍam and arranged for the festivals and the worship in the temple, must have been a Toṇḍamān chieftain of Tiruvēngaḍakkōṭṭam and the localities near about; and this is supported by the fact that Māmūlanār could speak of the celebration of festivals in Tirupati. This must have been even earlier than the bringing of all Toṇḍamaṇḍalam under one authority that central authority being placed at Kānchi. We have therefore to take it that Toṇḍamaṇḍalam was one ethnical unit; but consisted of a certain number of chieftaincies, whether it be actually 24 or not, and had been gradually politically united to be regarded as one kingdom under the rule of the chieftain at Kānchi. That is the stage in which we find it under Toṇḍamān Iḷam Tiraiyan, and the opening period of the inscriptions when the authority of the Āndhra dynasty was still in full force. We see one or two Āndhra governors in the locality probably coming after the Toṇḍamaṇḍalam had been unified as stated above. This unification followed perhaps the Chō̤la conquest involving as a consequence, the systematic introduction of agriculture and of an agricultural civilisation consequent thereon. Just about this time, we have inscriptional evidence for a line of rulers, who may be father and son, and perhaps the second came two generations after the first. The first of these rulers is credited with having carried out a policy of promotion of agriculture by the gift of the means of agriculture, plough-oxen, and ploughs themselves together with money. The son seems to have followed in the same course, and was probably the acknowledged ruler of the whole region. It is an inscription of his daughter-in-law Chārudēvi which records a gift to the temple of Vishṇu-Nārāyaṇa, thereby putting it beyond a doubt that temples to Vishṇu were in existence, and worship of Vishṇu in temples was not unknown. If Chārudēvi could do it, be it remembered that she did not build the temple but merely made a grant to an existing one, what is there to prevent another ruler who may have been previous to her by a few generations having constructed a temple and arranged for worship and the conducting of festivals through the year ? With the appearance of these we seem to arrive at the establishment of Pallava rule in Kānchi, and of Pallava dominence in Toṇḍamaṇḍalam. Of course, when well established the Pallavas also called themselves Toṇḍamāns, and kings of Toṇḍaiyar (*Toṇḍaiyarkōn*) and so on. This could be explained by the fact that, having succeeded to the rule of the country of the Toṇḍaiyar, Toṇḍamaṇḍalam, they could very well describe themselves as Toṇḍamāns. Whether the term Pallava actually took its origin from the Toṇḍai creeper with which, according to the story, the Toṇḍamān prince born to the Nāga Princess by the Chōḷa king, was decorated was what gave the name, is perhaps more than we can say definitely although some of the early inscriptions would give that explanation. Be that as it may, we find Pallava rule beginning betimes, almost immediately after the rule of Toṇḍamān Iḷam Tiraiyan, and we could mark three separate groups of rulers, as indicated before, from that period down to the later years of the 6th century. The point for consideration at present is why these rulers who have left some inscriptional records of their own in various other places, have left none in the shrine of Tirupati. We cannot say exactly why. Tirupati must have been in the age of the Pallavas as inaccessible as in the earlier, and even down to the much later period of the Chōḷas, and the practice of recording in inscriptions gifts to temples had not become so much a vogue as yet. That seems to be enough explanation, and, at any rate, that is all that we are in a position to offer. The absence of inscriptions therefore cannot be held as an argument against the existence of the temple itself. The temple may have existed without as yet having become sufficiently important, or sufficiently popular to merit that recording, and, as we have stated already, that way of recording itself has been comparatively rare in these early days. When we come to the great Pallava dynasty, we are able to see that temple worship had become popular and a well recognised institution. Numbers of temples both to Vishṇu and Śiva and to many other gods of the Hindu Pantheon do find mention in the Pallava territory. We find the statue of Simhavishṇu and his queens, and his son Mahēndravarman and his queens in the Varāha cave in Mahābalipuram, and, in all probability, the Vishṇu shrine in the locality was perhaps already in existence, not in the form of the present temple, but perhaps in the form of a smaller shrine. It is the great Narasimhavarman that attempted the laying out and beautification of the city which perhaps was not carried to completion because of a political revolution. The great Nandivarman Pallavamalla was the builder of a great temple to Vishṇu in Conjeevaram itself, and his son has left records of his benefactions to the temple at Triplicane and at Tirupati. Nandivarman of Teḻḻāṟu, his grandson was the parton of Perundēvanār, whose work Bhārataveṅbā, we already mentioned, makes prominent mention of Vēngaḍam and Kānchi. So before we come to Nṛpatungavarman we have more or less indirect references to Vishṇu temples and Vishṇu worship, and just a few occasional references to the temple at Vēngaḍam itself. In the light of the works of the Āḻvārs alone, we ought to hold that Vishṇu worship was prevalent and popular. We have enough of secular evidence in what has been stated above. We need not therefore, be unnecessarily sceptical about the statements of the Āḻvārs in regard to the matter.

THE GENERAL COURSE OF SOUTH INDIAN HISTORY TO A.D. 800. The general trend of South Indian History during the first eight centuries of the Christian era may be set down in general terms as follows. The Āndhra rulers, whose authority during the best periods of their history extended over the region beginning southwards from

Ajmer and Pushkar in the north down to the western districts of modern Mysore, had an alternative capital in the basin of the lower Krishna at Amarāvati wherefrom they stretched southwards, and, perhaps at one time, made an effort to extend their authority successfully even down to the southern Peṇṇār. It is perhaps this effort of the great Āndhra Yagñaśrī that set up a vigorous opposition from the Tamils. When ultimately the Āndhra power collapsed at the beginning of the third century, some of the enterprising governors of these eastern provinces of the Āndhras probably made an effort to gradually fix their hold upon the territories of Toṇḍamaṇḍalam. The gradual pressure from the Āndhra empire seems to have set up a popular movement resulting in the migration of the somewhat less civilised people who seem to have completely upset the governments of South India and introduced what may well be regarded as the period of anarchy to which the later inscriptions refer in unmistakable terms. This is the movement of the pepole called *Kaḷvar* or *Kaḷavar*, and they must have moved down from the region round and about Vēngaḍam, if not from the whole of the Toṇḍamaṇḍalam. The subversion of the Chōḷa dynasty seems to have been more or less complete, and the Pāṇḍya power suffered substantially, if not exactly to the same degree, so that there seems to have been something like a break in the established order for a number of generations, say six to eight. Emerging from this a new Pāṇḍya dynasty had to re-establish its claims to what normally belonged to them, some time about the end of the 6th century, and through a course of struggle lasting for more than two centuries restored themselves to their former position. The materials at our disposal generally give evidence of another such recovery on the part of the Chōḷas. It looks as though the Chōḷa power had not been completely destroyed, although for the moment it was so thoroughly crippled that it failed to show itself during these centuries. It was in the course of this movement that the so-called Pallava state of Kānchi came into existence and successfully established its authority over the territory extending from the river Krishna down to the southern Peṇṇār. In the course of this effort, they seem to have shifted their capital. Kānchi was certainly an important city and was regarded as the capital of Toṇḍamaṇḍalam in an earlier period. During the next following centuries the dominating power of South India became the ruling power at Kānchi known as the Pallava, generally referred to in Tamil works relating to the period, as the kings of the "northern territory", as distinct from the three crowned kings of the south. The period of struggle which culminated in the establishment of this dominent position of the Pallavas is the period covered by the Pallava dynasty of the Sanskrit charters, as the epigraphists call them, beginning almost with Vishṇugōpa of Kānchi referred to in the Samudragupta inscription and coming down to Simhavarman II, the father of Simhavishṇu. The two centuries and more therefore of this dynasty is the period of the building up of the Pallava power in the south.

PALLAVA KINGS.

I.

Bappa—c. A. D. 225-250.

Śiva Skandavarman I of Kānchi.—c. 250-275.

Buddhavarman—275-300. Md. Chārudēvi.

Buddhyankura—300-325.

Vishṇugōpa I—325-350.

Skandavarman II—350-375.

Kumāra-Vishṇu I *alias* Kālabhartṛ—375-400.

- Buddhavarman II—400-425.
  - Kumāra Vishṇu II—425-450.
- Skandavarman III or Chūṭu-Pallava.
  - Vīravarman or 'Vīrakūrcha.'
    - Vijaya Skandavarman IV *alias* Skandaśishya—450-475. (Fleet makes reign end in 436).
      - Simhavarman I*—475-500 (Fleet makes his accession as in the year following August 25, 436). This king crowned the Ganga Harivarman or Ayyavaram for the purpose of crushing the Bāṇa chiefs, about A. D. 450.
        - Skandavarman V *alias* Chaṇḍa-daṇḍa—500-525 (c. 460 Fleet) Installed the Ganga Mādhava I about 470 (Fleet).
          - Nandivarman I—525-550.
      - 'Yuvamahārāja' Vishṇugōpa II or 'Kumāra Vishṇu' Did not reign. Recaptured Kānchi from the Chōḷas.
        - Simhavarman II—Did not reign.
          - Vishṇugōpa III—Did not reign.

---

* For Fleet's date see *J. R. A. S.* 1915, p. 471 f, especially p. 485.

PALLAVA KINGS—(*Continued.*)

II.

Simhavarman II—550-575.

|

Simhavishṇu or 'Avanisimha-Pōttarāja'

|

Mahēndravarman I—600-630.

|

Narasimhavarman I—630-668.
Captured Bādāmi from W. Chāḷukyas, 642

|

Mahēndravarman II—668-670.

|

Paramēśvara Pōtavarman I—670-690.
'Destroyed the city of Ranarasika.' Won battle of Peruvaḷanallūr.

|

Narasimhavarman II—690-715.

Paramēśvara-Pōtavarman II—715-717. The line ended with him.	Mahēndravarman.

III.

Simhavarman II—550-575.

|

Bhīmavarman.

|

Buddhavarman.

|

Ādityavarman.

|

Gōvindavarman

|

Hiraṇyavarman. Md. Rōhini.

|

Nandivarman II—717-779.
Won battles at Maṇṇaikkuḍi and Śankaramangai against the Pāṇḍyas.
Pāṇḍya records however claim the victory, prior to A. D. 769.

|

Dantivarman—779-830 Vanquished by Rāshṭrakūṭa Gōvinda III,
to whom he became feudatory, about 804.

|

Nandivarman III—830-854.
Md. Śankhā, dau. of Rāshṭrakūṭa Amōghavarsha I.

Nṛpatunga—854-880. The Bāṇa chief Bāna-Vidyādhara was his tributary.	Vijaya-Kampa.

|

Aparājita—880 c. 898 crushed by the Chōḷa king
Āditya I, and territory annexed.

THE PERIOD OF PALLAVA ASCENDENCY STILL LEAVES TIRUPATI IN OBSCURITY. With Simhavishṇu the son of Simhavarman II, we come to the period of the Pallava history when a great dynasty of Pallava rulers, as set forth in the tables above, held rule over South India and established a dominence which they had to make good as against the Chāḷukyas of Bādāmi, the contemporary Dakhan power whose southern frontier was more or less continuously in touch with the northern frontier of the Pallavas; the whole block of territory between the Krishna and the Tungabhadra in the upper part of its course, and the northern Peṇṇār in the lower, happened to be the debatable land between the two powers. It was more or less the rivalry between the Āndhras and the Tamils of the earlier period carried forward almost undiminished during the period of the great Pallavas. The first South Indian power to recover from the devastating irruption of the Kaḷvars was the Pāṇḍya, and naturally the Pāṇḍyas challenged the title to supremacy over the Tamil land set up by the Pallavas. The struggle seems to some extent somewhat embittered not merely by the political rivalry of the dynasties, but by racial bitterness, and, to some extent, even cultural hostility. This great dynasty of Pallavas, from Simhavishṇu almost down to the end of the reign of Nandivarman II may be said to have held their own. Their title however was seriously challenged by the rising power of the Pāṇḍyas who, almost about the same time as the beginning of this dynasty, recovered to some considerable degree their original position and prestige to make a successful attack on the Pallavas. This Pallava-Pāṇḍya struggle was a feature of this period of Pallava history, and culminated almost in the simultaneous extinction of both the powers as dominating South Indian politics. We have already stated that the Pallava sovereigns of this dynasty though engaged primarily in war were not negligent of their duties as civil rulers. Their achievement is on the whole very considerable both in useful public works and in the pious acts of benefactions to religion. Notwithstanding this we do not find them to have done anything worthy of record to the holy shrine at Vēṅgaḍam, notwithstanding the fact that the shrine had attained to great fame early in its history. This can be explained as due more or less to Vēṅgaḍam being on a frontier in dispute between the Pallavas and their northern neighbours for one reason. Almost the first Chōḻa to establish his authority over the territory of the Pallavas has had to do a good deal of fighting on this frontier—in fact, as his inscriptions state it—he laid down his life in battle at a place called Toṇḍamānāṛṛūr, not far from Kāḷahasti on the Svarṇamukhi river. This was the great frontier of dispute between the Āndhras and the Tamils at one period, and the Pallavas and the Chāḷukyas in the succeeding period. Vēngaḍam, ordinarily accessible only with difficulty, has had this further difficulty added to it, and therefore was not as much frequented as a place of pilgrimage as other places within the frontiers of the Tamil land.

ABSENCE OF RECORDS EXPLAINED. The visit of a pious pilgrim, a mendicant or a poor family-man, would not lead to the leaving of records in the temple. It must be a visit of ruling families, either royal or feudatory, or powerful and important officials which would lead to placing their bequests on record. The reason stated above would make such visits almost impossible when the frontier was in dispute. Then again the practice of recording inscriptions had not yet become so common as we have already noticed, and therefore the absence of records of this period in the temple need not surprise us, and certainly will not justify the inference that the temple either had ceased to exist or ceased to be of importance. Either inference would be unwarranted on the mere basis of this fact. The two centuries following proved to be again a period of transition, and therefore it is that even during this period we are not likely to have such records in volume to furnish much information regarding the temple. We shall have to come into the full light of the period of Chōḻa ascendency before we get any useful inscriptional information.

VISHNU-WORSHIP AND TEMPLES TO VISHNU. Before closing this section, however, we may note down such inscriptional references as have come down to us in regard to Vishṇu shrines and Vishṇu worship in this region of the country. The first inscriptional reference, in point of time, is the record known as the British Museum plates of Chārudēvi. * This is a Prākrit charter issued by the queen-regent in the name of her minor son Vijayabuddhavarman, sometimes read as Buddhyankura, son of Mahārāja Vijayaskandavarman. It is a grant to a temple of Nārāyaṇa at a place called Dālūra. The next one is what is known as the grant of Simhavarman.† The record opens frankly with an invocation to Vishṇu in the name of *Bhagavat*, and purports to have been issued from the camp at Mēnmātūra, and is a grant of Simhavarman, son of Mahārāja

---

* *Epig. Indica*, VIII. p. 143.

† *ibid*, p. 159.

Vishṇugōpa, who in turn is stated to have been the son of Mahārāja Skandavarman. The next one is what is known as the Uruvappalli grant * of Yuva Mahārāja Vishṇugōpavarman who is described as a worshipper of Vishṇu (*Parama Bhāgavata*). It is a grant to the temple of God Vishṇuhāra at the village of Kandukūra. The next one is what is known as the Mahēndravādi inscription † of Guṇadhara. It is an inscription of the great Mahēndravarman and the shrine is called Mahēndra Vishṇugṛha on the bank of the Mahēndrataṭāka in the city of Mahēndrapura, all of these names having reference to Mahēndravāḍi. The next one is Manḍagappaṭṭu ‡ of Vichitrachitta, another name of Mahēndravarman. It refers to the construction of a cave-temple to Brahma, Īśvara and Vishṇu by Mahēndravarman. The next one is the series known as the Vaikunṭhaperumāḷ inscriptions in the temple of Vaikunṭhaperumāḷ constructed by Nandivarman II, Pallavamalla. § The temple is in Conjeevaram, and the inscriptions describe the circumstances under which Nandivarman came to the throne of Kānchi. The next one is what is known as the Tanḍan-

* *Ind. Antiquary*, V, p. 50.

† *Ep. Ind.* IV, p. 152 ff.

‡ *Ep. Ind.* XVII, p. 14.

§ *South Ind. Ins.* IV, p. 10 ff.

tōṭṭam plates of Kōvijaya-Nandivikramavarman.* This makes provision for the conduct of worship in the local Vishṇu and Śiva temples, and for the reading of the Mahābhārata in the temple. A similar provision for the reading of the Mahābhārata in the temple is referred to in the Kūram plates of Paramēśvaravarman I, three or four generations earlier. The next reference is the inscription of the temple of Ādivarāha at Mahābalipuram † dated in the 65th year of the same sovereign Nandivarman II, Pallavamalla. The next one is what is known as the Tiruveḷḷaṛai inscription ‡ of Dantivarman in the Puṇḍarīkāksha Perumāḷ temple near Trichinopoly. The next one is an inscription of the 9th year of Dantipōttaraśar in the Vaikuṇṭhaperumāḷ temple at Uttaramallūr, § which is much nearer. Then we come to the Triplicane inscription of the same sovereign in the *garbhagṛha* of the temple. This is dated in the 25th year of Dantivarman Mahārāja ¶ and refers to a donation to the temple. The next one is one of the 21st year of the same king in the Vaikuṇṭhaperumāḷ temple

---

* *S. Ind. Ins.* II, p. 517.

† *Epig. Colln.* 666 of 1922.

‡ *Epig. Coll.* 541 of 1905 *Ep. Ind.* XL, 156.

§ *Ep. Coll.* ·74 of 1898.

¶ *Epig. Ind.* VIII, p. 291.

at Uttaramallūr.* The next one is a reference in the 51st year of Vijaya-Dantivikrama to the Perumānaḍigaḷ at Tiruviḷangōvil in Tirucchōhinūr in Kuḍavūr-Nāḍu, a sub-division of Tiruvēngaḍak-kōṭṭam. † If this Vijaya-Dantivikrama is the Dantivarman son of Nandivarman II this would be the earliest record in this region of the Pallavas. The next is a record in the Ulagaḷanda-Perumāḷ temple at Conjeevaram dated in the 18th year of Nandipōttarayar, victor at Teḷḷāru obviously Nandivarman III.‡ The next one is in the Venkaṭēśapperumāḷ temple at Tirumukkūḍal in the Madhurāntakam Taluk of the 24th year of Nṛpatungavarman. § It is a gift of gold to the temple of Vishṇu, which was taken charge of by the assembly of Śiyyapuram, the modern Śīvaram near Conjeevaram. This spread of the inscriptions, and the number of Vishṇu shrines coming under reference would indicate the prevalence of Vishṇu worship, at least as one of the popular religions of the country. But in all these there is still the remarkable omission of Tiruvēngaḍam as a Vishṇu shrine, which omission may be

---

* *Ep. Coll.* 61 of 1896.

† *Ep. Coll.* 262 of 1904.

‡ *Ep. Coll.* 12 of 1895; *Madras Christian College Mag.* VIII, p. 102.

§ *Ep. Coll.* 179 of 1916.

explained as being due to causes already indicated above.

THE TELUGU CHOLAS AND TONDAMANDALAM. The region with which we are concerned, which, for convenience, we may call the region of north Toṇḍamaṇḍalam extending northwards of Kānchi and taking into it all the territory almost up to the river Krishṇa, has always been the debatable frontier of history for the Tamil country. We have already noticed that it was so between the Āndhras and the Tamils before the Pallavas came into power. In the days of the early Pallavas this constituted their territory principally, their expansion taking place generally towards the south. With the advent of the great Pallavas in the latter half of the 6th century, a change had come over this region also. In the earlier period this was included in the great Bāṇa country, Perumbāṇappāḍi as it was called in Tamil, to the west of which lay the land of the Gangas. But at this period a new power sprang up in the region to the north-west which early acquired possession of the south-western viceroyalty of the Āndhras. These were the Chāḷukyas who early acquired this region and established themselves at their capitl in Vātāpi, the modern Bādāmi in the Bijapūr taluk. Their expansion into this region itself was something of an aggression into territory to which the Pallavas felt themselves entitled legitimately as the successors of the Āndhras. There sprang up a natural rivalry between the two powers and the frontier line moved to and fro according to the exigencies of the wars between the two. While there were two great powers well balanced one against the other and contending for mastery indecisively, the districts in the middle changed possession; but still in their own interests they had to remain attached to the one power or the other, but subordinate and feudatory. When these powers showed a tendency to weaken by the exhausting wars, the natural tendency to independence would show itself more prominently, and so it did. While the empire of the Chāḷukyas was weakening towards its fall, and before the establishment of the powerful dynasty of the Rāshṭrakūṭas in their place, the central powers seem to have found an occasion to assert themselves. The Bāṇas seem gradually to disappear from the scene, while the bulk of their territory got absorbed into the empire of the Pallavas; the northern portions seem to have remained in the hands of a feudatory dynasty which claimed Chōḻa descent. Probably they sprang from a family of Chōḻa rulers who might have been planted in the north in early times; but they came into prominence only in the 7th century. Their territory was "a seven thousand country" with the Cuddapah district for its centre, and these were known as the Telugu Chōḷas later on. They ruled over Mahārājavāḍi Seven-thousand extending from Cuddapah eastwards to take into it the district called Pottappināḍu round Kāḷahasti, the region with which we are directly concerned. The territory of these Chōḷas who at a particular period came to be more closely associated with Pottappi, was one new state which comes to notice when the Pallava power wore away.

RISE OF NEW POWERS ON THIS CHOLA-CHALUKYA FRONTIER. In the course of a struggle we already adverted to, between the Chāḷukyas and the Pallavas success lay with the Chāḷukyas in the earlier period. They were able to take so much of Pallava territory that the great Chāḷukya ruler Pulikēsan felt justified in appointing a younger brother Viceroy over the eastern districts extending from the Pallava frontier right on to the Krishna and beyond, thus laying the foundation, unconsciously it may be, of the kingdom of the Eastern Chāḷukyas. When the Rāshṭrakūṭa usurpation took place in the middle of the 8th century in the Chāḷukya kingdom itself, this viceroyalty remained by itself alone without being absorbed into the Rāshṭrakūṭa territory not only to maintain its independence but to become so aggressive as to be a source of weakness and danger to the Rāshṭrakūṭas. When after two centuries of expansion and empire, the Rāshṭrakūṭas suffered a usurpation by a Chāḷukya feudatory of theirs, setting up another state and founding the later Chāḷukya dynasty, the Eastern Chāḷukyas had begun somehow or other to collapse simultaneously and become a minor power; but still they held the territory immediately north of the Telugu Chōḻas, sometimes claiming suzerainty over them, so that they were oftentimes in contact with the Pallava frontier in the north. So during the period when the Pallava power was actually overthrown and the Chōḻas established themselves as the leading power, these states were also coming into notice, along with the Gangas of Mysore proper and of the Noḷambas, a dynasty which claimed relationship with the Pallavas in the Ceded Districts; so that when the Chōḻas effected the conquest of Toṇḍamaṇḍalam, they had to deal with all these powers and bring them one after another under their influence either by peace or by war to assure peace to their empire. We shall see that these, particularly the first two, the Tamil Chōḻas and the Chāḷukyas showing themselves prominently in the history of the region with which we are directly concerned.

THE CHOLAS BECOME THE LEADING POWER IN SOUTH INDIA. From the end of the 6th century onwards, as we have already noted, the Pallavas had to maintain a two-faced struggle for existence: one all along their northern frontier against the Chāḷukyas, and the other practically all along their southern frontier against the Pāṇḍyas. Sometimes the southern power and the northern joined to the great detriment of the Pallavas in between. Notwithstanding the difficulties of the position and the successful wars that their enemies conducted against them, the Pallavas managed to hold their own from the days of Simhavishṇu who laid claim to have conquered the Chōḻas down to comparatively late in the reign of Nandivarman Pallavamalla. Pallavamalla had to fight hard against the Pāṇḍyas, and succeeded in maintaining himself ultimately by perhaps getting into a marriage alliance with the Rāshṭrakūṭas who superseded the Chāḷukyas in the middle of the 8th century. It is from thence that the Pallava decline may be said to begin. On the northern frontier the usurpation of the Rāshṭrakūṭas and their preoccupations with the rulers of Mālva on the one side and the Eastern Chāḷukyas on the other, gave the Pallavas the much-needed respite on that side. But simultaneously the vigour of the Pāṇḍya wars increased. They were able to keep the Ceylonese out of the struggle, and succeeded in pressing the Pallavas close till finally the Pāṇḍyas were able to march victoriously through much of the South Arcot District under their great ruler Varaguṇa II. About this time a civil dissension within the Pāṇḍya territory brought the Ceylonese into the struggle. Taking advantage of this, the Pallavas managed, with the assistance of their feudatories all round, particularly the Gangas, in pressing the Pāṇḍyas south from the banks of the Kāveri which had become the scence of this Pallava-Pāṇḍya wars generally. It is in this engagement that the name of the Chōḻa power figures on the side of Pallavas naturally. Very soon after, in fact within a decade of this victory, the Chōḻa somehow found the position wholly unsatisfactory and took upon himself to lead the forces of the victorious power allied with the Pallavas against the last Pallava himself, and won a decisive victory against him, and put himself in the position of the leading power among the southern states. The Pāṇḍyas, being otherwise occupied in their home struggles and against the Ceylon invasions, left these very much to themselves. The Pallavas who managed to hold their own even as against the powerful Pāṇḍyas seem, after their last great struggle against the Pāṇḍyas, to have weakened considerably, perhaps owing to the dissensions within the family aided by the disloyalty or the changeable loyalty of the feudatories. We are not able to see clearly the details of the struggle, but the fact that the inscriptions of the Pallavas are scattered all along the territory, and three or four Pallava names occur as rulers without any reference to a common authority at the centre, seem to indicate that there were dissensions in the Pallava succession after Aparājita, or while yet he was holding rule. This, together with the disaffection of the feudatory states, naturally paved the way for the assertion of his authority by one of the feudatory states, with the prestige of former greatness and perhaps the present power, acquired through two centuries of careful piloting of their policy and the building up of their resources. The first Chōḻa of this modern dynasty, Vijayālaya stands out thus the most powerful among the feudatories of the Pallavas who does not seem yet to proclaim himself as the successor of the Pallavas in their position as the leading Southern power. The advent of his son Āditya puts a new vigour into this kind of a struggle, and one plain fact which emerges out of the darkness of the period is the signal achievement of his, that he brought the whole of the Toṇḍamaṇḍalam under Chōḻa authority. That is a clear statement. The

TIRUCHANUR-TEMPLE AND TANK

(To face page 229)

achievement of his predecessor fell short of a supersession of the Pallavas all round although he established the position of the Chōḷas as a rising South Indian power. When Āditya came into possession of his father's conquests matters were ripe for him to advance northward and take possession of the home territory of the Pallavas, which would set the seal upon the succession of the Chōḷas to the leading position of the Pallavas in South India.

TEMPLE ORGANISATION AS REVEALED IN THE PALLAVA INSCRIPTIONS. Among the inscriptions so far published by the Tirupati Dēvastānam there are just eleven inscriptions which relate to the Pallavas. Of these the first two inscriptions refer themselves to the reign of a king Dantivikramadēva. The first of them belongs to the 51st year of the reign. This would bring us to somewhere about A. D. 833-34, that is, just the generation following that of the latest Āḻvār, Tirumangai Āḻvār. The inscriptions both of them are gifts of money for the purpose of maintaining a perpetually burning lamp for the image of the temple at Tiruvēngaḍam installed in Tiru-Iḷankōvil. Iḷankōvil is a term we have come across with in the works of the *Mudal Āḻvārs* as referring to the temple on the hill at Vēngaḍam. Whether we should interpret Iḷankōvil here also that way may be regarded open to doubt, as the record is in the temple at Tirucchānūr. It is however probable that the gift was made and put on record here for the service on the hill shrine. These two inscriptions already indicate the existence of a complete organisation of the administration of the country that we find much more fully described in the large number of records of the following period. Here Tirucchōhinūr is referred to as belonging to Kuḍavūr Nāḍu in the Tiruvēngaḍakkōṭṭam. The gift is made by an officer of the Chōḷa country who made the donation. From this and a number of inscriptions in the group we find Tiruvēngaḍakkōṭṭam belonging to the Toṇḍa-maṇḍalam, or, as it was later called Jayaṅkoṇḍachōḷamaṇḍalam, divided into four *nāḍus*, of which Kuḍavūrnāḍu comprised the villages round Tirupati, while the villages round the town of Chandragiri, a few miles to the west are grouped in Vaikuṇṭhavaḷanāḍu. Farther west the country dependent upon Chittoor now, are grouped together in the division Tuyyānāḍu. The country to the east of Tirupati and round about Kāḷahasti goes by the name Āṟṟūrnāḍu, obviously from the Toṇḍamānāṟṟūr or Toṇḍa-mānpērāṟṟūr, not far from Kaḷahasti itself on the river Svarṇamukhi. Apart from these we see the temple already under an organisation under which people at distances could make their donation and deposit their capital with properly constituted authorities in the confidence that the maintenance of a perpetual lamp, extending over a long period of time, would be safely attended to. The village is already under an organisation with something like a Secretary (*Śrī-kāryam*) to carry on the actual work. Inscription 4, also from the Tirucchōhinūr temple, refers to a deposit in gold with the *Śrī-kāryam*, and the gift was to be announced publicly and should be maintained in the register as the *Ūrniyōgam*, that is, the command of the people of the town. This is intended for the benefit of the god in Iḷankōvil, of the god installed in *Mantraśāla*, and the god in Tiruvēngaḍam. No. 6 is a provision for feeding two Brahmans in the temple. No. 7 is a record of Śaka 820, A. D. 898, and refers to the revenue *puṟavu* of the village of 1,000 *kāḍi*, and whatever was due to the government of the village, giving us clearly to understand even in this imperfect condition of the record, that the rural organisation was pretty much the same as what we find described more fully in later records. Records 8 and 9 which are included among the Pallava inscriptions ought really to belong to the next following period. These refer to the 14th year of Kō-Pārthivēndravarman, which seems to be the designation of the Chōḻa prince Āditya II, Karikāla, as he is called. We cannot say for certain that he lived on to the 14th year of his reign. But anyhow the number of records that have recently come to light would show that the prince Āditya II of the Chōḻas probably had this title and held the government of the northern region under his father Sundara Chōḻa. These two records relate to gifts by a certain lady, Śāmavvai, the wife of a Kāḍava (Pallava) chief named Śaktiviṭankan (Śaktiviḍangan in Tamil), a subordinate of Pārthivēndravarman. The lady herself is described as the daughter of a Pallava *Pērgaḍai*, which means a high officer under a Pallava chief, or it may be interpreted as a Pallava chief who held the high office. Śakti-viṭankan is a name merely, and he was of Pallava descent who had married apparently, a Kannaḍa chieftain's daughter who held the high office under the Pallavas of *Pērgaḍai*, a Kannaḍa title like the Tamil *Perundaram*. The title of the lady was Kāḍavan Perundēvi, and the gift is made to "the god standing at Vēngaḍam". She made an image of silver with a number of jewels and ornaments, of which a list is given, the value of which is set down at 47 *kaḻañju* of gold. She made this gift, and, after having performed an ablution of the God, made over to the temple authorities, 3,000 *kuḻi* of land as measured by the rod of the *ghaṭikā* (a settlement of learned Brahmans) of 16 spans, making up three *paṭṭi* of land. These were acquired from various parties, of which the *Sabhā* of Tirucchōhinūr is one. A Lakshmaṇa Nambi, the manager of a *Maṭha* is another. The god of Iḷankōvil is the third. These were acquired by the payment of the prices to the parties concerned. A further payment was also made to the *Sabhā*, and the God concerned for making it tax-free, and the land was then made over to the temple for certain purposes of service on particular occasions of the year. The proper carrying out of these is entrusted to the managers of the *Maṭha* in Tiruvēngaḍam. The lands would have to be taken care of and looked after by the *Sabhā*, and this disposition was to last as long as the sun and the moon, and the whole arrangement is put under the direction of the Śrī Vaishṇavas. The next following grant is altogether similar and refers to the gift of 4,176 *kuḻi* of land made over similarly to the managers of the *Maṭha* for use for the purpose of the festival on the occasion of the *Mārgaḻi-Dvādaśi*, the *Dvādaśi* or the 12th day of the growing moon in the month of *Mārgaḻi*, December—January. The two other records included in this section really belong to a much later period though they were grants by Pallava rulers, and may be held over for a later stage for consideration. These two should perhaps be so treated; but, as coming so close to the Pallavas and as indicating fully the organisation at the time, it is of advantage to take them over here. It will thus be seen that from these few inscriptions we find that the temple is provided already, in the days of Dantivarman Pallava of the Triplicane inscriptions, with the organisation for the management which we find in regard to these temples generally in the period following. Not only is the temple provided with the requisite machinery of management, but we find already the administration of the division in full swing with the assemblies of the villages, with various departments of accounts, the *Sabhā* managing lands, selling them to parties, taking payment and making them tax-free, and administering them as trust lands for the purposes for which they were dedicated by the donors. We could not well regard the temple organisation as having been just then brought into existence, as we find it in these records. Notwithstanding therefore the paucity of information, we would be justified in taking it that the organisation and worship in the temples had already been sufficiently well established and long in use.

CHAPTER X.

INSCRIPTIONS OF THE CHOLA DYNASTY.

CHOLA INSCRIPTIONS IN TIRUCCHANUR: PARANTAKA I AND PARANTAKA II. Passing on to the dynasty of the Chōḻas we have two records of Parāntaka I, both of them in the temple at Tirucchānūr. We have already mentioned before that, on the establishment of the Chōḻa power after the overthrow of the last Pallava by Vijayālaya, it took another campagin under his son and successor Aditya to bring the whole of the Toṇḍamaṇḍalam under the Chōḻa authority, and that this Chōḻa ruler Āditya successfully brought the whole of it under the authority of the Chōḻas. From one of his titles, it is inferable that he died at Toṇḍamānāṟṟūr near Kāḷahasti, probably in a campaign in the northernmost border of this territory. We may infer from this that, before his death, he had successfully brought the whole of the Toṇḍamaṇḍalam under his authority including the most northerly Tiruvēngaḍakkōṭṭam. His son and successor Parāntaka came to the throne in A. D. 906, and had a long reign of 48 years which would take his reign to A. D. 952–3. Under Parāntaka therefore we may take it that Toṇḍamaṇḍalam formed part of the Chōḻa empire. The existence of two of his records in Tirucchānūr is not surprising. The first of them belongs to his 29th year, that is, about A. D. 935. The document refers to the agreement by the *Sabhā* of Tirucchānūr to burn a perpetual lamp in the temple as long as the sun and moon last, that is, for all time, on behalf of an officer apparently, who paid the money. This officer is described as belonging to Malaināḍu (Chēra country) and to Koḍungalūr (Cranganore). He deposited 40 *kaḻañju* of gold as weighed by the current weight of the town. The whole charge is placed under the protection of the devotees of our Lord God (*Emberumān Aḍiyār*). The other record relating to the reign is again for the burning of a lamp. It is too far gone to make anything more out of it. The two records already referred to as belonging to a Pārthivēndravarman, the son of Parāntaka II, indicate that the state of things that the two inscriptions of Parāntaka I exhibit, continued pretty much the same under his successors for two or three generations, so that we may take it that, notwithstanding the wars of which we have records in this part, the Chōḻa authority was maintained more or less continuously. Parāntaka's queen was a Chēra princess, and that an inhabitant of the Chēra kingdom should have come all the way from Koḍungalūr to make this charity would not be anything surprising. This *Koḍungalūrān* was probably an officer in the service of the Chōḷa monarch, and felt called upon to make this charity in the course of his official tours. In this and the earlier inscriptions, the place is called Tirucchōhinūr as the name of the place. One would infer from this that the name was derived from Jōgimallāvaram, a part of Tirucchōhinūr, the *Jōgi* being transformed in Tamil *Śōhu*. Sanskrit *Yōga* assumes the form *Yōgu* in Tamil; in fact the term in that form occurs in the *Prabandha*, and a further transformation from that into *Śōhu* is not impossible. But the possibility is not enough in this case. We must know first of all that Jōgimallāvaram had been a place known by that name earlier than Tiruchukanūr. That place seems to be called Tiru-Parāśarēśvaram corrupted into Tiru-Palādhīśvaram. We should also know beforehand that the place came to be called Jōgimallāvaram in Telugu, and when and why it was so called. The Pauräṇic association of the one place with Parāśara and the other with his grandson Śuka both of them Rishis, would be quite all right. But we have to demonstrate that the more popular names had the anterior vogue before making this important inference. My recent visit to the temple goes to confirm what

I thought was the true explanation. The Śiva temple is actually a few furlongs from Tirucchānūr, and the temple is much shrunk from its original dimensions in a hamlet containing a few houses. The sanctum and the vestibule in front are all that are left over, and serve as the general stow-away for all the extra things of the few houses, that of the temple priest and a few others, immediately adjacent to the temple. I found a few cattle also being stalled quite close. The sanctum does contain the *lingam* over the usual pedestal. I was pointed out that there was a representation of a *lingam* and a *yōgi* performing penance just in the pedestal. Śiva is always represented by the *linga*; what the particular *mūrta* or figure is intended to be has necessarily to be indicated otherwise, and the indication is given in this fashion in one of the cornices in the stone pedestal. That gives the name Yōgimallāvaram for the place, that is, God Śiva presenting himself to the *Yōgi* Arjuna in the form of a *malla* or wrestler, to test his strength before granting him the boon of Śiva's *Pāsupata*, for which he performed penance. If this is the *mūrta* intended to be indicated there according to the temple tradition, the name Yōgimallāvaram among the people would be perfectly clear. While therefore one might admit that this

PADIKAVAL GOPURAM, TIRUMALAI (To face page 239)

designation, having regard to the character of the image, is possible from the beginning of the temple, it is always open to sacerdotal tradition to give the temple a name, even at the outset, as Parāśarēśvaram, so long as the local tradition connected the locality with Parāśara, and Śiva's presence there is taken to be due to the penance of this venerable *Rishi* in the locality. It is quite possible that the two villages were connected with each other, as even now the space between the two is not worth mentioning. They might have gone together into the same unit for administrative purposes.

INSCRIPTIONS OF RAJARAJA I A. D. 985—1016. Passing down we come to the reign of Rājarāja of whom we have a number of records, namely five, Nos. 14 to 18 of the Dēvastānam Inscriptions, Volume I. Of these a certain number happen to be copies made of the older inscriptions under the orders of Vīra Narasimha Yādavarāya when the inner shrine of the Venkaṭēśvara temple was either repaired or renewed by a certain Tiruppullāṇi Dāsa. We shall refer to this fact again. But for the moment we are concerned with the records as documents referable to the reign of Rājarāja I. The first of these, No. 14, refers to the 16th year of Rājarāja, that is, the year A. D. 1001, and registers a gift of an ornamental plate for the forehead for God Tiruvēngaḍadēva by a Dēvi Ammanār, meaning queen. She is described as a daughter of a Chēramān, a Chēra king, the wife of a king who died in the golden hall, *Ponmāḷikai*. This designation is given to Parāntaka II, Sundara Chōḻa, father of Rājarāja I, who had married a Chēra princess, although she was not the mother of Rājarāja. She lived in the reign of Rājarāja, and apparently as a respected member of his household as the queen-mother for 31 years at least. The gift referred to weighed 52 *kaḻañju* of gold, and had set in it four rubies, and six diamonds and 28 pearls. As if to make clear any doubts, she is called Parāntakadēvi Amman, the queen of Parāntaka. No. 15 also refers to Rājarāja I, and gives a part of the historical introduction which had become the fashion in his reign; and this document contains one of the *praśastis (meykkīrtti)* associated with Rājarāja I's inscriptions, and details his conquests. It refers to the gift by an officer who belonged to the Chōḻa country, and to Āvūrkkūṟṟam on the southern side of the Kāveri. His name is given as Aruḷākki, with an official title Mūvēndavēḷān. The rest of the inscription is gone. No. 16 seems to refer to the 29th year, and has reference to the donation of a perpetual lamp to Tiruvēngaḍamuḍaiyān, the God on the hill. There is the figure 29 which cannot be said to refer to the year of the ruler, as it is not quite in place for that. The next following is an inscription which comes from Tirucchānūr where the same officer paid 40 *kaḻañju* of gold, apparently for the burning of a perpetual lamp. Even that document is imperfect. The next one belongs to the 23rd year of Rājarāja, and is found in the Parāśarēśvara temple at Jōgimallāvaram. This is a gift by a Brahman officer of the Chōḻa country who belonged to Nenmali Nāḍu, and the Brahman village of Aruvaikkōvai. His name is given as Kōḍinambi Angāḍi with a title Gangaikoṇḍa Śōḻa Brahma Mārāyan (Mahārāja Gangaikoṇḍa Chōḻa Brahmaṇa). He deposited 26 *kaḻañju* of gold weighed by the measure, specifically in use in regard to charitable gifts, for the purpose of an ablution to God on the occasions of the Uttarāyaṇa Sankarānti, the first of day of Uttarāyaṇa every year coming about the middle of January. These inscriptions of Rājarāja refer to donations by his officers to the God on the hill, and to the Vishṇu and Śiva temples at Tirucchānūr. Two of them attempt to record the official introduction, one by a plain recital, that is No. 15, and the other, No. 18, by a mere reference in the terms "with the usual prefatory *meykkīrtti*", or historical recital of his glorious deeds. That is so far as the reign of Rājarāja is concerned, A. D. 985 to A. D. 1016.

RECORDS OF RAJENDRA CHOLA I: A. D. 1011-1044. Then follow two inscriptions of Rājēndra Chōḷa, his son. One of them from the temple on the hill, and the other at the foot of the hill in the Kapilēśvara temple. This does not contain the *praśasti* or the official laudatory passage, and begins straightaway with the 7th year of Rājēndra, the number of days in the year, omitted probably by inadvertence of the sculptor who engraved the inscription. That is, however wrongly read as the 7th day of the first year. The usual way of specifying these dates is, first to give the year, and then proceed to mention the date. The record here therefore mentions the year 7, followed by the day. The number which has to follow this is omitted. This would correspond to the year A. D. 1018. This is a very interesting document and refers to an official enquiry conducted in regard to the arrangements for the conduct of worship in the temple of the God at Tiruvēngaḍam. The officer concerned is the lord of Kottamangalam. Tiruvēngaḍakkōṭṭam is here referred to as a part of Perumbāṇappāḍi in Jayankoṇḍachōḷamaṇḍalam. He held the enquiry in Tiruchukanūr belonging to Kuḍavūrnāḍu, and Tiruchukanūr is here described as a *dēvadānam*, gift to God. The officer held his court in the front hall of a building that he presented on a previous occasion, and held an inquisition into the management of the temple affairs. He made the enquiry from an officer of the survey and classification (*vakai śeyvadu*) of land of Kuḍavūrnāḍu. He is described as a *Śirudanattu Perumakan*, which would mean the chief official belonging to the class *Śirudanam*, and his name is given as Kaḍappañ-koḍaiyan, which would ordinarily mean belonging to Kaḍappañ-kuḍai, the name of a village or a town, and the servants of the temple *Dēvar Kaṇmi*. It came out on the enquiry that the *Sabhā* of Sirumunḍiyam, another village gifted to the temple, took possession of the gold offered, according to inscriptions recorded in stone, and agreed to burn 24 perpetually burning lamps including one to be burnt with camphor. Of these the *Sabhā* of Tirumunḍiyam was burning only two lamps and could not burn the rest according to agreement, and requested that 20 *kaḻañju* belonging to the capital be recovered from the inhabitants of Tirumunḍiyam, and, along with three more *kaḻañju* from the temple treasury, should be made over to the *Sabhā* of Tiruchukanūr, so that they may, without fail, burn the total number of lamps in the temple on the hill. This was the decision given by the officer (*Adhikāri*) and this decision was accepted by the *Sabhā* of Tirumuṇḍiyam, which was again accepted by the treasury of the temple at Tiruchukanūr, and the requisite number of lamps was undertaken to be burnt by the officials of the temple and those engaged in the religious service to the temple as long as the sun and moon should last. This was the accepted decision of the Śrī Vaishṇavas. The other record refers to the Kapilēśvaram temple at the foot of the hill known as the Kapilatīrtham; and refers to the raising of a building by the Lord of Kōṭṭūr with the title Rājēndra Chōḷa Brahma-Mārāyan with the official title *Munayadaraiyan.* From this time on to the date of Kulōttunga I we have no records forthcoming. This would leave an interval between the year A. D. 1018 and the third year of Kulōttunga I, A. D. 1073, the date of the earliest record of the ruler, which would mean a period of about half a century.

INSCRIPTIONS OF KULOTTUNGA I, THE CHALUKYA-CHOLA: AND HIS SON VIKRAMA CHOLA. With the inscription No. 21 in the Parāśarēśvara temple at Jōgimallāvaram, we come upon the reign of Kulōttunga Chōḷa, whose reign period is counted from A. D. 1070 to A. D. 1148. This Kulōttunga, as he called himself afterwards, was a prince of the dynasty of the Eastern Chāḷukyas, and was the son of the Chōḷa princess Madhurāntaki, the daughter of Rājēndra

Chōḷa I, who was married to the Eastern Chāḷukya Rājarāja, who was again the son of Rājarāja's daughter married to the Eastern Chāḷukya prince Vimalāditya, so that Kulōttunga was a Chōḷa Chāḷukya prince, heir to the throne of the Eastern Chāḷukyas by birth, and became king of the Chōḷas by an act of usurpation. He was a remarkable Chōḷa sovereign and is counted among the great Chōḷas deservedly. It is, however, noteworthy that, in the records round Tirupati and in several others of his earlier years, he is given all the Chāḷukya titles, some of which are titles of feudatory princes. Among them peculiarly the title "*Samadhigata Panchamahāśabda*", was assumed by the Eastern Chāḷukyas from the time of Kubja Vishṇuvardhana, the first member of this dynasty. It began as a title of the feudatories entitled to go about with the band playing, the band being composed of musical instruments, the sounds produced emanating in five ways, according to the ancient classification of the various instruments constituting the band. The privilege of going about with the band playing was generally conferred upon those newly raised to dignity, as a mark of distinction. The first of these, No. 21 of Volume I describes him as a *Mahāmaṇḍalēśvara* (lord of a great division only), as an ornament of the

Chāḷukya race, as the lord of Vengi, as the beloved of the Gōdāvari river, and the supreme lord of Kānupākka, etc. All these my be regarded as peculiarly Eastern Chāḷukya titles· What follows is a matter for personal distinction, the fearsome one with the use of the sword *(Karavāḷa Bhairava)*. Then follows the title *Vēnkaṭanātha Purandhara* which seems to imply that he was a ruler over the region dominated by Vēnkaṭanāthapura (Tirupati). He is said further on to have destroyed the stronghold of Kaṭakapura, probably Cuttack in Orissa, the capital of the ancient Kalingas. With all this follows what is generally a feudatory title *Mahāmaṇḍalēśvara*. He is given the further title *Mahārāja Śri Vīra* Rājēndra Chōḷa, and refers itself to the third year. He is given the title *Rājēndra Chōḷadēva*, to which sometimes is added the prefix *Vīra*, which, in the few instances in which it occurs in his age, ought to be interpreted as a mere attribute meaning valiant, and not as forming a part of the name, if for no other reason, for the simple reason that this is not uniformly given as his title, as in the case of the uncle whom he succeeded, Chōḷa Vīra Rājēndra. The record is nothing more than a grant made for the purpose of maintaining two perpetual lamps. No. 22 is a record in Tirupati which is too far gone to make anything out of, except that it mentions Śrī Rājēndradēva referring in all probability to this Rājēndra Kulōttunga. The next following document which is in the Śiva temple at Jōgimallāvaram is a document of importance, as it gives one of those usual *praśastis* of Kulōttunga recounting all his exploits both as a prince and as a ruler. It is a record of the 24th year of Kulōttunga which would mean A. D. 1094. It is a grant made by somebody for burning four perpetual lamps in the temple for which, at the rate of 32 cows a lamp, 128 cows were taken possession of by a certain number of Śaiva Brahmans engaged in service in the interior sanctum of the temple; and that is the purpose of the record. The province concerned is described as Rājēndrachōḻamaṇḍalam instead of the usual Toṇḍamaṇḍalam or Jayankoṇḍachōḻamaṇḍalam, and the sub-divisions are mentioned as usual. No. 24 is a record of the same temple. The first part of it is gone. It refers itself to the 35th year, and records a grant made by one Kaṇṇan Vāsudēvan who is given the title *Śōḻa Brahma-Mārāyan*, who destroyed darkness and acquired something by his own strength. He acquired a certain piece of land in the *dēvadāna* village Munnaippūṇḍi, otherwise called Śivapādaśēkharanallūr by paying five *māḍai* of gold, and getting the particular bit of land tax-free. The importance of the record consists however in the procedure that is indicated. This Kaṇṇan Vāsudēvan made the request of the superintendent of the *Māgāṇi*, a small revenue sub-division. He apparently got the order from the king himself who, by word of mouth, sanctioned the transformation of the village into a tax-free temple-gift land, in evidence whereof a number of officers of the settlement department affixed their signatures. Seven or eight such names are mentioned in detail. The land became a free-gift land to the temple from the 35th year of Kulōttunga onwards. The next one No. 25 comes from the same temple and refers itself to the 41st year of Kulōttunga. The record is in an imperfect state of preservation and refers to the sale of a certain bit of land to the Mahādēva, that is, to the temple. Among the other details mentioned are the temple, the digging of a tank in the near vicinity of Kāḷahastīśvara. The signatures are also gone. No. 26 is in the temple on the hill. But enough of it is left to show that it begins with one of the *praśastis* of Kulōttunga whose name itself is mentioned. No. 27 is in the same temple and the bit of the *praśasti* itself clearly refers unmistakably to the reign of Kulōttunga. It refers to the gift of milk and curds for the God by a lady, the wife of an officer who had a title beginning Rājēndra. The interesting point to note in this is the God in the temple is referred to as "Tiruvāyppāḍi Tirumalai Āḻvār", which would mean the lord of Tiruvāyppāḍi (cowherd village) on the hill. It is a clear recognition in the reign of Kulōttunga I that the God was regarded as an aspect of Krishṇa-Vishṇu, as by the early Āḻvārs. Unfortunately the precise date is not available in the record that the temple on the hill was recognised to be a temple of Krishṇa on the hill. No. 28 again in Tirupati can be taken to be a record of Kulōttunga. The next following one is also his, but there is nothing of importance in it, and so also No. 30. Almost the same might be said of 31 and 32. In these records of Kulōttunga amounting in all to 12 records, we are given the indication that, in the days of Kulōttunga, the region was directly under the Chōḻa government undoubtedly, from the days while yet Kulōttunga was only a Chāḷukya prince down to a comparatively late period in his reign. The shrines in the locality, a Vishṇu shrine at Tirupati, the Śiva shrine at Tiruparāśarēśvaram near Tirucchānūr, the temple even of Kāḷahasti find mention. The Śiva temple at Tiruparāśarēśvaram comes in for great benefaction. There is only one record of his successor Vikrama Chōḻa, who came to the throne in A. D. 1118 and ruled for about 17 or

18 years, so that his reign period would be A. D. 1118 to A. D. 1135. In this one record, Vikrama Chōḻa is given all the Chāḷukya titles almost exactly as in the records of Kulōttunga, even though the record happens to be one of his 16th year, that is, A. D. 1134. The division is again referred to as Rājēndraśōḻamaṇḍalam, and relates to a gift to the Tiruparāśarēśvaram temple of oil for lighting the lamps on the occasion of the festival in the month of *Vaikāśi*, May—June. The piece of land in gift is referred to as being to the north of the *Dēvadāna* village, Munnaippāḍi.

During the period therefrom, A. D. 1017 to A. D. 1135, we have a fairly large number of inscriptions referring to the temple on the hill, and the Śiva and Vishṇu temples at Tirucchānūr as also a reference to the great Śiva shrine in the neighbourhood, Kāḷahasti. We may therefore take it that these were certainly all of them in existence and received donations from various people, some of the more important donors being actually officers of government under the Chōḻas. The more important donations seem, however, to have been to the Śiva temple at Yōgimallāvaram (Tiruparāśarēśvaram), and hardly any important one by way of major donations of large gifts or additions to buildings, etc., to the Vishṇu temple on the hill, or at

Tirucchānūr. Being more or less donations by private individuals we can hardly argue that it indicates partiality, one way or the other, of the government. The fact may, however, bear the inference that enthusiasm for Śiva worship was rising perhaps among the people generally, but certainly among those occupying positions in life. On the basis of these facts it would be difficult to go further and say that there was anything like a movement of a Śaiva character which could do damage to Vishṇu worship and Vishṇu temples as such. There is one noteworthy point, however, that, since the days of the great Gangaikoṇḍa Chōḻa, the region seems to have passed out of view of inscriptional information for half a century, and then when it does come into view, it comes into view as the territory of the Chōḻa-Chāḷukya prince Kulōttunga, and the character of his earlier inscriptions in the locality would seem to warrant the impression that it ceased to be, if not formally, at any rate practically, intimately associated with the Chōḻa empire as such. We might perhaps account for it by the keen contest between the Chōḻas and the Chāḷukyas of the west during the period.

We stated already that it was the policy of Rājarāja to bring about peace between the empire and its neighbours on all frontiers with a view to the coming struggle between the Chōḻas and the Chāḷukyas, the two imperial powers face to face on the somewhat indefinite frontier of the north-west of the Chōḻas, and south and south-east of the Chāḷukyas. The peace with the Eastern Chāḷukyas sealed by a marriage alliance, probably had this coming great struggle in view; but that Rājarāja anticipated this and made his arrangements accordingly is not left to us in doubt at all, as he put his son and heir-apparent the Gangaikoṇḍa Chōḻa in charge of this north-western frontier and the war, thereby creating him a sort of a superior viceroy, not so much in charge of the territory, but in charge of the war on this frontier. Rājēndra, the Gangaikoṇḍa Chōḻa had to do a good deal of fighting on this frontier, and the war continued almost with the same vigour under his sons, three of whom succeeded one after the other on the Chōḻa throne, before the Chōḻa-Chāḷukya Prince Kulōttunga, we might almost say usurped the empire. During this period of war, the frontier districts, among them the region with which we are directly concerned, must have been constantly liable to attacks and invasions, and required special provision to guard against the enemy incursions; and one way of doing that perhaps was to include it in the sphere of the wardens of the northern frontier of the Chōḷas, the more so, as that particular frontier was in charge of a dynasty of rulers intimately related to the Chōḷa family. It is not so much the transfer of this division or *Maṇḍalam* to the Eastern Chāḷukyas, as a mere transfer of charge and the guardianship to whomsoever was in charge of the southern portion of the Eastern Chāḷukya territory. It seems to be thus that the Chōḷa-Chāḷukya prince Kulōttunga came to be in charge of it in the earlier years of his reign as these districts were a centre of the war zone. We can understand from the fact that the immediate successor of the Gangaikoṇḍa Chōḷa had to march across the whole of the Mysore territory, which then was more or less under Chōḷa control, to Kampli in the Bellary district, not far from Hampi where are the ruins of Vijayanagar, and thence all the way through the Chāḷukya territory proper to Kolhāpur in the heart of the Chāḷukya dominions. He fell in battle and his younger brother, who brought up reinforcements and beat back the enemy, had to fight hard to maintain his position. When he was succeeded by Vīrarājēndra, he had to continue the same war; but we find that that war had to be continued over more extensive fields. Vīrarājēndra claims a victory over the *Kuntaḷas*, the Western Chāḷukyas, at Kūḍalsangamam, wherefrom he is said to have marched successfully to Bezwada (Vijayavāḍi, as it is called in these inscriptions) and went further north. We find inscriptions of about this time in the Telugu country proper at Drākshārāma, and elsewhere in the neighbourhood, of the prince Vikramāditya, son of the Chāḷukya emperor Sōmēśvara who was the reigning monarch. There is also the additional fact that the Chāḷukyas about this time, appear to have created a new viceroyalty in charge of a prince of the blood round the region of Kampli. These facts taken together would indicate clearly that the war between the two empires was quite as active in the region across Tiruvēngaḍakkōṭṭam of the Toṇḍamaṇḍalam. It would therefore be nothing surprising if the peaceful activity of people moving about on their normal official duties, holding enquiries and making donations, by the way, to temples and recording them in inscriptions remain suspended. That perhaps is the reason why between the comparatively early date in the reign of Rājēndra, the Gangaikoṇḍa Chōḻa, down to the third year of prince Kulōttunga, we find no inscriptions in this locality, and this distraction must have continued even when Kulōttunga had succeeded as the Chōḻa emperor. Kulōttunga and his contemporary the Chāḷukya Vikramāditya VI had both of them alike to make war the prime concern of their policy. It was rather late in their reigns, after a continuous struggle lasting for a whole generation as it were, that they realised that this war was likely to prove interminable, and as such detrimental to the actual interests of everybody concerned. Then they came to an understanding, implicit or expressed, we do not know for certain, to let the Mysore plateau remain with the Chāḷukyas; and the two emperors contented themselves with keeping within their own frontiers and pursuing the arts of peaceful administration, for the remaining period of their lives. Kulōttunga died somewhere about the year A. D. 1120 and Vikramāditya followed six years after. While there was a succession of capable rulers in the Chōḻa empire, the Chāḷukya empire was not lucky to the same extent, and gradually weakened away towards its decline. Vikrama Chōḻa had to be a viceroy of the Chōḻas in the ancestral territory of the Eastern Chāḷukyas, from where he had to march south to take over the Chōḻa empire. All this period therefore was a period when the empire was preoccupied with war.

CHAPTER XI.

THE AGE OF THE VAISHNAVA ACHARYAS.

INTERVAL OF ABSENCE OF INSCRIPTIONS. The period extending from the death of Vikrama Chōḻa down to the early years of the reign of Rājarāja III, must have been for this region a period of the rise to prominence of the feudatory chieftains to power and authority. There were two sets of those who play a prominent part in the later years of Kulōttunga III and throughout the reign of Rājarāja III, becoming independent rulers of the locality afterwards. Whether we could consider this activity on the part of the feudatories gradually to make themselves independent, is the actual cause of the absence of inscriptions, we cannot say for certain; but it seems likely, as, early in the reign of Vikrama Chōḻa, that region was to some extent distracted between loyalty to the Chōḻas and the Western Chāḷukyas. That disturbance must have been the cause of the ultimate establishment of independence by the local chieftains. This was made possible by the preoccupation of the imperial Chōḻas with their wars in the south, and the activity of the Hoyśālas, who acquired a firm hold on the Chōḻa territory in the period immediately following.

THE ACHARYA NADAMUNI, THE FIRST ACHARYA: The two centuries since the end of the Pallava ascendency early in the 10th century, almost down to the beginning of the period with which we are concerned happen to be the period of active life of the Vaishṇava Āchāryas, as distinct from the Āḻvārs. The teachings of the Āḻvārs could not have been anything particularly systematic, and even the works which have come down to us could not have been known so widely in those early times. There is, however, a tradition which finds mention in the *Guruparamparas*, the traditional accounts of the lives of these Āḻvārs and Āchāryas, that Tirumangai Āḻvār during his life-time arranged for the recitation of these once a year on the occasion of a particular festival in Śrīrangam in December—January of each year. Apart from the mere work of individual teachers, teaching a few pupils of theirs, there seems to have been no particular provision for the propagation of the Vaishṇava teaching in any organised form. The need, however, seems to have been felt to some extent, and provision had to be made sooner or later. The credit for organising such is due to the first Vaishṇava Āchārya known by the name

Nādamuni. He seems to have belonged to the village of Mannārkōvil in the South Arcot District where he lived most of his life, spending some time also in the adjoining village called Kurukaikkāvalappan Kōvil in the South Arcot District, just about a mile off the Chōḻa capital Gangaikoṇḍaśōḻapuram. He probably was a practitioner of Vaishṇavism, and a teacher of local reputation like so many others. It so happened that a set of Vaishṇava pilgrims were going about worshipping in the Vaishṇava shrines, and they came to the latter place where Nādamuni was engaged for the time being in teaching his pupils, and practising *Yōga*. When he heard them recite just one of the tens of the *Tiruvāymoḻi* of Nammāḻvār, he was struck with the verses, and he asked the pilgrims to repeat them; and, having learnt from them the ten, he also learnt from them that it was only a ten taken from out of the 1,000 of Nammāḻvār, and the pilgrims heard it recited in the temple at Kumbhakoṇam. They learnt it off from there and knew no more about the work or the author. Nādamuni was naturally curious to secure the whole if possible, as he had heard probably of Nammāḻvār and of his *Tiruvāymoḻi*. He went down to Kumbhakoṇam, and got from there no more information than he already possessed and the one ten which he had already taken down or got by rote from the pilgrims. He learnt however that it was possible that at Nammāḻvār's native place, Āḻvār Tirunagari as it is called, in the Tinnevelly District, it is possible he could find people who knew the whole of the work. So he started on his pilgrimage to Aḻvār Tirunagari. After futile attempts to gain information from anybody who knew anything about the whole work, he went into the temple and sat in *Yōgasamādhi* in front of the sacred tamarind tree under which Nammāḻvār is said to have practised *Yōga*. He then chanced upon some one who had learnt this from Madhurakavi, the direct disciple of Nammāḻvār, and he is said to have secured the whole work. He brought it over to Śrīrangam and there revived the annual festival instituted by Tirumangai Āḻvār, which since had fallen into desuetude owing to the impossibility of bringing the image of Nammāḻvār all the way owing to heavy rains and floods. Having done this, he started on a pilgrimage to the holy shrines. It is said in the *Guruparamparas* that he travelled north as far as the Himalayas visiting some of the Vishṇu shrines in these regions, and passing down southwards therefrom, he visited Ahōbalam, and then Tirupati. He went away from Tirupati feeling that the arrangements for worship there were not as good as they should be. We are told nothing further than this in his life so far as Nādamuni is concerned. He is said to have been born in the year of *Kali* 3684, which would mean A. D. 582-83. This obviously is too early a dating for him, having regard to the dates of the others given in this very account, if nothing else. There is further the fact that the *Guruparamparas* have to make up the dating in a way which perhaps gives us an idea roughly of the actual period in which he lived. He is said to have been 340 years in *Yōga* to acquire the *Tiruvāymoḻi* from Nammāḻvār himself direct. The 340 years, or say roundly three or four centuries, perhaps prove the gap between the Āḻvār and the first Āchārya Nādamuni. Perhaps this may indicate roughly the time in which he flourished, some time early in the 10th century A. D.

THE SUCCESSORS OF NADAMUNI: ALAVANDAR AND RAMANUJA. His grandson Āḷavandār Yamunaitturaivar or Yāmunāchārya), is said to have been born almost at the fag end of the life of Nādamuni, and lived on to see Rāmānuja as a young man, made a similar pilgrimage to the shrines of holy reputation among the Vaishṇavas and visited Tirupati similarly. He found apparently the same defect in regard to the arrangements for worship, particularly the fact that there was no satisfactory arrangement, such as, providing for a flower garden, for the supply of flowers, etc., for the daily worship of God in the temple. As that was considered one of the necessary objects for the offer of worship, he wanted to know if any among his disciples would brave the rigours of a life on the hill, and do what was necessary to provide this essential need of daily worship. One of his own grandsons who had attained to manhood and had reached the stage of householder volunteered for this service, and moved himself away with two of his young and unmarried sisters to set up life on the hill. This is Tirumalai Nambi, as he is called, and that is perhaps more a title than an actual name. He settled down there, laid out a garden, and cultivated such flowers and plants required for worship, and further took it upon himself to provide water daily for the ablution of the image from the waterfall some distance away on the hill known by the name *Ākāśagangā*. One of the young sisters that he took with him was married to one Kēśava Sōmayāji of Śrīperumbūdūr. The offspring of this marriage was Rāmānuja. Rāmānuja's date of birth, according to the traditional account of his life, is *Kali* 4118, A. D. 1017. The other date given of course is Śaka 937 by a chronogram. So Rāmānuja's life would be cast in the 11th century mostly, extending, it may be, into the 12th to some extent. Among the cardinal events of Rāmānuja's life happen to be at least two visits to Tirupati which in the nature of the case would be nothing very unusual, although according to other accounts, he is said to have paid as many as four visits. We shall have to consider this matter in some detail later. One of his visits was for the purpose of being taught the *Rāmāyaṇa* by his own uncle Tirumalai Nambi, who had received this exposition from Āḷavandār specifically. During another visit, he is said to have got the local ruler to build the Gōvindarāja shrine at Lower Tirupati, and set up the image of Gōvindarāja, which was cast out of its place in the great temple at Chidambaram into the sea. During the time of Rāmānuja, and while he was still teaching in Śrīrangam, he felt the need again of an enterprising young man going and settling down in the temple for the flower service, probably because Tirumalai Nambi was growing too old for it, although the *Guruparamparas* do not state it so. One of his disciples who happened to be an arrival from the district round Tirupati volunteered for this service, and this person is Anandāḻvār, who figures in the accounts of the Tirupati temple, of which one prominent one is the *Vēnkaṭāchala Itihāsamāla* by one Anantārya. We shall examine this work in some little detail later. In the time of Rāmānuja there seems to have been considerable improvement in the kind of organisation and the requisite agency for looking after the general management of the temple which already existed, and for the conduct of worship in the proper form. For this period we have some inscriptional information also which we shall have to consider together with the traditional information.

MANAGEMENT OF TEMPLES AND ORGANISATION OF WORSHIP; THE BUSINESS OF WORSHIPPERS. In these accounts of the lives of the Āchāryas, Tirupati gets to be mentioned as already a holy place of reputation which the Achāryas felt called upon to visit in the course of their pilgrimages. There is no mention of any ruler of the locality, either governors under a higher or a suzerain authority, or even rulers of the locality who claim to be ruling on their own account. Temple worship and provision therefor seem to have been more or less a matter for the devotees to provide for, and it seems to be only private generosity, whether of the ordinary people or those in authority, that made provision for this. In this period that point must be clearly noted. When the assistance of local rulers was sought, and when these rulers intervened, there again in the great majority of cases, the donations, made by these very rulers for various purposes, seem to have been made in their personal capacity and not as rulers exercising authority, except where they interfered to correct a wrong or do justice between different parties disputing for privileges or other matters connected with the temple.

RAMANUJA'S CONNECTION WITH TIRUPATI ACCORDING TO SRI VENKATACHALA ITIHASAMALA. The above account is as far as the *Guruparamparas* go. But Śrī *Vēnkaṭāchala Itihāsamāla*, a work compiled by one Anantārya contains a detailed account of Rāmānuja's doings in Tirupati. Rāmānuja's connection with Tirupati may be said to begin with Tirumalai Nambi, whose sister Rāmānuja's mother was. As was stated above, on the authority of the *Guruparampara* account, Tirumalai Nambi went and settled down at Tirupati with his two young unmarried sisters for doing service to the God on the hill, as desired by his grandfather and teacher Āḷavandār. He remained there almost as a permanent resident, and it is from there that the hand of his sister was sought and obtained by Rāmānuja's father whose own native place was Śrīperumbūdūr, not far from Tirupati in point of distance. Apart from such visits as he might have made on occasions of domestic functions where the mother's presence may have been called for in Tirupati, the first visit of Rāmānuja to Tirupati, in his character as a Vaishṇava teacher at all, was when he went there to get from his uncle the esoteric teaching of the

Rāmāyaṇa as one among the several cardinal items of learning that he had to acquire to equip himself for the high office of the chief Vaishṇava teacher of the day. On that occasion he is said to have stayed for a year with Tirumalai Nambi, and learnt the Rāmāyaṇa from him and returned to Śrīrangam.

RAMANUJA'S SECOND VISIT TO TIRUPATI: The second occasion that necessitated Rāmānuja's visit to Tirupati was later. The worship originally organised at Tirupati was in accordance with the system of the Vaikhānasa Āgama, and was being conducted by a descendant of the first temple priest Gopinath. In the course of years, in fact centuries after, there seems to have been some irregularity in the conduct of worship, for which the local ruler punished the priests in charge, who, in consequence took themselves away from the place; and there seems to have followed as a result a certain period of neglect of this work. In consequence the temple seems to have remained without a recognised guardian, and some Śaivas in or about the locality seem to have got into possession of the temple; at any rate, set up claims to it. There apparently was not a sufficient community of Vaishṇavas to resist this claim effectively, and the local ruler, described as a Yādavarāja, with his head-quarters at Nārāyaṇavaram, wished to put the matter on a satisfactory footing after due enquiry. It was on that occasion, probably on the representation of a few Vaishṇavas in the locality, that he sent for Rāmānuja from Śrīrangam to come to his court and meet the Śaiva divines who set up claims to the temple, and enable him to arrive at a correct judgment as to the fact whether the temple at Tirupati was a Vishṇu shrine or a Śiva shrine. Rāmānuja responded to the invitation, and explained the matter satisfactorily at the assembled court, meeting the arguments of the Śaivas in support of their claim, and ultimately established, to the satisfaction of the Rāja, that Venkaṭēśa at Tirupati was beyond doubt a representation of Vishṇu and not of Śiva. He created a favourable impression upon the local ruler, the Yādavarāja, so that he was able to make use of the good offices of the Rāja for the purpose of installing, in a temple at the foot of the hill, the image of Gōvindarāja, whose shrine in the great Śiva temple at Chidambaram had been ordered to be destroyed, and the principal image thrown into the sea, by the Chōḻa monarch for the time being, a zealous Śaiva. Some of those connected with the temple however, managed to get away from the place carrying the movable images of the shrine, and had arrived in Lower Tirupati for safety. Through

Rāmānuja's influence, the Yādavarāja set apart an unoccupied portion of the town at the foot of the hill, built the shrine of Gōvindarāja there, and laid out an *Agrahāra* (Brahman settlement) round it, making the necessary arrangements for the conduct of the service in the temple. The removal of the Gōvindarāja image from Chidambaram is said to have taken place in this account just a little before Rāmānuja's successful mission in connection with the character of the shrine of Venkaṭāchala at Tirupati. He is said to have done several other things in connection with the worship and festivals in the temple at Tirupati before he returned from there. If the *Vēnkaṭāchala Itihāsamāla* is to be believed, Tirumalai Nambi was still alive and active in Tirupati as well as Anantārya, his own disciple whom he had deputed for the service of God at Tirupati. Anantārya was to look after the affairs of the temple under the direction of Tirumalai Nambi, now very old.

RAMANUJA'S LATER VISITS: Rāmānuja is said to have visited Tirupati again at a very advanced age, and that is said to have been his last visit on account of the great age to which he had attained by the time. The actual age is given as 102 years, and this is equated with the *Kali* year 4,220, and the Śaka year 1,041. He took advantage of his being there on this occasion to make certain improvements in the arrangements that he had already made by giving the one *Sanyāsin*, who was to look after the affairs of the temple disinterestedly, two or three assistants who were to be bachelors looking after certain departments of work. He also instituted the chanting of the *Prabandha* hymns in the proper form, and for that, he arranged that a special person should be appointed to be in charge. This became afterwards the head *Sanyāsin* with the title Śaṭakōpayati. He was assisted by four bachelors who had the management of the temple. This was to be supervised and controlled by the Yādavarāja, who, in all matters relating to the temple, was to act with the advice of Anantārya, Rāmānuja's own disciple, who is, in this account, said to have attained to the age of 66. On the basis of this arrangement, we may take it that Tirumalai Nambi had passed away.

There are one or two items of further arrangements spoken of in connection with matters more general, and not exclusively in regard to Tirupati, which would indicate that he had come to the last years of his life. That is about as far as we are concerned with the history of the temple at Tirupati with respect to

Rāmānuja. But what we have noted already from the *Guruparamparas* that Nādamuni paid a visit as did his grandson Yāmunāchārya, are borne out by the account in the *Vēnkaṭāchala Itihāsamāla* as well. In the absence of confirmation from inscriptions we have to make the best of these accounts, and arrive at our own conclusions as to the historical character of these incidents.

EXAMINATION OF THE GURUPARAMPARA AND ITIHASAMALA ACCOUNTS: We have already noted that there are no inscriptions in Tirupati and the places dependent on it, during the period, and, among the valid reasons for this absence was one that probably this region was gradually passing under the authority of local chiefs who were rather inclined not to recognise the central authority and who wished to set themselves up in independence ultimately. The Yādavarāya who figures in these accounts was probably a chieftain who belonged to the family of Yādavarāyas, some of whom became famous later on in this locality, the best known name being the powerful chief Vīra Narasimha Yādavarāya, feudatory of Kulōttunga III and his successor Rājarāja III. But before we proceed to examine this, we must study one or two preliminary questions in regard to the statements in the *Vēnkaṭāchala Itihāsamāla*, and clear the position so far as these statements are concerned. According to this authority, the first visit to Tirupati was undertaken for the purpose of the Rāmāyaṇa teaching of Tirumalai Nambi. Another detail is mentioned in connection with this, and that is a reference to the grant of an *Agrahāra* called Bālamaṇḍya a village in the vicinity of Tirupati by a Viṭṭhalarāja, a disciple of Rāmānuja, which would mean that this, the first visit of Rāmānuja to Tirupati, should have taken place after Rāmānuja had returned from what is now Mysore, to which he had to betake himself in fear of the Chōḷa monarch's anger, because of the Vaishṇavas of Śrīrangam, the disciples of Rāmānuja, not subscribing to the Śaiva doctrine that "Śiva is the Supreme Deity." Then the second visit comes in rather close to the destruction of the Gōvindarāja temple at Chidambaram, and for the third visit the *Itihāsamāla* gives specific dates. We shall have to examine this carefully in the light of what is known of the life of Rāmānuja with a view to appraising the actual value of these statements for purposes of history. The *Guruparampara* date for Rāmānuja's birth is the Śaka year 939, in the Christian era A. D. 1017. The same *Guruparamparas* give us the date that, in the Śaka year 1021, the temple at Tirunārāyaṇapuram was built, and the image duly installed with the countenance of this Viṭṭhalarāya, who had already become a disciple of Rāmānuja. This date would correspond to the year A. D. 1099. Of course, the actual date given for his third visit is based apparently upon this *Guruparampara* date, and therefore works out correctly for this date. But our difficulty centres round certain known historical facts, two of which relating to Rāmānuja are established facts of history. The first of these two facts is as to when Rāmānuja had to take himself away from Śrīrangam for safety, and in consequence, came into contact with, and secured the good-will of, Viṭṭhaladēvarāya, the ruler of that territory at the time. Viṭṭhaladēvarāya is obviously the name of Biṭṭidēva, which is the Kannaḍa form of the Sanskrit Vishṇudēva. Of course after getting into association with Rāmānuja, he is given the Vaishṇava form of the name Vishṇuvardhana, which is not altogether far from the original name of the monarch, the addition merely indicating that he had become a Vaishṇava and promoted the cause of Vaishṇavism. Taking the *Guruparampara* account itself, it mentions this Viṭṭhaladēva as the ruling monarch at the time, and he is brought into contact with Rāmānuja while he was still in residence at the village Toṇḍanūr, a few miles from the railway station of French Rocks of to-day, in connection with a domestic matter of Viṭṭhaḷadēva's family. It seems a daughter of this ruler was possessed, and all the Jaina divines at court and elsewhere, were not able to raise the ghost and free the young lady from its clutches. Rāmānuja is supposed to have effected this successfully, and in gratitude therefor the ruler became a disciple of Rāmānuja giving up Jainism which was his former religion. It is after this incident that Rāmānuja got to know of the image buried at Melkōṭṭai and installed it in a temple built for the purpose in the locality. The precise date given for that is, as we have already noted, at the commencement, the equivalent of A. D. 1099. It is this date that actually runs against what is known from inscriptions and history. At this date A. D. 1099, Viṭṭhaladēva was yet a prince, and his father who gives himself the titles of a feudatory of the Chāḷukya empire under Vikramāditya VI, had just died. He was succeeded in the position by an elder brother of Biṭṭidēva holding only a subordinate position like that of his other brother. It was about A. D. 1106 at the earliest that he became ruler in his own right, even in a subordinate capacity as a feudatory of the Chāḷukya empire. We have inscriptions of date A. D. 1117 stating that the temple of Nārāyaṇa at Bēlūr was completed,* and

* *Epigraphica Carnatica*, Hassan, Vol. *Bēlūr*, 58 and 41.

the image of God was installed in it. The year before that A. D. 1116 Vishṇuvardhana's general Gangarāja successfully drove the Chōḻas out of Mysore and captured Talakkāḍ. * If Rāmānuja met him as ruler in the locality in which he is said to have spent his time of exile in Mysore, it must have been after A. D. 1106. It is very probable that Biṭṭidēva was in no position to do anything for Rāmānuja or Vaishṇavism till much later when his whole attention was centred on releasing Southern Mysore from the grip of the Chōḻas. There seems to be therefore a discrepancy of about 15 or 16 years in regard to this particular date.

THE CHOLA CONTEMPORARY OF RAMANUJA: There is one other detail in connection with this matter which we get from the *Guruparamparas*, namely that Rāmānuja returned to Śrīrangam, from this locality where he had resided for about 25 years, on hearing that the Chōḻa monarch for the time being, having had an attack of carbuncle, died from the effects of it. Of course, the Vaishṇavas regard this as a visitation from God Vishṇu for his disservice, and dub him *Krimikanṭa* Chōḻa. The Chōḻa contemporary of Rāmānuja at this period, and the Chōḻa who was responsible for Rāmānuja's taking himself away

* *Epigraphica Carnatica*, Vol. for Mysore, *Maḷavalle* 31.

from Śrīrangam to the Mysore country, could have been no other than Kulōttunga I, who was by no means a fanatic Śaiva. He may have been a Śaiva and he may have been zealous in the pursuit of his religion; but we have indubitable records that he was anything but a fanatic, as arrangements were made for the worship of God Ranganātha at a particular festival at Śrīrangam, and the inscription is dated in his reign *, and mentions him as the ruling sovereign. This would mean that in very Śrīrangam, which was the place of Rāmānuja, Kulōttunga allowed the freedom to the Vaishṇavas to make their own arrangements for worship even to the extent of providing for the recital of certain sections of the *Prabandha*. Notwithstanding this, it is not impossible to conceive that he invited Rāmānuja for a discussion, or religious disputation, as against a Śaiva controversialist, and punished the two Vaishṇavas who went instead, in the manner described by putting their eyes out, not so much on account of differences in religion as to punish the impertinence of the answer that was actually given by the stout-hearted disciple of Rāmānuja, Kūrattāḻvān, who met the thesis that "Śiva is the Supreme" by an almost blasphemous play upon words that the measure

---

* *South Ind. Ins*, III, 70, pp. 148-152.

Drōṇa was higher than the measure *Śiva*, Śiva being the name of God and of a grain measure alike. Then it was felt that Rāmānuja's position in Śrīrangam was dangerous, and he had to get away from there. If he remained anything like 25 years out of Śrīrangam and returned thereto only after the death of the ruler, the ruler under reference could be no other than Kulōttunga I, who died some time about A. D. 1118–20, A. D. 1118 being the earliest known year of his successor Vikrama Chōḻa, who was a Vaishṇava. It is probable that Rāmānuja's building of the temple at Mēlkōṭṭai may have been some time after A. D. 1106 and before A. D. 1116. The date A. D. 1099 for this seems impossible.

DATE OF FOUNDATION OF TIRU-NARAYANAPURAM-MELKOTTA BY RAMANUJA. In the traditional accounts of the *Guruparampara*, while it is possible that there should be errors in regard to the precise dating of events, as these were compiled generations later, the general trend of the story is likely to be more or less correct. On this assumption we may take it that Rāmānuja went away to what is now Mysore, and remained there for a period of about a quarter of a century more or less as the accounts state it. He might have remained there, and even gone about teaching and collecting together a number of disciples devoted to him. It would be impossible for him to have constructed a temple like that at Mēlkōṭṭa, not a big temple that it now is, but even a comparatively small shrine, without the countenance of the local authority, and therefore we may well take it that that was undertaken after Rāmānuja had gained the good-will and perhaps even the esteem of a devotee of Vishṇu in the person of Viṭṭhaladēvarāya. As we have a specific date for his building the Vishṇu shrine at Bēlūr in A. D. 1117, we may perhaps safely take it that the temple at Mēlkōṭṭa was founded just a few years earlier, say, about A. D. 1015, when certainly Biṭṭidēva was the ruler, and was actively engaged in the locality round Mysore in the course of his conquest of that part of the country from the Chōḷas. This would mean a discrepancy of about fifteen or sixteen years in the date given by the *Guruparampara* for the foundation of the Mēlkōṭṭa temple. This event perhaps happened somewhere about A. D. 1115, rather than A. D. 1099. It is the *Guruparampara* of the Tritīya Brahmatantrasvāmin that gives the date Śaka 1021 precisely for this. But the other *Guruparampara* of Pinbaḷagiya Jīyar sets down the date as Śaka 1012, making the year *Bahudānya* like the other one, which is impossible, as *Bahudānya* equates with Śaka 1021, and cannot therefore with Śaka 1012. A discrepancy in the precise date therefore seems not merely possible, but is proved by this difference between the authorities. If Rāmānuja returned to Śrīrangam soon after hearing of the death of the Chōḷa, who was responsible for sending him away from there, it must have been at the earliest after A. D. 1118, it may be after A. D. 1120, which would agree fairly well with the date somewhere about A. D. 1115, for the foundation of the Mēlkōṭṭa temple.

THE PERIOD OF RAMANUJA'S EXILE FROM SRIRANGAM. The statement in the *Vēnkaṭāchala Itihāsamāla*, which seems to couple Rāmānuja's first visit to Tirupati, to learn the secret teaching of the *Rāmāyaṇa* from his uncle, with the fact he had already got the grant of land of Bālamaṇḍya, a village near Tirupati from Viṭṭhaladēvarāya seems highly improbable. Rāmānuja was, under the instruction of his great grandfather Āḷavandār, being gradually equipped for the position of the chief Vaishṇava teacher at Śrīrangam by acquiring from the eight disciples of Āḷavandār who each one had been entrusted with the esoteric teachings of the one or the other of the main Vaishṇava scriptures, had begun acquiring these comparatively early in his life, after having been duly installed in

Śrīrangam. It seems unlikely that this took place so late as after his return from Mysore. It was probable that he had acquired this before his name could be put forward as a Vaishṇava teacher of reputation, whose subscription to the Śaiva doctrine could be regarded as of decisive importance. So Rāmānuja's first visit to Tirupati must have been pretty early in his life soon after he left Conjeevaram and went and settled down in Śrīrangam as yet not quite the chief Vaishṇava teacher; while Anandāḻvār's going over to Rāmānuja to be his disciple might well have been after his return from Mysore. That an *Agrahāra* had been established in Bālamaṇḍya at his request by Viṭṭhaladēvarāya, is itself improbable as this village was near Tirupati which was not then in the Hoyśāla territory. Anantārya may have been one of the principal Vaishṇavas who might have settled in that *Agrahāra*. The *Itihāsamāla* statement seems to confound the two as apparently Anantārya was asked to go and settle down in Tirupati, probably because Rāmānuja's uncle, Tirumalai Nambi, had reached to ripe old age and could not be expected to continue his service, which involved a considerable amount of physical strain, for long. Counting therefore the 25 years' stay of Rāmānuja in Hoyśāla territory backwards from the date A. D. 1120, it would bring us to some time about A. D. 1095, for him to leave Śrīrangam under fear of death through the ill-will of the Chōḷa emperor. There is no obvious objection to this date from the circumstances of Rāmānuja's history, which would mean that he left the Chōḷa country about A. D. 1095 and returned to it soon after A. D. 1120.

RAMANUJA'S EPOCH-MAKING VISIT TO TIRUPATI. His second visit is the really epoch-making visit to Tirupati. We stated already that he was invited to go there by the Yādavarāja for the time being, as his name is not specifically mentioned to us, to argue on behalf of the Vaishṇavas against the claims set up by the Śaivas that the temple on the hill was a Śiva temple. It was also stated that this contention was raised, as worship in the temple had been neglected for some considerable time by the *Vaikhānasa* priests having abandoned the place, and the prescribed worship in the temple having been given up. It was this that gave the opportunity for the Śaivas to take over the worship and claim possession of the temple. That might well have happened in the latter part of the reign of Kulōttunga I, and in consequence of the same wave of Śaiva fanaticism which turned out Rāmānuja from the Chōḷa country. It was about that time that Kāḷahasti had become a great centre of the

Śaivas. Rāmānuja's cousin, the son of the other sister of Tirumalai Nambi, who, as Gōvinda Bhaṭṭa, was a fellow student of Rāmānuja who had afterwards become a fanatical Śaiva and was in residence in Kāḷahasti. He was so fanatically attached to Śaivism that Tirumalai Nambi found it very difficult to wean him from his attachment to Śiva, and reclaim him to the fold of the Vaishṇavas as the story has it. He had just then been reclaimed and Rāmānuja was able to take him with him after completing his *Rāmāyaṇa* studies with Tirumalai Nambi, according to the *Guruparampara* account. Therefore there was a considerable amount of Śaiva fanaticism in the locality, and, if the actul Vaishṇava priests at Tirupati failed to discharge the functions, it was possible for the Śaivas to step into their place, and claim the shrine as their own. Since Rāmānuja moved away from Śrīrangam, the body of Vaishṇavas at the place had been somewhat cowed down and could not put forward or sustain a claim to speak for the Vaishṇavas as a whole. It was probably the return of Rāmānuja to Śrīrangam, and the accession of a Vaishṇava ruler like Vikrama Chōḷa to the Chōḷa throne, that put new heart into the Vaishṇavas and made them claim the temple on the hill as their own. This must have happened some time after Rāmānuja returned to Śrīrangam, and had sufficient time to install himself in his place and make his position secure there. As a matter of fact the *Vēnkaṭāchala Itihāsamāla* states it that while Rāmānuja was still in Tirupati, the news of the removal of the image of Gōvindarāja in the Gōvindarāja shrine in Chidambaram reached Tirupati. Rāmānuja heard of this from those who had run away for shelter to Tirupati, carrying the movable images from the shrine. For this event a precise dating is possible, as it is actually mentioned in Tamil literature in three separate works of the poet Oṭṭakkūttar, who was tutor and governor to Kulōttunga II, the son and successor of Vikrama Chōḻa who ascended the throne in A. D. 1135, and whose *abhishēka* must have taken place probably that year. So about A. D. 1135 ought to be the time when the images should have reached Tirupati. At that time Rāmānuja was high in influence at the court of the local ruler, Yādavarāja, and had been ordering things at Tirupati, largely not only for the conduct of worship as of old, but even to provide the temple with all that was necessary to carry on regular worship throughout the year, the periodical worship, provision for festivals, improvement of the town itself with a view to these, and much else that went to improve the amenities of the town to make it possible for the people there to live comfortably all the year round and render the services to the temple which must have become much more constant and regular. It was then that the Yādavarāja undertook the building of the Gōvindarāja shrine and lay out the *Agrahāra* which he called *Rāmānujapura*. Therefore then the second visit of Rāmānuja to Tirupati should have taken place some eight or ten years after his return to Śrīrangam, say, after A. D. 1130. If the Yādavarāya, whose capital is said to have been Nārāyaṇavaram not far from Tirupati, had been a ruler of such influence in the locality as to have helped Rāmānuja, we can well expect some record of his doings, which would normally be set up in the temple in the form of inscriptions. There is no inscription referable to the time of any Yādavarāya, and the only record of the period is the one inscription of the 16th year of Vikrama Chōḷa dated A. D. 1117, and this has reference to the Śiva temple at Tirupalādīśvaram, Śrī parāśarēśvara, in lower Tirupati. We shall have to find an explanation for this.

GHATTIDEVA, THE YADAVARAYA CONTEMPORARY OF RAMANUJA. We have records of a Yādavarāya of the time with whom we can, in our present state of knowledge, safely equate all these doings to assist Rāmānuja to put the daily and annual functions in the temple on a footing of assured purpose from time to time. The actual circumstances under which this was called for has already been stated. From all that was said before, it would be clear that, so far, the organisation for conducting worship in the temple of Tirupati seems to have been more or less of a private matter and left entirely to the community concerned to manage. It seems to have been entirely the doing of the Vaishṇavas of the locality interested in the matter as actual worshippers of the deity installed in the temple. Except the earliest incidents connected with the almost legendary Toṇḍamān Chakravarti, there is no mention of any state authority or royal personage having done anything towards this organisation of worship in the temple, or provision therefor, through all the long period of history that we have covered. It seems to have been left entirely to the *Vaikhānasa* priestly family, or it may be a few families, who had been brought in there for conducting the worship according to that school of Vaishṇava Āgama worship. In our comparatively scanty, and broken pieces of, information which are put together, there is no reference to this particular so far. Such grants as have been made to the temple—and there have been a number—were more or less private grants which were allowed to be managed by the residents of the locality,

Stānattār as they are called, who had the management of the temple in their own hands, as in fact was the case actually in respect of shrines in villages right up to the end of the last century almost. Royal or official interference of a necessary or compulsory character, would be invoked only on occasions of extraordinary trouble, or dissension beyond the power of the local people to settle. The intervention sought of the local ruler, Yādavarāya was in this case of that particular character, on the basis of such information as we have access to for the present. There is an inscription of the 17th year of Vikrama Chōḻa, which would bring us to the date A. D. 1135, of a Yādavarāya by name Ghaṭṭidēva who was ruling in this locality, very probably as a governor—it may be a feudatory—of the ruling Chōḻa for the time being, and that is, Vikrama Chōḻa. In the records just a few years later, he assumes the title—probably he was given that title—Kulōttungaśoḻa-Yādavarāya, which would mean he continued to hold the office under Kulōttunga II, the son and successor of Vikrama Chōḻa. More than that, he apparently continued to be conducting the administration loyally, and earned the appreciation of his sovereign so far as to have been conferred this title of honour. This is a point of some importance in this context, as that would go a great way towards explaining why he did not put on record any inscriptions in the temple of what he did by way of organising worship, and even making benefactions to the temple. This Ghaṭṭidēva seems to have been the actual ruler during the period with which we are concerned, as his records seem to go down to A. D. 1150. He is said to have had the title Yādava Nārāyaṇa, which perhaps need not be given a Vaishṇava significance. Some time later we hear of a son of his, a Rājamalla Yādavarāya, otherwise Bhujabala Siddharasa; but his records take him to rather late in the reign of Kulōttunga III. Therefore we may take it safely that it was this Ghaṭṭidēva, the feudatory of both Vikrama Chōḻa and Kulōttunga II, that was actually the Yādavarāya who called in the assistance of Rāmānuja to settle the dispute in the Tirupati temple. Not only that, he interested himself further in putting the whole course of temple management and worship in order through Rāmānuja and the community of Vaishṇavas in Tirupati. We may perhaps take it that he did not, as rulers of his standing before him did, think of putting on record what he did to the temple at Tirupati, as he might have felt such a thing might have been displeasing to the sovereign, who showed himself to be an enthusiastic follower of Śaivism personally, and what is really more, what he did to the Vishṇu temple both at Tirupati on the hill, and the town below, were acts which might have been regarded as going against some of the acts of the suzerain. It is just possible that Kulōttunga II as a Hindu sovereign might not have actually objected to his doing what he actually did, but it would be justifiable if the Yādavarāya felt shy that these acts of his may not be actively approved at headquarters. This Ghaṭṭidēva Yādavarāya therefore, the first name among the Yādavarāya rulers to come to our notice in inscriptions early in the 12th century A. D., seems to have been the actual ruler, who was contemporary with Rāmānuja.

THE PROBABLE TIME OF THE SECOND VISIT OF RAMANUJA. Having regard to all these various circumstances, we are entitled to infer that the most active part in the life of Rāmānuja in Tirupati must be the years following the accession of Kulōttunga II to the Chōḷa empire. This was his second visit. According to the *Vēnkaṭāchala Itihāsamāla*, he paid a third visit when he was 102 years of age, and then regarded it as no more possible for him to be visiting Tirupati as frequently as hitherto, and made certain arrangements in order to assure permanence to the arrangements that he had made, and returned to Śrīrangam. The same work says that he paid afterwards two or three flying visits before he died. In the traditional *Guru-parampara* accounts, he is supposed to have lived 120 years, the length of a *mahādaśā*. Without taking it too literally, we might regard Rāmānuja's was a long life running past a century, it may even be some years more than that, and whithout attempting to be too precise where perhaps too much precision may not be possible, we may say roughly that the active period of Rāmānuja's life covered a century from A. D. 1050 to A. D. 1150. Going by the precise statements given above, his 102nd year would correspond to the year A. D. 1119 which we have shown to be impossible for the precise events recorded, of which we can be certain in regard to dating If in A. D. 1119, he was 102, he must have lived on 18 years longer which would mean that he passed away some time about the year A. D. 1139, which, having regard to the precise dating of the accession of Kulōttunga II, would make it much too early. But if we take in the 15 or 16 years of discrepancy by way of antedating that we have noted already, it would mean that he actually passed away in A. D. 1155, and this date, it is just possible may be correct.

CHAPTER XII.

ORGANISATION OF WORSHIP AT TIRUPATI BY RAMANUJA.

THE OCCASION FOR RAMANUJA'S WORK IN THIS LINE. The main items of his arrangements for the conduct of worship in Tirupati, and what he did for the improvement both of the shrine and the town, may be summarised as from the *Vēnkaṭāchala Itihāsamāla*. The purpose for which Rāmānuja was invited to Tirupati on this occasion was to meet the arguments of the Śaivas at the Court of the Yādavarāya, in justification of their claims to the possession of the temple on the hill, as a shrine dedicated to Śiva and as such entitled to Śaiva guardianship. They put forward that certain peculiar features of the temple, both in the features of the image itself and in the details of the worship conducted, constituted a claim to the image being regarded as that of Śiva, and the shrine therefore a Śaiva shrine. It is hardly necessary, for our present purpose, to go through the whole series of arguments which Rāmānuja urged in reply to give satisfaction to the Śaivas, quoting largely from the Paurāṇic and other authorities, and drawing largely on the *Prabandha* works also. He was therefore able completely to satisfy the Yādavarāja that the features pointed out were features by no means peculiar to Śiva alone, and forms of Vishṇu with those features are not impossible either of contemplation or of representation. But even then, the Śaivas had recourse to this final argument that the Yādavarāja had been prejudiced against them, not by force of the arguments of Rāmānuja, but by some kind of an occultic influence which they actually averred Rāmānuja exercised over him. To put the matter beyond all doubt, it is said that Rāmānuja suggested that the ultimate decision might be left to God himself, and it was then that they got prepared the weapons peculiar to Śiva and Vishṇu which were to be placed in the sanctum of the temple when the night worship should be over, and the sanctum locked up and sealed, so that nobody might have access to the place. It was agreed that whichever of the weapons the image of the God had assumed when the shrine should be opened in the morning, would indicate the nature of the deity there. Certain accounts, of a popular character generally say that Rāmānuja assumed the form of a serpent, as he was himself an emanation of Ananta, the serpent, and set the conch and the disc in the hands of Vishṇu overnight. But the *Vēnkaṭāchala Itihāsamāla* is quite content with merely saying that Rāmānuja spent the night in contemplation upon the deity, and in prayer that the deity might prove the truth by assuming the Vaishṇava weapons, as he had no honest doubt whatever that the deity was a Vaishṇava deity, and had been so regarded almost from the time that the image was found and a temple was erected to house it. That done, it was his responsibility as head of the Vaishṇavas, and of the Rāja, who was the ruler of the locality, to see to it that whatever had to be done in the temple had been laid down, with proper arrangements made for carrying them out through the year. Naturally this would involve arrangements for the worship as it had so far been conducted continuously, and wherever necessary to revive items of temple ritual, which may have fallen into desuetude. Some few new items which seemed to Rāmānuja very appropriate were also introduced in his time and continued ever since.

THE DETAILS OF RAMANUJA'S ORGANISATION. Of the seven divisions of the work, *Śrī Vēnkaṭāchala Itihāsamāla*, the first three sections or *stabakas* as they are called, are concerned with the discussion as to the Vaishṇava character of the image. The remaining four *stabakas* are taken up with what Rāmānuja did for the temple, and, after him, his disciple Anantārya. Since inscriptions of the next following century do mention the gardens and other features named after Rāmānuja and Anantārya, we may take it that Rāmānuja's doings there and Anantārya's presence are matters which need not be regarded as historically doubtful. Nos. 171 and 173 from the Tirupati temple mention, without a doubt Anandāḻvān, and No. 175 mentions equally clearly the *Tirunandavana* (flower-garden) of Rāmānuja. Rāmānuja's effort therefore as to what he should do consisted first of all in the publication of the Yādavarāya's award that the shrine was a Vishṇu shrine, and to restore to it the rituals of worship, etc., according to the Vaikhānasa Āgama as of old, after performing the initial purificatory rite of the great ablution of the temple, etc. He is said next to have repaired the tower rising over the temple called Ānanda Nilaya in accordance with the prescriptions of the same Āgama. He is said to have made a gold necklet containing an image of Padmāvatī, and put it round the neck of the God and restored the image to its position. This is the first part. The next item that called for his attention was the performance of the weekly ablutions, and the kind of face-mark with which the God's image was to be decorated. The ablution given to the God on every Friday was in accordance with the Ānanda Samhita of the Āgamas of the Vaikhānasas. The upright face-mark for the God (*Ūrdhva Puṇḍra*) was prescribed to be of the camphor mixture called *Pacchaikarpūram*, and for three days from Monday onwards, of the white earth generally called *Nāmam*. All the jewels and wearing apparel of the God were to be removed on Thursday, and the God was to be dressed only in flowers completely. He instituted, that during this process the *Nācchiyār Tirumoḻi*, one of collection in the *Prabandha* was to be recited. For the continuance of the worship in the proper form, and, according to the practices of the Vaikhānasa Āgama, he entrusted the work to such of the descendants of the early Vaikhānasa priest Bimbādhara, who, having received the purificatory ceremony of Vaishṇava initiation from himself, were to conduct worship. He made arrangements for the installation of images of the Āḻvārs ; but, as several of these by themselves, had stated that it would be profanation to walk up the hill, Rāmānuja arranged to install their images in Tirupati at the foot of the hill in the shrine of Gōvindarāja which had recently been constructed.

THE BUILDING OF THE GOVINDARAJA TEMPLE. The most important item of Rāmānuja's work on this occasion, was the building of this

TOWN OF TIRUPATI

(*To face page 293*)

Gōvindarāja shrine. The temple on the top of the hill was dedicated to Vishṇu in the form in which he is believed to reside in *Vaikuṇṭha* (Vishṇu's Heaven). There the God is in the standing posture, with all the attributes and attendants usual to him, in Vaikuṇṭha. The Gōvindarāja in Chidambaram was believed, and the belief continues even now, was the representation of God as he sleeps on Ananta, the great serpent, on the 'ocean of milk'. It is upon this feature that the young Chōḻa monarch made a pun in his remark that the natural home of that God was the sea, not the front yard of the temple of Naṭarāja. So when the movable images from Chidambaram had been brought by the Vaishṇavas, and the Yādavarāja undertook to build a temple to house them, Vishṇu, as he lay abed on 'the ocean of milk', was installed in the temple at the foot of the Tirupati hill. The Yādavarāja not only built the shrine at the end of the town, but built houses round it on the four sides, and, presenting them to good Brahmans, made an *Agrahāra* round the temple calling the place Rāmānujapura, which became thereafter an important locality, as he took care to provide everything that was required to constitute a good town out of it. Rāmānuja arranged for a small shrine for Gōdā within the temple, and taking that occasion the Yādavarāja instituted two annual festivals in that temple, one in *Āni* (August—September) and the other in *Mārgaḻi* (December—January). Having done this, the Yādavarāja invited Tirumalai Nambi and Anantārya to come and reside in the houses which he had built in Lower Tirupati.

THE TEMPLE WATER SUPPLY. The temple on the hill had been provided, soon after the foundation of the temple, with wells for the temple services and for the purpose of the garden by one Rangadāsa. They had fallen into disrepair and got partly destroyed. Rāmānuja restored these two wells. On the bank of the step well, he set up images of Śrīnivāsa and Bhūdēvi, and arranged that the flowers etc., used in the temple service should be thrown into the well as sacred to Bhūdēvi. Then there seems to have been a difficulty for the supply of good water, and one of the services rendered by Tirumalai Nambi ever since he settled down there, was to bring the supply of water from Pāpanāśa, some distance away. On the occasion of Āḷavandār's visit, Tirumalai Nambi was not able to bring the water owing to illness, and, to avoid the inconvenience for the future, Āḷavandār obtained divine sanction to use the water from the kitchen-well dug by Rangadāsa within the temple premises for the kitchen service. This

PAPANASA-TIRTHAM

(To face page 294)

which he had undertaken to Rāmēśvaram. Finding that the temple was without a tower, he wanted that a great tower should be built, and, having ordered the building, he went forward on his pilgrimage, and when he returned to Tirupati, work on the tower had already reached the first stage. At this stage, he had a dream, when he was in Tirupati, that Ananta, the great serpent, appeared before him and complained that, by way of devoted service to God, he was overloading him, as the whole hill was his own body, and wished to be spared the trouble. After taking advice, he stopped the tower at the stage which it had reached, and in token of Ananta's appearance before him, got a representation of him made as a jewel, and placed it on one of the arms of the God which the God himself had accepted. At the same time he was also informed that not one but a pair of *Nāgā* jewels were presented to God Venkaṭēśa on the occasion of his marriage with Padmāvatī by his father-in-law Ākāśarāja. Having regard to this Rāmānuja asked that the gold *Nāgā* jewels should be on both hands of Venkaṭēśa.

SHRINES TO NARASIMHA. Another of the institutions of Rāmānuja is said to be the Nṛsimha shrine within the premises of the temple. The Paurāṇic story in regard to this is that God

Śankara performed a penance to Vishṇu-Nṛsimha who appeared before him and granted his prayer. This is said to have taken place on the west bank of the *Svāmi Pushkaraṇi*, and an attempt was made later to build a temple to Śiva on the spot. The Vaishṇavas of the locality objected on the ground that a Śiva shrine should not be built there as God himself had ordered otherwise, on the authority of the *Purāṇas*. According to their story, when the original temple was constructed and subsidiary shrines made for Vishṇu and his attendant deities, Śiva requested that he might also be allowed accommodation on the hill. God Vishṇu himself, to whom the request was preferred, allotted to Śiva a place at the foot of the hill on the banks of the *Kapila Tīrtha*, and hence they argued it would be sacrilege to build a shrine to Śiva anywhere within the limits of the hill. Rāmānuja agreed, and, in order to solve even future difficulties arising therefrom, provided a shrine within the walls of the temple for Nṛsimha as this aspect of Vishṇu was fearsome and frightening to ordinary people. He therefore provided a shrine within the sanctum of the temple under the tower *Ānanda Nilaya* for Nṛsimha, and ordained worship there. He also arranged for the setting up of an image of Nṛsimha where Mārkanḍēya was supposed to have had a vision of Nṛsimha himself in front of the Nṛsimha cavern which led by a secret passage to the hill. Rāmānuja set up an image of Nṛsimha and built a shrine for the image, and arranged worship for that also.

MIRACLES IN FAVOUR OF ANANTARYA AND THEIR PERPETUATION. Then follows the story of two miracles that God Śrīnivāsa is supposed to have performed in respect of Anantārya. The first has reference to a hollow in the chin of the image, which, according to the story, is said to have been caused by Anantārya in the following circumstances. Anantārya was engaged in digging a small tank for watering his garden. He used to make his wife, then pregnant, carry the baskets of earth on her head to be thrown at a distance. God took pity on her, and, in the form of a young bachelor, used to carry the basket on his head and relieve Anantārya's wife of the labour. Anantārya felt displeased that this impertinent bachelor was depriving him and his wife of the merit of service to God. When the bachelor would not give up what he was doing, notwithstanding several requests, he became wild and hit him with the butt-end of the shovel with which he was digging. The bachelor disappeared, and when Anantārya went into the temple for worship in the evening as usual, he noticed the bleeding wound on the spot where he hit the bachelor. Taken aback by this, he immediately ran out and brought in a herb to stop the bleeding, and making a powder from out of it filled in the wound and thus stopped the bleeding. Pleased with this service of Anantārya, God agreed that, as an item of daily worship, that depression should be filled with the camphor mixture, which is used for his face-mark, and ordered that the shovel itself should be hung up in a prominent place in front of the temple. The other miracle was that Anantārya was cultivating a flower-garden with the greatest care near the temple. He found that at the flowering season, the flowers were all collected and used and thrown about, leaving comparatively little of it for his own purpose in the morning. Being very wroth that somebody should be doing this, he kept watch to discover who it was that was actually doing it. After six or seven failures, he discovered one night a princely young man and a young lady to match, were disporting themselves in the garden and playing with the flowers, etc. The old man ran about to capture the young man who dodged him and disappeared into the temple. But he managed, however, to catch the young lady and tied her up to the next *champaka* tree. As became her, she begged of him to release her, and pleaded that he should take hold of the man and punish him, and not her, whom he might regard as his own daughter, and let go. Anantārya would not let her go. When the day dawned, and the temple servants entered the sanctum, Śrīnivāsa intimated to them what actually took place, and when the story reached Anantārya, he was transported beyond bounds; and, taking the flower basket full of flowers and carrying Padmāvatī, the goddess, on his head, he entered the temple, and set both of them before God. This story is said to have been related to Rāmānuja, and he ordered that thereafter on the occasion of the *Puraṭṭāśi* festival, the God may be taken to the garden on the seventh day, and that Anantārya may be presented with a garland of flowers, etc., on the eighth day on the occasion of the festival of the car.

FOOTMARKS OF SRINIVASA UNDER THE TAMARIND TREE. The next institution of Rāmānuja is the footprints of God under the tamarind tree half way up the hill. It was stated already that Rāmānuja went to Tirupati to learn the orthodox teaching of the *Rāmāyaṇa* from his uncle Tirumalai Nambi, who under direction of Āḷavandār had been in residence on the hill serving God. Since Rāmānuja would not go up the hill and resided in Lower Tirupati, the Nambi had to come down from the hill, and they so arranged it that they met somewhere half way up the hill where there was a big shady tamarind tree. The *Rāmāyaṇa* teaching went on under this tree. Tirumālai Nambi was sorry however that the discharge of his duty to Rāmānuja and the community deprived him of the afternoon worship of God, a duty which he regarded as due from him. In this perplexing position, God appeared before him in a dream and told him that He would appear before him at the mid-day worship where he was, and while Rāmānuja and the Nambi were engaged in the *Rāmāyaṇa* lesson, and, at the correct moment of worship in the temple on the top of the hill, the footmarks of God appeared in front of these two with the smell of flowers and basil, and such other articles of worship as were thrown at the feet of God. Rāmānuja thereafter arranged that the spot should be held as a place of worship and everybody who goes up the hill, on reaching this spot should offer worship to Śrīnivāsa, crying out the name of Gōvinda. Even *Chaṇḍāḷas* were allowed to go and offer worship there, after having bathed in a tank called *Chaṇḍāḷa-tīrtha*.

ARRANGEMENTS FOR WORSHIP OF RAMA, VARAHA, ETC. Rāmānuja was also responsible for installing within the temple of Śrīnivāsa an image of Śrī Rāma as He offered refuge to Vibhīshaṇa just before the war of the *Rāmāyaṇa*. This manifestation of God was made in response to the prayer of a certain *Yōgi* by name Viśvambara who lived on the banks of the river *Vaigai* (Sans. Kṛtamālā) to the south-west of Madura, at a place called *Kalavinkam* in Sanskrit (Tam. *Kuruvitturai*). Owing to disturbances in the locality later on, the Vaishṇavas were directed to carry the image for protection to Vēnkaṭāchalam. The image was brought to Tirupati as Tirumalai Nambi and Rāmānuja were engaged in the study of that part of the *Rāmāyaṇa.* Happy at the coincidence, Rāmānuja arranged to set up the image of Rāma as He appeared on that occasion, with the addition of an image of Sīta also, and provided a place of worship for these in the temple.

The next item in this line is Rāmānuja's enforcing the old-time worship of Varāha on the west bank of the *Svāmi Pushkaraṇi* before offering worship at the temple of Śrīnivāsa. In ordering worship at the temple of Gōvindarāja, Rāmānuja also ordained that, as in Vēnkaṭāchala, the temple priests, after the performance of the last item of worship overnight, should be presented with garlands in the shrine of *Vishvaksēna,* the guardian deity before locking up the door for the night.

FESTIVAL IN MEMORY OF TIRUMALAI NAMBI. The sixth section of the work has reference to the association of Tirumalai Nambi and Anantārya with Tirupati. In regard to Tirumalai Nambi

VARAHASVAMI-TIRUMALAI (To face page 302)

AKASAGANGA-TIRTHAM (To face page 505)

we have already stated how and when he went to Tirupati, and what service he was rendering there on the hill. One of the items of service to which he devoted himself was the carrying of water from the *Pāpanāśa*, a few miles away, for the daily ablution of the God. He used to carry the water-pot on the head reciting the *Periya Tirumoḻi* of Tirumangai Āḻvār on the way. One day he noticed suddenly that the weight on the head was diminishing gradually, and discovered when he looked at it that the pot was empty. Turning back he discovered a young hunter was drinking off the water by deftly making a small hole in the earthern pot by means of an arrow. To the Nambi's angry question whether it was proper that he should do what he did, as the water was intended for God's service, the hunter answered with a provoking nonchalance "O, Grandfather, do not be distressed about the water. Here a little way down is a holy pool of water, from which you can carry the water for the temple service". So saying he went a little way ahead and pointed to the *Ākāśagangā*, and said "This is the holy Ganges water itself, and you might bring this daily for Our service". So saying the hunter disappeared. Wondering at the exhibition of God's grace to his devotees, he became even more devoted than before, and was thereafter carrying water from the *Ākāśagangā* instead of the more distant *Pāpanāśa*. Since God himself chose to call him grandfather (*Tāta*), the term *Tātārya* was added as a cognomen or title. His descendants thereafter were entitled *Tātāryas* or *Tātāchāryas* in consequence. Tirumalai Nambi had a son whom he had named Rāmānuja. On his premature death, he adopted a son whom he named Kumāra Tirumalai Nambi, whom the Nambi used to call *Tāta* for brevity. It would appear that this young man was extremely friendly to everybody and received the sobriquet of *Tōḻappa* (the friendly one). Hence the family came to be known as *Tōḻappa Tātāchārya*. When Tirumalai Nambi passed away, Rāmānuja instituted the festival in his honour on the day following the *Adhyayana Utsava* during which the *Prabhanda* used to be recited. The festival consisted in bathing the image of God, seating the image in the *Mangaḷagiri* hall, with water brought by Vaishṇava Brahmans from the *Ākāśaganga* chanting the *Prabhanda* of Tirumangai Āḻvār all the way in procession, and presenting *Śaṭakōpa* (the sin-destroying crown surmounted by a pair of sandals).

THE PAVILION OF YAMUNACHARYA. In regard to Anantārya we have already stated that he came to Rāmānuja as a disciple from his native place

Bālamaṇḍya in the country near Tirupati, and that he volunteered service to go to Tirupati on Rāmānuja's requisition. His service consisted in making a flower-garden and supplying flowers for the purpose of the daily worship of the God. Having heard that Yāmunāchārya during his stay there at Tirupati had a little cottage near the temple from which he supplied flower for the God, Anantārya built a *maṇḍapa* there in which he set up an image of Yāmunāchārya. Anantārya used to bring the flowers there, string them up and take them over for service to the temple. He had a son whom he named Rāmānuja who used to assist his father in this service.

RAMANUJA'S REGULATIONS AS TO RESIDENCE AT TIRUPATI, ETC. The other festivals instituted by Rāmānuja are collected together in the 7th section. Rāmānuja had to make certain regulations in regard to residents at Tirupati, as that was considered an act of desecration on the authority of the *Purāṇas* and the *Prabandhas*, which he adopted in his own conduct. So he laid down that those who were engaged in the immediate service of God should alone reside on the hill, all else even among the devotees living at the foot. The second regulation was that those resident there, and the pilgrims that go there, all of them should take for food what was provided by the temple after the temple service was over. The third regulation was that those resident on the hill should not grow flower-plants for purposes of household worship, but should use only those used for worship in the temple. The next regulation was that when one of the residents on the hill is about to die, he should be taken down the hill before death. The next regulation laid down is that the animals and birds on the hill should not be killed in hunting as they were regarded as creatures specially devoted to God. The next rule laid down is that those going up the hill should not use vehicles for carrying them, and should not wear sandals or other protection for the feet. The whole precincts of the hill were marked as all the distance from the *Kapila Tīrtha* at the foot of the hill to the *Svāmi Pushkaraṇi* on the top, with a radius all round the *Svāmi Pushkaraṇi* of one *yōjana*, seven to eight miles. It was also laid down that, within this area, no temples should be built for any other God. These regulations that Rāmānuja made were put before God himself for His approval by Tirumalai Nambi and Anantārya, and promulgated accordingly.

APPOINTMENT OF BACHELOR SUPERINTENDENT. For the purpose of carrying out these regulations and seeing to the regular conduct of worship,

SVAMI PUSHKARINI

(*To face page 306*)

etc., Rāmānuja wanted a disinterested person as superintendent. He therefore arranged that a bachelor of good qualifications should be nominated for the purpose. The person chosen must be a man of learning, should be capable of advising the local ruler, and should be free from any desire. He therefore nominated a bachelor accordingly, as prescribed in the *Paramēśvara Samhita*, gave him the image of Rāma for worship, and entrusted him with the Hanumān seal, a seal with the device of Hanumān on it for sealing up the treasury, and was given the key with which to lock up the temple for the night. In ordering the affairs regarding the temple, he was to take advice of Tiumalai Nambi and Anantārya all the time that their advice was available. This bachelor was also given a pennon with a bell-mark as his ensign, and the Yādavarāja was to support his authority.

FINAL ARRANGEMENTS OF RAMANUJA DURING HIS LAST VISIT. When again he visited Tirupati for the last time almost, he found this arrangement working satisfactorily so far. Tirumali Nambi had passed away some time since, and Anantārya was getting old; and he therefore found the work too much for the bachelor *Sanyāsin*. He thought it was necessary to give him two or three assistants, as there was work enough for three or four. He also wanted that a special service should be instituted such as is described in the *Tiruvāymoḻi* of Nammāḻvār. With a view to this in particular, he set up a *Sanyāsin* under the name Śaṭakōpa *Yati*, who was given charge of what the bachelor had hitherto been doing. Then choosing four bachelors from among the disciples of Anantārya, he appointed them to assist this *Sanyāsin*. Advising the Yādavarāja to see to the affairs of the temple being managed satisfactorily and instructing him to act according to the advice of Anantārya, Rāmānuja left Tirupati finally for Śrīrangam. For the future he ordained that the management should be Anantārya's as long as he lived, and after him some one of his descendants. The Śaṭakōpa *Yati* representing Rāmānuja himself, and some representatives of Tirumalai Nambi together, should have the whole management. He also wanted that one of the representatives should be of the Śaṭamarshaṇa *Gōtra* as representative of Nādamuni and Yāmunāchārya.

ARRANGEMENTS FOR THE RECITAL OF THE PRABANDHA. Some time later Rāmānuja passed away, and, on hearing this, Anantārya set up an image of Rāmānuja with the permission of God Śrīnivāsa, and instituted a festival with the recital of *Rāmānuja Nūṟṟandādi* (the centum on Rāmānuja) during the *Adhyayana Utsavam*. On one occasion one Śrīrangarāja who used to recite the *Prabandha* in Śrīrangam and was also accustomed to instructing Rāmānuja himself in the *Prabandham* went on a visit to Tirupati. On the occasion of his worship in the sanctum, he sang the *Tiruvāymoḻi* of the Āḻvar. At the end of it, God commanded him to sing a few verses from the first Aḻvārs, and, having received the holy water and *prasāda*, he returned to Tirumali Nambi and Anantārya. Since his visit the *Adhyayana Utsavam* in Tirupati was organised, and the chanting even of Periyāḻvār's *Tirumoḻi*. He then left for Śrīrangam. To continue this work a special man was appointed who came to be called *Śrī-Śaila Vigñapti Kārya* (the official to make petitions to the God of the hill) on the analogy of a Śrīrangarāja Vigñapti Kārya, whose function was the recital of the *Tiruvāymoḻi*.

CRITICAL REVIEW OF THE ACCOUNT. These, according to the *Itihāsamāla*, were the arrangements that Rāmānuja made in Tirupati for the conduct of worship in the temple. As would naturally be expected there is in these things a certain amount of miracle mixed up with several matter of fact arrangements. It would be rather difficult to rationalise over the miracles where we are actually concerned with the devotees who believed in them. Any process of rationalisation of these would seem therefore to be out of place. We may or may not believe in these. We have nothing by means of which to say categorically whether Rāmānuja and his companions believed in them or not. We shall have to leave them there. Even where they are miracles, the institutions based on them remain. Therefore we might pass over the miracles side of it without further notice, and consider, so far as the history of the temple is concerned, whether Rāmānuja did or could have done all that is ascribed to him. We have already indicated that, in less than a century of time, some of these institutions get to be referred to in inscriptional records in parts of the Tirupati temple which may not be altogether late structures, Tirupati having received comparatively little addition till much later times. From what we have already stated above, we have enough justification for taking it that Rāmānuja did play an important part in the organisation of worship in the temple at Tirupati, and that he had occasion to do it at the time indicated. The *Vēnkaṭāchala Itihāsamāla* seems to be a work composed at a period much later than Rāmānuja, it may be; but even so, it records the traditions coming down to the time, and, at the very best, it would be a mere effort at explaining the institutions that actually existed in the temple. So the institutions were there, whether the origin of these had anything miraculous to support it or not. For instance, the miraculous occurrences in connection with Anantārya a modern reader may well consider could not have been readily believed in the time of Rāmānuja. Even this would be taking too much for granted. Devotees do believe in miracles, and, if they do believe in them and set up institutions in consequence, it is none of our business to call the institutions of festivals themselves unhistorical. We shall perhaps see, in the course of the whole history of the temple, that these institutions existed, at least there are records mentioning them—almost from a century after the date of Rāmānuja. We shall discuss those details when they come before us in our further consideration of this history. For the present we may take it that many of these institutions had either been in existence before Rāmānuja, or had been newly brought into existence by Rāmānuja, or were by him, put on a footing of permanence.

CHAPTER XIII.

THE LAST CHOLAS AND THEIR SUCCESSORS.

A GAP IN OUR KNOWLEDGE, A. D. 1150-1235. The period of active life of Rāmānuja comes to a close in the middle of the 12th century, and the last date for him may therefore be taken to be roughly A. D. 1150. The first Chōḻa inscription of this period that we come upon in the region of Tirupati is that of Rājarāja III referable to the year A. D. 1235. Between these two dates, there seems to be a gap, as it were, of about three generations. We have seen already that a Yādavarāya ruler of the locality was of great assistance to Rāmānuja, and had rendered valuable services both to Rāmānuja and to the temple at Tirupati. According to the inscriptional records of the period, we find a Yādava Ghaṭṭidēva holding a position both under Vikrama Chōḻa and his successor Kulōttunga, and the available records of his do not seem to go much beyond A. D. 1140. But these records indicate that he had sons, one of whom has left records referable to a period somewhat late in the reign of Kulōttunga III which would take us to the eighties of the 12th century. These records have reference to one son. Possibly he had others who may have held the subordinate government in succession to the father, although no records of them have so far come down to us. The history of the locality therefore seems to be deeply associated with the fortunes of these Yādavarāyas, as we see one Vīra Narasimha Yādavarāya, with the Chāḷukya titles, wielding great power and exercising authority over an extensive area including the region with which we are concerned. The names of a number of Yādavarāyas, including that of Vīra Narasimha, occur in a large number of inscriptions in Tirupati itself and places dependent upon it and adjacent to it. To understand the history of the Tirupati temple therefore it would be necessary to understand the history of these Yādavarāyas.

RISE OF THE FEUDATORIES: YADAVARAYAS AMONG THEM. But the Yādavarāyas were not alone exclusively connected with this region. There are a few records of Telugu Chōḻas as they claim descent from the ancient Chōḻa Karikāla, sometimes called Pottappi Chōḻas, and another dynasty which goes by the name Telugu Pallavas, as they claim descent from Mukkanṭi Kāḍuveṭṭi, sometimes Trinētra Pallava, giving themselves the *gōtra* and the titles of the Pallavas of Kānchi. It is in this tangle that we find the intrusion of a certain number of records connected with the Hoysālas—and two or three of the greater officers of the Hoysāla Vīra Ballāla figure even in the inscriptions at Tirupati—a fairly clear indication of the extension of Hoysāla influence, if not of actual suzerain authority, over the region. This complication has to be clearly analysed before we can deal with the history of Tirupati during this period. Very unfortunately our information for the period from inscriptions generally is comparatively scanty. We do not know much about what was taking place in the Chōla empire itself under the Chōlas, Kulōttunga II and his successor Rājarāja II occupying between them the period A. D. 1133 to 1163, when the succession passed to a collateral branch of the Chōla dynasty under Rājādhirāja II, whose period of reign was A. D. 1163 to 1178. He was followed by the great ruler Kulōttunga III, A. D. 1178–1216, followed by his son Rājarāja III, A. D. 1216 to 1246 followed by Rājēndra III, whose records reach up to A. D. 1267 as active ruler, and A. D. 1279 nominally. We have noticed already that the territory with which we are particularly concerned had been associated with Vikrama Chōla as a prince, more or less intimately, and perhaps opened the way by virtue of his special connection as viceroy of this region for the accession to power of a new family of rulers certainly related to the Eastern Chāḷukyas, and may have belonged to a collateral branch of the ruling family. They very probably continued to hold the region in a feudatory capacity, but like feudatories generally, not keenly regardful of the suzerain authority, when the holders of that authority themselves got involved in a struggle for existence. This attitude seems to have come about more or less gradually, as a new feudatory power began to assert itself in the region of South Arcot District. They come into prominence somewhat later in this period, but were gradually building up that position in the region round Cuddalore. The most distinguished member of this dynasty who contributed very largely to the decline of the Chōḻa authority under Rājarāja III was a person known by the name Kō-Perunjinga. The rise of this feudatory power immediately to the North facilitated to some extent the assumption of independence or semi-independence in the feudatories farther north. Hence it is that we find the Yādavarāyas gradually giving up all references to the suzerain authority in their records, from the reign of Kulōttunga Chōḻa II onwards, though not always and uniformly. Tirupati and its history got therefore in a way peculiarly associated with the fortunes of the Yādavarāyas, whose history we shall have to consider as a necessary preliminary.

THE ACTUAL FEUDATORY FAMILIES. We suggested already that the Chōḷa-Chāḷukya war between Kulōttunga I of the Chōḷas and the Chāḷukya Vikramāditya VI, which perhaps came to an end in the last years of the 11th century, and perhaps received a definitive determination of the frontier between the two by A. D. 1116, helped to bring into prominence these feudatory families. The names of several of these could be traced in the inscriptions of the reign of Vikrama Chōḷa definitely. Under his successor Kulōttunga II almost the same families are found mentioned prominently. They occupy positions, no doubt of importance, but there is one little noteworthy feature in connection with them; they seem as yet capable of being transferred from one sphere of activity to another. While therefore they might be regarded as feudatories holding portions of land under the rulers in different localities, so long as this transfer was possible they must be regarded more or less as officials. But we could see, in the course of the generation following the early years of Kulōttunga II, the gradual change that the families get associated with their territories, and their authority being even confined to the actual territories over which they wielded authority. This it is that transforms them from a body of officials, however great, into regular feudatories holding particular portions of territory and changing their fealty to their suzerain as circumstances changed. This transformation is undoubtedly a gradual process, and was taking place, during the reigns of both Kulōttunga II and Rājarāja II—a period, which is essentially one of peace. While the Ganga frontier thus got definitely settled as was stated before, the frontier immediately to the north of the Chōḻa territory was not exactly in that condition. Over the Eastern Chāḷukya territory proper, the power of the Western Chāḷukya Vikrmāditya spread rapidly during the period of the war; and while considerable success had been attained in the reign of Vikrama Chōḻa in the recovery of all these territories where Chōḻa officers held rule during his reign acknowledging his authority without question, a number of families gain prominence as feudatories. The families that figure in the inscriptions of this reign are the Pallava family of Kūḍal (Cuddalore) in the South Arcot District; immediately to the north of them, the family of the Śambuvarāyans was coming into prominence in the Pālār basin between Vellore and the farther north; then there was the family of the Malayamāns round Tirukkōvilūr, sometimes called Śēdirāyans. We also hear of a lord of the Śenjiyar, people in the territory of Śenji (Ginji). Further north of these a number of chieftains are referred to under Vikrama Chōḷa named the Śāḷukkis of Toṇḍamaṇḍalam. Further north of these were the Pottappi Chōḷas. Then figure the names of a certain number of chieftains called Gāngēyas. Then comes the *Mahāmaṇḍalēśvara* Ghaṭṭidēva. Even farther north the lord of Koḷḷipākka happens to be mentioned. This Ghaṭṭidēva belonged to the family of the Yādavarāyas, who claim descent from the Śaśikula Chāḷukkis. One of them by name Nāraṇadēva is traceable in the records of the reign of Vīrarājēndra. All these families in the locality continued more or less in the reign of Kulōttunga, and his successor. Only we see certain changes due to transfers. But otherwise it becomes clear that, in this period, there were a large number of powerful feudatories who interposed themselves between the Chōḷa headquarters and the local administrations, which gradually developed so as to make themselves intermediate powers, more and more identifiable as local rulers, throwing the authority of the Chōḷa rulers into the background.

THE YADAVARAYA FAMILY IN THIS PERIOD. Of these feudatory families the one that is most frequently associated with Tirupati is the family of the Yādavarāyas who seem to have been imperial officers of great importance to begin with, and exercising authority over a vast extent of the empire of the Chōḻas. Among them Vīra Narasinga Yādavarāya with various titles, indicating more or less his gradual rise to importance, is the most distinguished. But there are a certain number of other Yādavarāyas besides, whose names also figure, as in fact the names of the members of other dynasties such as the Gaṇḍagōpālas, the Telugu Chōḻas and even others. These various names appearing in the inscriptional records of Tirupati during the same period would go to indicate that they were all officers of dignity, under the empire of the Chōḻas or Pāṇḍyas according to time, who made donations to the temple, perhaps without being necessarily associated with the rule of the locality containing Tirupati. But the records of the Yādavarāya Vīra Narasinga and just one or two others would indicate that, in their particular case, the association was very much more than that of officials who were donors of importance. We may therefore take note of the names of this dynasty that figure in this connection, with their dates as far as they are ascertainable, so as to be able to locate them properly.

We referred already to the Yādava ruler Ghaṭṭidēva as probably the Yādavarāya who assisted Rāmānuja in various matters connected with the hill-shrine of Tirupati in connection with the claim of the Śaivas, and the arrangements, that he made subsequently. It was also probably he who assisted Rāmānuja to build the shrine of Gōvindarāja in Lower Tirupati and who laid out the *Agrahāra*, Rāmānujapuram round it in honour of Rāmānuja, although we have not come upon any record of these associations of Ghaṭṭidēva. His known dates, the 17th year of Vikrama Chōḷa and the 6th year of Kulōttunga, or A. D. 1135 to 1139, would leave but little doubt in regard to the matter. From this last date A. D. 1139 almost to the year A. D. 1235 there is a gap in these inscriptional records which we could hardly fill. That is just the period of the rule of Rājarāja II succeeded by Rājādhirāja, and then again by Kulōttunga III. The whole of the reign of Rājādhirāja and the first years of Kulōttunga were occupied completely with the war of Pāṇḍya succession in which the Chōḷas took one side and the Ceylonese the other. So the imperial preoccupation was altogether this, and we might almost say the face of the Chōḷa monarchs remained set towards the south during the whole of this period, with the exception of the few years of Rājarāja II, whose reign appears to have been one essentially of peace. Then the name of a

Yādavarāya that we come upon with dates in the 7th year of Kulōttunga III, and in the 11th and 15th years of Rājarāja III or the period A. D. 1185 to 1231, is that of a Tirukkāḷattidēva Yādavarāya, not to be mistaken with the Telugu Chōḷa of the same name. We have a son of his by name Śiriyapiḷḷai with the title Vīrarākshasa Yādavarāya, and date A. D. 1193. A son of Ghaṭṭidēva by name Rājamalla Yādavarāya appears with dates in the 31st year of Kulōttunga III and the 21st year of Rājarāja III, A. D. 1209 to 1237. He is followed by a son of his with the date in the 19th year of Rājarāja, A. D. 1235 by name Kāśāṇmai, rather a peculiar name, and then we come to Vīra Narasinga Yādavarāya.

YADAVA VIRA NARASINGA AND HIS SUCCESSORS. This name occurs as that of an important officer of the Chōḷa empire under Kulōttunga III and the earlier years of Rājarāja III, his authority extending practically all over the region of Toṇḍamaṇḍalam. The authority that he exercised perhaps would bear the inference that he was something of a superior governor, whose authority prevailed over that of local governors of the divisions under him, which, in his time, would have been practically the northern half of the Chōḷa empire. The earliest record of his that we know of refers to the 31st year of Kulōttunga III, that is A. D. 1209, and the latest takes us on to the 14th year of Rājarāja III which would mean A. D. 1230; and then there is one of the 12th year of Jaṭāvarman Sundra Pāṇḍya I which would mean A. D. 1262—63, so that he seems to have wielded his authority and held his position during the long period A. D. 1209 to 1263 at least. His inscriptions are numerous in the temple of Tirupati itself, and he had undertaken and executed some large works in connection with the temple. There are three other names of Yādavarāyas that occur, Ghaṭṭidēva II, during the period A. D. 1224–27 in the reign of Rājarāja III, Tiruvēngaḍanātha Yādavarāya, whose dates are from the 8th to the 12th year taken to be his own. But these dates might as well be those of Vīra Narasinga, whose son-in-law he sems to have been from an expression in one of the inscriptions, *Maruhanār* occurring in inscription No. 102, which ought to be applied to him. We shall revert to that later. He is followed by another Śrīranganātha Yādavarāya, whose dates are comprised between the years A. D. 1336 and 1355. It will be seen that, considering merely the dates, these last three Yādavarāyas figure in the period in which Vīra Narasinga's authority prevailed, as was stated above. While these may have been princes of the royal family of the Yādavas, their spheres of office must have been those of local governors under the supervision of the higher officer Vīra Narasinga Yādavarāya. We shall now proceed to consider what light the inscriptions throw upon their associations with Tirupati.

INSCRIPTIONS OF THE YADAVARAYAS UNDER CHOLA RULE. Notwithstanding the fact that several of these Yādavarāyas were contemporaries of Kulōttunga III, and could be ascribed to his reign, there are no inscriptions in Tirupati which refer themselves to the reign of Kulōttunga III explicitly. This is probably to be accounted for by the fact that, in the earlier years of Kulōttunga and for the far greater part of his reign clearly, he was occupied in the south with wars against the Pāṇḍyas and the Ceylonese; and, though subsequently we know that he was very active and brought the empire back substantially to allegiance to him, it is just possible that the northern portions of the empire had not been so completely brought back again to the same sense of duty as the other portions of the empire. Consequently these northern chiefs conducted themselves as if they were their own masters. We shall refer, as we proceed, to such inscriptions as may be referable to his reign from the mere dating whenever it is possible. But among the inscriptions included in Volume I of the Dēvastānam Inscriptions, the first is No. 34 referring itself plainly to Rājarāja III, and probably to his 5th year, which would mean A. D. 1221, and refers to the digging of a tank in Tirucchānūr, where the inscription is found, by an officer of the treasury by name Pāṇḍyataraiyan. The grant itself refers to the gift of a piece of land to the temple. No. 35 refers to the 7th year of Rājarāja, and refers to the temple at Yōgimallāvaram, and refers to the same officer as above, whose son-in-law Vīra Narasingadēva Yādavarāya is said to have been. It refers to a grant by this officer in honour of one Nārāyaṇa Piḷḷai, who fell in the battle of Uraṭṭi, fighting on the side of the Yādavarāya, and seems to imply that he laid his life in defence of the Yādavarāya. The Pāṇḍyataraiyan bought the piece of land for gold under the new tank Nārāyaṇa, and made it over to the temple for the offer of worship at *Ardhayāma* (overnight), and for taking out the God in procession. This was made over, under sanction of a letter from Piḷḷaiyār Yādavarāyar, that is, Vīra Narasinga Yādavarāya, and acknowledged as such by the Vaishṇava Brahmans in charge of the temple. Vīra Narasinga Yādavarāya, it should be remembered, figures here as the son-in-law of the officer concerned. The battle

VISHNU'S DISCUS AT THE FRESH WATER TANK
AT TIRUPATI TOWN

(*To face page 324*)

of Uratti must have taken place before the 7th year of Rājarāja, and probably was fought for by the Yādavarāya on the one side as against enemies. The next one, No. 36, comes from the same temple and is dated the 9th year of Rājarāja. This is an interesting grant and refers to an arrangement made in the 23rd year of Rājarāja I by a Jayaṁkoṇḍa Chōḷa Brahmamārāyan, who paid 26 *kaḻañju* of gold for the purpose of celebrating an ablution on the *Uttarāyaṇa Sankramaṇa* (about the middle of January) day every year. This had apparently not been done. When the matter was brought to the notice of Vīra Narasinga Yādavarāya, he made the necessary enquiry, and, finding the facts as stated, ordered that the money might be taken over into the treasury of the temple, and arrangements made for the celebration of the festival by the *Sabhā* of the village. The next inscription has reference to the same year, and seems to refer more or less to the gift in the previous grant for the ablution of the God on the *Uttarāyaṇa Sankramaṇa*, and gives details of how the income had to be expended, and is an acknowledgment by the *Sabhā* of their responsibility in regard to this matter. The next one No. 38 belongs to the 14th year of Rājarāja, and refers to the same temple and the same officer Pāṇḍyataraiyan, who is described as a treasurer, son of one Anḍār, who was a lion to those of other faiths, and as holding the office of the Superintendent of the *Maṭha* attached to the temple, and refers to a gift of land under the tank Vīra Narasingadēva, in whose name it was repaired and put in order by his father-in-law, the Pāṇḍyataraiyan referred to. The revenues in paddy and in gold from some of this land was made the capital for the celebration of certain festivals in the temple. The land was made over to the *Ūravar*, the governing body of the town, who agreed to conduct the festival for all time from the income. This was agreed to by the governing body of Munnaippūṇḍi, and attested by the accountant of the temple under the *Mahāsabhā* of Yōgimallāvaram. The next following inscription has reference to the temple accountant, mentioned in the above record, who is said to have set up an image of *Gaṇēśa.* The document is incomplete. That again is a document in Yōgimallāvaram. With No. 40 we come on to the Gōvindarāja shrine, which, it will be remembered, was actually constructed, at the instance of Rāmānuja, by a former Yādavarāya to house the images carried away from Chidambaram when the ruling Chōḻa ordered the Gōvindarāja shrine to be removed from there. The document is prefaced, "in accordance with the oral orders of the King," and is dated in the 19th year of Rājarāja III. It states that on a particular day in the month of *Kārttika* of the year, the *Periyanāṭṭavar* (the big assembly of the division) assembled in the Iḷangōvil of the locality, what is now the Alamēlumangā shrine, and refers to a resolution that they came to. The resolution had reference to the provision by the *Periyanāṭṭār*, for the daily offerings to Tirumangai Āḻvār, who is described as *Kārāḷar Karpakam* (the wish-giving tree among the Kārāḷar), Kārāḷar being an agricultural Kaḷḷar community. A shrine had been built for this Āḻvār in the Gōvindarāja temple, and, as a provision for the daily worship had been omitted to be made, this omission had been made good by a certain number of people. It is interesting to note the first name is Śrī Śaṭakōpadāsa, (a devotee of Nammāḻvār) and Kolli Kāvalidāsa (the first part has reference to Āḻvār Kulaśēkhara). The third name is one Aruvar-anayakōvil Pillai, and the last is a Kalikanṛidāsa (the first part being one of the names of the Tirumangai Āḻvār himself). A certain amount of land was made over for the purpose, the cultivators of which had to make over a certain measure of paddy for each *paṭṭi*. This was made over in the name of Gōvinda Perumāḷ to the managers of the treasury of Tiruvēngaḍamuḍaiyān, the God on the hill.

This was the order of the governing body of Tirukkuḍavūr, and was to be a perpetual grant. This charitable gift received the approval of the *Periyanāṭṭavar*, the governing body of the *Periyanāḍu*, and was attested by their *Vēḷān*, that is, the hereditary writer of the division. No. 41 is an imperfect document, but refers itself clearly to the days of Rājarāja, and makes mention of the Yādavarāya as well as the Nārāyaṇan 'who fell formerly', apparently referring to the Nārāyaṇa Piḷḷai who fell in the battle of Uratti. No. 42 is an inscription in the temple at Tirupati, and refers to the 6th year of Allun Tirukkāḷattidēva. The other details are gone, but what is left is enough to indicate it was a grant by Madhurāntaka Pottappi Tirukkāḷattidēva. From this we pass on to the documents referring to Sundara Pāṇḍya I.

THE REIGN OF RAJARAJA III AND THE DECLINE OF THE CHOLA POWER. We have already stated that the Chōḷa Kulōttunga III ceased to rule in A. D. 1216 or somewhat later, but was succeeded by Rājarāja III in that year, either as joint ruler or in his own right. Rājarāja's rule extended from that date to the year A. D. 1346 without a doubt, and there are documents referring to his reign for a number of years afterwards even. We come upon inscriptions of a certain

Rājēndra III from A. D. 1246 onwards, or even somewhat earlier. Whether he succeeded Rājarāja III and what his actual relation to Rājarāja was, we do not know for certain. But from what we gather from the inscriptions of the time, it looks as though he were a brother of Rājarāja III, who played his own part in the last years of Rājarāja III's feeble reign to regain to some extent the power and prestige of the ruling family of the Chōḻas. The Pāṇḍya wars, which had remained the preoccupation of Kulōttunga III through practically the whole length of his reign, seem to have continued more or less notwithstanding the drastic punishment inflicted upon the defeated Pāṇḍya by Kulōttunga. The great humiliation the Pāṇḍyas suffered only whetted their appetite for revenge, and, throughout the reign of Rājarāja III, he had to suffer humiliation at the hands of the Pāṇḍya, almost from the outset of his reign. Jaṭāvarman Kulaśēkhara Pāṇḍya was the last contemporary of Kulōttunga III, and was succeeded by Māravarman Sundara Pāṇḍya, who came to the throne in A. D. 1216. Māravarman almost immediately set out on an invasion of the Chōḻa country and claimed to have conquered it, burning the capitals of Tanjore and Uraiyūr. All through his reign and that of his successor Māravarman Sundara

Pāṇḍya II, the Chōḷa territory and Chōḷa authority were alike reduced to the lowest position. This attack from outside was taken advantage of by the discontented feudatories within, among whom the Kāḍavas with their head-quarters, first at Cuddalore and then at Śēndamangalam, played the chief part. There were some loyalists among the feudatories farther north, who fought against the Kāḍavas and their allies. Among them figure the names of Vīra Narasinga Yādavarāya, and a certain number of other chiefs in his neighbourhood. This war against the Kāḍava was not so very much to restore the authority of the Chōḷa emperor but to prevent the Kāḍava lording it over them, and showed respect for the central authority as a matter of form more or less. The position of the Chōḷa emperor became precarious in the 2nd or 3rd year of his reign, and it was the timely intervention of the Hoyśāla ruler Narasimha II, who was related to the Chōḷa family, that saved the situation for the time being, by releasing Rājarāja from prison into which he was thrown by the Kāḍava. The attack therefore from the south by the Pāṇḍya, and from the Kāḍava in the interior immediately to the north of the country alike, made the position of the Chōḷa monarch precarious in the extreme, and, in the next following years, the

Hoyśālas found it necessary to be constantly on the alert in his defence. They felt it necessary therefore to establish themselves near Śrīrangam where, on the northern bank of the Coleroon, they fortified the town of Kaṇṇanūr, and erected for themselves a capital which they named Vikramapura. It was through the good offices of the Hoyśāla that Rājarāja was able to maintain some semblance of power. When Rājēndra III comes to notice we see him acting as if he were impatient of this tutelage of the reigning Chōḷa monarch, and, as if he were exerting himself to vindicate the Chōḷa prestige and authority, as against the Hoyśāla and the Pāṇḍya together. But the years were years of constant war and turmoil, so that there was not much chance of the Chōḷas being left in peace.

JATAVARMAN SUNDARA PANDYA. In these circumstances Jaṭāvarman Sundara Pāṇḍya I ascended the throne in succession to Māravarman Sundara Pāṇḍya II. He was a powerful ruler and very warlike. He started on a campaign against the Chōḷa territory, but primarily against the Hoyśāla monarchs who seem to have been, at the time related both to the Chōḷas and the Pāṇḍyas. In the course of a decade, he had succeeded in defeating the Hoyśālas, and along with them the Chōḷas, the Kādava feudatory of the Chōḷas and even the more powerful among the feudatories farther north who held possession of Kānchi and the territory dependent thereon. Marching farther north, he brought into subordination to him, the northern provinces of the Chōḷa empire reaching as far as the Krishṇa and celebrating the anointment of heroes in as far north a place as Nellore. So during his reign he had successfully brought the Chōḷa empire under his authority; and those of the feudatories of the Chōḷas who were prudent, had to acknowledge his authority and pay allegiance to him. The inscriptions referring to his time naturally therefore have to be issued more or less with his countenance, if not his authority almost. The inscriptions in Tirupati which refer to him give evidence of the completeness with which he imposed his authority over the Chōḷa empire.

SUNDARA PANDYA'S INSCRIPTIONS. The first record in this volume of inscriptions ascribed to him is No. 43 in the hill shrine at Tirupati. There is nothing in the record to indicate that it was of Sundara Pāṇḍya's, the only reference being that it was a letter (*ōlai*) written by a Yādavarāya, on the authority of a communication from the *Nāyanār*. Presumably therefore the Yādavarāya referred to is Vīra Narasinga Yādavarāya, and the Nāyanār is probably Sundara Pāṇḍya. The despatch was received by the governing body of Kuḍavūr Nāḍu, Toṇḍapāḍi Paṟṟu, Aharappaṟṟu, and a person described as Vāriya Vimānattān who exercised supervision over something. Then it records the action that they took, with effect from the third year, in connection with the Tiru-Iḷankōvil, the Vaishṇava temple at Tirucchānūr. It is the grant of the revenues to the temple, the details of which are gone. The next one, 44, is from the same place. It refers, of course, to a communication from Nāyanār Vīra Narasinga Dēva, and refers to the grant, as dating from the 12th year of Sundara Pāṇḍya, a clear indication of the recognition of his authority. It is the granting of the land as *sarvamānya*, detailing the revenue derivable therefrom, to constitute the funds from the income of which a certain kind of food-service was to be made to the God in the temple. No. 45 of the same place begins with a clear *Praśasti* in Sanskrit of Sundara Pāṇḍya, which credits him with the achievements usually ascribed to him in his inscriptions. They may be set down as some of them seem to be not quite so usual. He is described as an ornament of the *Sōmakula* (dynasty of the moon), a *Mādhava* of the city of Madura, destroyer of the family of Kēraḷa, one who caused the destruction of the city of Lanka, a second Rāma, a hammer that broke the hill of the Chōḷa family, a *Kūṭapākalā* fever to the Kāṭaka (this word is gone in the inscription), the destroyer of the various hill forts of enemies, a wild forest-fire burning to destruction the forest of Vīra Gaṇḍagōpāla (Vīra here being perhaps a general epithet as the person who suffered in this event is known as Vijaya Gaṇḍagōpāla), lord of the excellent city of Kānchi; and then follow the general titles, Mahārājādhirāja, Paramēśvara, and Tribhuvanachakravarti followed by the name Sundara Pāṇḍya. The document refers itself to the year opposite to the 14th year of the Perumāḷ, that is, Sundara Pāṇḍya. The grant portion is gone. No. 46 gives a different kind of *Praśasti*, only speaking of the prowess of Sundara Pāṇḍya. But the point of importance here is that it makes a distinction between Vijaya Gaṇḍagōpāla, whom he killed, and Vīra Gaṇḍagōpāla to whom he gave the kingdom of the other. The grant portion here is gone. No. 48 refers to Sundara Pāṇḍya having killed a certain Āndhrēśvara. This is followed by a *ślōka* that he established Vijaya Gaṇḍagōpāla; probably this Āndhrēśvara is no other than Vijaya Gaṇḍagōpāla. No. 49 refers to Sundara Pāṇḍya setting up a *kalaśa* on the temple at

Kānchi. No. 50 is too far gone to make much out of it, except that he had an anointment of heroes after killing an Āndhrēśvara. No. 51 is a Tamil verse giving almost the same idea as No. 50 and refers to *Vaḍa Kānchi-maṇḍalam*, the equivalent of *Ādhi Kānchi* in the previous record. It seems to refer almost to the same event. No. 52 also is similarly gone except of course for a reference to the Kūṭaka, that is, the ruler Kōpperuṇjinga of Cuddalore and Śēndamangalam, and a reference to a *Vīrābhishēka*. No. 53 is a reference to a Gaṇapati, certainly the Kākatīya ruler Gaṇapati. No. 54 refers to Chakravarti Sundara Pāṇḍya, and gives a part of the *Praśasti* containing the name Vīra Gaṇḍagōpāla. No. 55 again is a fragment of the *Praśasti* in which his putting to flight a Karnāṭaka Rāja, and the re-establishment of some other king are mentioned. These are the records that have any reference to Sundara Pāṇḍya. The fact that they are all found on the hill shrine and are built in various parts of the temple indicates clearly that Jaṭāvarman Sundara Pāṇḍya's rule was well acknowledged by the rulers of this region who found it to their interest to declare openly their allegiance. So Sundara Pāṇḍya's authority prevailed in a real sense over the region of north Kānchi as it is described.

The next two inscriptions Nos. 57 and 58 in this Section of Volume I of the Dēvastānam Inscriptions have reference to the building of the Āḻvār shrine on the banks of the tank called *Kapila Tīrtham* at the foot of the hill. The first document merely says that the tower, the pavilion and the hall for the Āḻvār were constructed by one Vānēḍuttakai Aḻagiyān of Tunjalūr in the middle division of Miḻalaikkūṟṟam in the Pāṇḍya country. The next one is a Sanskrit *ślōka* referring to the Āḻvār being established there, of the great services to humanity that he rendered by making accessible in Tamil the recondite teaching of the Vēda, obviously a reference to Nammāḻvār; but the name is gone, as the document is not complete. It is not quite clear why these two documents are grouped in this section. It is likely that they refer to the time, although there is nothing to warrant that.

INSCRIPTIONS OF GANDAGOPALA IN TIRUPATI. The next section of this volume of inscriptions has reference to a number of chieftains belonging to the various families such as the Telugu Pallavas, Yādavarāyas, and others. These have to be brought in here as from such detail as may be available in regard to time, they are referable to this period and undoubtedly to this region.

KAPILA TIRTHAM

(To face pags 336)

The first family is that of the Telugu Pallavas, two members of which figure prominently during the period. They seem to be, from certain Tamil records, undoubtedly brothers, namely, Vijaya Gaṇḍagōpāla and Vīra Gaṇḍagōpāla. They seem to have been rulers associated with Kānchi, and the districts north of it. Of these two Vijaya Gaṇḍagōpāla was put to death, as the result of a battle, by Jaṭāvarman Sundara Pāṇḍya in the year A. D. 1250–51, and his territory, a number of records say, he made over to his younger brother, Vīra Gaṇḍagōpāla. Records of Vijaya Gaṇḍagōpāla extend over a period of more than a decade previous to his death. His successor Vīra Gaṇḍagōpāla ruled for a long period after A. D. 1251 continuing almost to the end of the century. The relation between these, and Vīra Narasinga Yādavarāya whose period was coeval, is not clearly stated in these records; but it seems to be more or less that these chieftains made their donations to the temple at Tirupati, although holding official positions which may not directly associate them with Tirupati. These documents when they give dates refer themselves to these actual rulers without any reference to a suzerain. The first of such documents is No. 59 in the hill shrine referring itself to the ninth year. The beginning is gone and we have got only

Gōpāladēva, presumably Vijaya Gaṇḍagōpāla as his name occurs immediately after. The grant has reference to the gift of 33 cows and a bull for the purpose of a perpetual lamp in the temple by one Ammaiyappan of the *Kaśyapa gōtra* who was on duty at the gate of Vijaya Gaṇḍagōpāla. No. 60 has reference to the ninth year, but the ruler's name is gone, and mentions a certain chieftain by name *Villavarāya* with possibly the name Tirukkālattidēva. No. 61 refers actually to Vijaya Gaṇḍagōpāla, and to what seems his fourteenth year. It is in the Gōvindarāja shrine, and makes provisions for certain food-service during the *Vaikāśi* festival to the God on the hill. The grant was made over to the treasury of the temple, apparently the temple on the hill. No. 62 belongs to the hill shrine, and refers to a Śingadēva *alias* Villavarāyan, an immediate attendant who made the gift of a lamp, by name, Sundarattōḷuḍaiyān. No. 63 belongs to the hill shrine as well, and refers to a *Perumānḍidēvi Araśiyār*, the princess (the consort of our Lord King), who made a gift. What that is, is gone. The record begins with Vijaya Gaṇḍagōpāla, probably in reference to the year, but that is gone. No. 64 again belongs to the hill temple and refers to a grant of cows for the lamp (same number of cows for a perpetual lamp). No. 65 in the same temple refers to a ruler Tripurāntaka. No. 66 similarly refers to a *Brahmaśeṭṭi* and a *Brahmamārāyan*. All else in the inscription is gone. No. 67 in the same temple refers itself clearly to Vijaya Gaṇḍagōpāla. Here again part is gone. A certain oilman Amarakkōn, probably a son of Kaṭṭāri, resident of Nārāyaṇapuram, made over 32 cows and a bull for the purpose of one perpetual lamp and a certain amount of money for a camphor lamp as well. No. 68 similarly refers to Vijaya Gaṇḍagōpāla, and refers to a grant of 450 *paṇam*, which was placed under the protection of the Śrī Vaishṇavas. No. 69 refers to a similar grant in the reign of Vijaya Gaṇḍagōpāla specifically. No. 70 is a similar grant also of a gift of 440 *varāhas* by the *Śāliyars*, dyers and weavers, of Vikramapura belonging to Ātrēya *gōtra*. No. 71 is a similar grant by the Śāliyars. No. 72 is the same and refers itself to the time of Vijaya Gaṇḍagōpāla, but the *gōtra* of the Śāliyars is given as Vishṇu *gōtra*. No. 73 is too far gone to make anything out of it. No. 74 is important as it refers to the festivals of *Chittirai* and *Puraṭṭāśi* of Tiruvēngaḍamuḍaiyān. These were both of them festivals of long standing, the latter of which is referred to by the early Āḻvārs themselves. It makes provision for a grant for a food-service as prescribed in the *Tiruppāvai of Āṇḍāḷ*. This festival was organised by Rāmānuja, and, according to the *Śrī Vēnkaṭāchala Itihāsamāla*, it was not in existence before. For the requirements of this service, a certain number of gold coins called *Gaṇḍagōpālan Māḍai* were made over from the interest of which the annual expenses were to be met. No. 75 is mutilated. No. 76 refers itself to the time of Vijaya Gaṇḍagōpāla as does the next one 77. The first refers to to a perpetual lamp on the day of the Uttarāshāḍa *Nakshatra*, and the next one refers to a money gift. The other details are gone. No. 78 refers to the fifth year and *Puraṭṭāśi* month, and a gift of three *māḍai*. The other details are gone. No. 79 refers itself to the days of Vijaya Gaṇḍagōpāla, and has reference to the flower-garden in the name of a Pāṇḍya, probably Sundara Pāṇḍya, and refers to the gift of 200 *kuḷi* of land. It refers in one of the following passages to Rāmānuja and Emberumānar, and makes the gift of 500 *varāhapaṇa* for certain items of expenditure. Record No. 80 is a Tamil verse glorifying Rāja Gaṇḍagōpāla, and says in so many words that there was nobody who did not benefit by the liberality of Gaṇḍagōpāla among those "who put their hands below" for receiving his gift. It thus becomes clear that the grants, Nos. 59 to 80, almost all of them being in the hill shrine, refer themselves to the time of Gaṇḍagōpāla, Vijaya Gaṇḍagōpāla obviously. As we already stated, his period of authority came to a close almost with the first year of Jaṭāvarman Sundara Pāṇḍya, and whatever the length of his reign we have records of about ten to twelve years. These records refer to a time before A. D. 1251. We pass on to the records of other rulers, those of the Yādavarāyas in particular.

CHAPTER XIV.

THE YADAVARAYAS.

YADAVARAYA INSCRIPTIONS IN TIRUPATI. The Yādavarāya inscriptions in Volume I of the Tirumalai-Tirupati Dēvastānam Inscriptions take up Nos. 81 to 117 followed by a batch of miscellaneous inscriptions going up to No. 177. The inscriptions thereafter refer themselves to the empire of Vijayanagar. We might take the Yādavarāya inscriptions first. The first record No. 81 comes from the temple of Tirupati, and is by one Tirukkāḷattidēvan, giving himself all the titles usual to the Yādavarāyas making it clear that he is not to be confounded with the Telugu Chōḷas of the name, and is the grant of a *sarvamānya* village to the temple of Tiruvēngaḍamuḍaiyān. This does not refer itself to any suzerain, Chōḷa or other, and does not even give a direct date, although it seems to refer to the nineteenth year of the reign. But one cannot be sure whether it is the nineteenth year of this Yādavarāya or any suzerain of his. We pass on to No. 82 in the same place, which seems to refer itself definitely, although the name is gone, to the reign of Tribhuvana Chakravartigaḷ Kulōttunga Chōḷadēva. The name of the Chōḷa, however, is gone, and refers to the fifteenth year. It is a gift by a Vīrarākshasa Yādavarāya, whose proper name, though given in the record, is gone. This probably refers to the Vīrarākshasarāya of other records, a son of Tirukkāḷattidēva, by name Śinga Piḷḷai, prince Śinga, who had this title. The fifteenth year of Kulōttunga would correspond to A. D. 1193. If the nineteenth year of the previous record is to be taken to be the nineteenth year of Kulōttunga, it would mean A. D. 1197, four years after that of his son. It would be nothing strange as the records of this Tirukkāḷattidēva range from the seventh year of Kulōttunga III to the fifteenth year of Rājarāja, A. D. 1185 to A. D. 1231. The next following, No. 83, refers itself to the reign of this Vīrarākshasa, and of his forty-first year. The word for forty is gone. If this forty-first year could be taken to refer to Kulōttunga III's reign, the actual date would be A. D. 1219. We cannot perhaps be quite sure about it, though the date of the previous record is explicitly in reference to the reign of Kulōttunga. Then we come to the most important name of the Yādavarāyas connected with this temple, namely, Vīra Narasinga Yādavarāya, whose records begin with his twelfth year, and take us down to his fifty-first year. We have records of his in other places beginning with the thirty-first year of Kulōttunga III, and going down to the fourteenth year of Rājarāja III. That is the period included between A. D. 1209 and 1230. We have also a record of his dated the twelfth year of Jaṭāvarman Sundara Pāṇḍya, corresponding to A. D. 1263, which would mean that his active association with the temple would cover the period A. D. 1209 to 1263, fifty-four or fifty-five years. But the highest date in his records happen to be the fifty-first year. While we may be sure that he lived in the reigns of Kulōttunga III, and Rājarāja, we cannot be certain about his dates. From No. 90 of this volume in the Gōvindarāja shrine, the year of reign is given as fifty-one, clearly as that of Vīra Narasinga, and the name of the year is given as *Rākshasa*. This would correspond to A. D. 1255. But the previous record No. 89 couples his fiftieth year with the year Vikrama, which is impossible. We have to take it that the year is named wrong. We are not enabled to go any further as the other *Panchānga* details are not given in these records usually, the records contenting themselves with referring to the year of the reign of the ruler ; and the month and date and further details which would admit of calculation are not given. If his fifty-first year corresponded to A. D. 1255, his reign must

SHRINE OF GOVINDARAJA, TIRUPATI

(*To face page 345*)

have begun in A. D. 1204, and as the last date is the twelfth year of Sundara Pāṇḍya, A. D. 1263, or a period of fifty-nine years, a length which may not be quite impossible, and would cover the three reigns practically of Kulōttunga, Rājarāja and even Sundara Pāṇḍya. The first record in Tirupati of this ruler refers itself to the twelfth year when his queen Yādavarāya Nāchchiyār made over sixty-four cows and two bulls for two perpetual lamps. This was placed under the protection of the Śrī Vaishṇavas of the temple. No. 85 is a record of the same queen, but of the fifteenth year, and is a gift for Gōvindarāja of one perpetual lamp for which she gave thirty-two cows and one bull. No. 86 again comes from the Gōvindarāja shrine and refers to the thirtieth year of Vīra Narasinga. It is again a grant by the queen. She made a *sarvamānya* of a village, part of which already belonged to the God of Tiruvēngaḍam, transforming the whole into a *sarvamānya* (free of all imposts) village. The part that was now given was for the purpose of the Gōvindarāja festival in *Āni* instituted by herself, and for the expenses of the big car of square formation constructed by herself for the God. She paid the sum due, making allowance for depreciation and destruction of property. No. 87 from the hill shrine is of the thirty-fourth year of the same ruler and is a gift for a perpetual lamp by one Malaikkiniya Ninṛān or Tiruvēngadanātha of Vīra Nārāyaṇa-chaturvēdimangalam. No. 88 from the hill shrine is of peculiar importance referring itself to the fortieth year of the Yādavarāya. It begins with the information that, in the year referred to, a *Dēsāntari*, that is, a foreign visitor by name Tiruppullāṇidāsa, undertook the rebuilding of the temple. He seems to have sought permission of the ruler for doing it, and got a communication permitting of his doing so, but ordering at the same time the copying out of all the inscriptions, in the part of the temple to be renewed, on the north wall of the shrine. This means it was only the inner shrine that was going to be put under repairs and the records found there were to be copied in the outer wall of the temple. Among the records so copied is a grant by the Chōḻa queen, the step-mother of Rājarāja, the queen of Parāntaka II, who died in "the golden hall", and a daughter of the Chēra. This again refers itself to the sixteenth year of Rājarāja when she made over fifty-two *kaḻañju* of gold set with six rubies, four diamonds and twenty-eight pearls. No. 89 is a record of date fifty, but the year is wrong, and refers to a gift of lamps and garlands by the Śrī Vaishṇavas. No. 90 is of the fifty-first year corresponding to A. D. 1255, as was said above. This, and the previous record, belong to the Gōvindarāja shrine. It refers to the making of a garden under the name Yādavanārāyaṇa, and for the purpose of this garden, a sheet of running water was to be impounded for growing the waterlily, and the water was to be drawn from the big tank in Tirupati. The document lays down that the water should be drawn by natural flow from the big tank as long as it was possible, and, when it became impossible, water should be drawn by water-lifts. The peculiar regulation is laid down that this should not be marked off by stones carrying the disc mark of Vishṇu. It is not clear why this unusual prohibition is made. There is reference to another flower-garden below the tank, and that was to receive the water supply as this one. The two gardens were to be under the management of those who were rendering service to the God on the hill, and the maintenance of this garden and the flower service were to be perpetual. The next one, No. 91, does not give any date, but mentions the Vīra Narasimha Yādavarāya, and refers to his weighing himself against gold, and making use of the gold to cover the temple *Vimāna* (tower over the sanctum) with gold; his victory over his enemies, and his bringing the whole world under his authority, are both mentioned in general terms. The weighing against gold was on the occasion of the repairs referred to in 88 above. No. 92 from the Gōvindarāja shrine contains a verse in praise of Yādavanāchchiyār, who is compared to the lotus-born Lakshmi. The rest of the record is gone. Obviously she made a gift to the temple. No. 93 of this ruler is from the hill shrine, and refers to the presentation of a perpetual lamp by a Dēvapperumāḷ belonging to Nellore, otherwise called Vikramasimhapura. He made over the usual number of cows and a bull. No. 94 is a mutilated inscription and refers to a gift probably by somebody belonging to Nellore. The record speaks of a *Nāyanār Piḷḷai Vīra Narasinga.* That would mean the lord Prince Vīra Narasinga. No. 95 comes from the temple at Tirucchānūr and refers to a gift of land, but the record is too far gone. No. 96 again comes from the same place and seems to refer itself to the Pāṇḍiyataraiyar, the father-in-law of Vīra Narasinga, whose name occurs in several other records, and refers to the reclamation of land under a tank. No. 97 is from the same place referring to the same person and seems to refer again to a gift of land. No. 98 refers itself unusually to a date 1230, the year *Kīlaka.* This could only be the Śaka year, and for Śaka 1230 *Kīlaka* is correct. It refers to an arrangement made by the Śrī Vaishṇavas of Vīraśikhāmukhacchēri of the Nārāyaṇa-

ANANDANILAYA VIMANA (*To face page 349*)

chaturvēdimangalam for feeding the pilgrims that came to worship at the temple on certain special days of the year. The record is in the Āṇḍāḷ shrine of Gōvindarāja, which is one of the small outer shrines built at the inspiration of Rāmānuja within the temple. This brings us to the end of the records of Vīra Narasimha Yādavarāya.

THE YADAVARAYA'S AUTHORITY WAS ONE OF SUPERVISION. We see from these records that this Yādava ruler Vīra Narasingarāya showed himself specially interested in the temple and arranged for a number of services both by himself and through his wife. These extended to the performance of a *Tulāpurusha*, which was made use of for decorating the temple *Vimāna*, probably after it was repaired by the pilgrim Tiruppullāṇidāsa. Betweeen them, the husband and the wife arranged for a certain number of festivals and services both in the hill shrine and in the Gōvindarāja temple at the foot of the hill, not excluding even the temple at Tirucchānūr. There is a reference to this Yādavarāya queen making a car for the Gōvindarāja. During the period of his authority, as we noticed already, he was not merely a local governor. He exercised authority over a far larger area of the Chōḷa empire than the region of Tirupati, and probably as such, made these gifts to the temple. The record of Sundara Pāṇḍya's twelfth year, which would be of date A. D. 1263, refers to the issue of an order by this Yādava Narasingadēva in regard to the grant of a *sarvamānya*, although the record does not say who it was that made the gift; but the order confirming this grant was issued by this Yādavarāya, which would mean that under the great Pāṇḍya he occupied perhaps the same position of authority as under the last two Chōḻas. With that we take leave of Vīra Narasinga. Great as his authority was, and his benefactions magnificent, we still see that he exercised no more authority than that of mere supervision and control over the affairs of the temple, the management having been really in the hands of those exercising it as of old, namely, the Śrī Vaishṇavas of the locality.

TIRUVENGADANATHA YADAVARAYA. We next come to a Yādavarāya whose records give only his years and do not refer themselves to any other authority, and make it difficult to fix his position. There are however some details in his few records which would enable us to locate him in point of time. The first record, No. 99, of Volume I of the Dēvastānam Inscriptions, comes from the hill shrine, and refers to the year opposite the eighth year of Tiruvēngadanātha Yādavarāya. The document records that the village of Pongaḻūr in the Illattūr-*nāḍu* was made a *sarvamānya* to God Tiruvēngaḍam-uḍaiyān. The order communicating this was made by the Nāyanār, apparently the Yādava-rāya, and was so conveyed by executing the document from the year nine and month *Āḍi* (July—August). The purpose of this *sarvamānya* was to carry out Śingayya Daṇḍanāyaka's institution of a festival in the month of *Āḍi* every year in the name of Rāchayya Daṇḍa-nāyaka, and a food offering also in his name. The usual number of feudal and other dues are given here, many of which are found in other documents as well. These are generally payments of gold, payments in grain for small dues etc., and among the gifts called *kāṇikkai*, we find things like *Tiruttāyār Kāṇikkai* and *Tiru-Maruhanār Kāṇikkai*, which would mean gifts in the name of the respected mother and the respected son-in-law. These seem more or less feudal dues of some kind; but who the *Tiruttāyār* and *Tiru-Maruhanār* are it is not clear from this record. But what is of importance to us, however, is who the Śingaṇa Daṇḍanāyaka was, whose institution of the festival is on record here. We shall consider that in connection with the following records as well, two of which have reference to these. The next record No. 100 coming from the Gōvinda-rāja shrine refers to the twelfth year of the same

Yādavarāya, and refers to an order received directing the gifting of certain land as *sarvamānya* for certain purposes, among others a Yādava-nārāyaṇan *sandi*, although the part Yādava is gone in the record. There are two interesting points in this record. Like the other two that we referred to in the previous one, here we come upon *Akkan Kāṇikkai*, gift for the elder sister, probably a payment similar to that of the others. Then there is one other which is perhaps more informing, a *vari* or tax going by the name Vaḷḷāḷadēva, that is, Baḷḷāḷadēva, which would mean a tax levied and collected for the purpose of Baḷḷāḷadēva, which could only mean payment to Baḷḷāḷadēva as a sort of a tribute or something akin to it. No. 101 also from the Gōvindarāja shrine is of the twelfth year and seems to be a communication, exactly like the previous one, and No. 102 comes from the temple on the hill. It is a document of some importance and refers to the *stānattār* of Tirumalai to whom a representation was addressed in person by Śrīman Mahāpradhāni Immaḍi Rāhutta Rāyan Śingayya Daṇṇāyakan. It was a request that a festival in the month of *Āḍi* and a food service called *Sitagaragaṇḍan* in the name of Singayya Daṇṇāyaka should be instituted. For this the *son-in-law* Tiruvēnkaṭanātha Yādavarāya made a *sarvamānya* gift of Pongaḷūr belonging to

Illattūr-*naḍū*, and renamed Singaṇṇanallūr free of all demands. It was also ordered that stones with the marks of the Vishṇu disc should be planted round the village to mark the boundary, and from the revenue drawn therefrom the expenses of these services be met from time to time. In addition to these two the food service for Vīra Narasingapperumāḷ and Tirumangai Āḻvār at Tirupati must also be arranged for. Further thirty-two Śrī Vaishṇavas should be fed in the *Sitagaragaṇḍan Maṭham.* After meeting all these expenses the rest of the income should be applied for the maintenance of a flower-garden and a water-shed in the hill, in the name of Singayya, as also any other charitable service that may be required. These were placed under the direction of the Śrī Vaishṇavas and the order was directed to be put in stone and copper as a permanent record.

SINGAYYA DANDANAYAKA, A HOYSALA OFFICER. Here Singayya Daṇḍanāyaka is given the title Immaḍi Rāhutta and the official position of Mahāpradhāni. The food service instituted in his name is to be called *Sitagaragaṇḍan*, which would mean that he had the title *Sitagara-gaṇḍa.* Who was this person, a Daṇḍanāyaka, a Mahāpradhāni with the titles *Sitagara* and Immaḍi Rāhutta, who figures in Tirupati in this prominence? The very name *Sitagaragaṇḍa* (one who kept the profligate under control) indicates his Kanarese origin. Daṇḍanāyaka is a well-known title popularised into Daṇṇāyak, the title given to all dignitaries of rank, both civil and military, in the Kannaḍa country. Mahāpradhāni is a well-known office under the Hoyśāla rulers which occurs sometimes even in Vijayanagar records, but is not found in the records of the Tamil country, as in fact even the title Daṇṇāyaka. Singayya Daṇṇāyaka certainly was an officer of the Hoyśāla ruler Vīra Baḷḷāḷa, whose reign covered the period A. D. 1292 to 1342. This Baḷḷāḷa ruler began his reign with his father's Brahman minister, Perumāḷa Daṇḍanāyaka, who was a very distinguished officer under Narasimha III, Hoyśāla. His son was a Mādhava Daṇḍanāyaka, who held similar high office under Vīra Baḷḷāḷa with dates early in the reign, A. D. 1310–11, while the father's date falls in about A. D. 1292. This Mādhava Daṇḍanāyaka had two sons, Kētayya Daṇḍanāyaka and Singayya Daṇḍanāyaka who similarly held office under Baḷḷāḷa III. It was Mādhava Daṇḍanāyaka, not his father, who acquired the *jāghīr* of Padinālku Nāḍu within the Mysore territory of the present day, and had made what is now the village Terukkaṇāmbi in the Guṇḍlepet Taluk of Mysore, his capital. They were all of them Brahman officers of rank under the Hoyśālas and the title Mahāpradhāni given to all of them is an indication that they wielded the highest authority in the state next the king. They became afterwards associated with Daṇṇāyakankōṭṭai below the Ghats, and came to be known as Daṇṇāyakankōṭṭai chiefs. That is, however, later. But as yet they were officers under Vīra Baḷḷāḷa III, the last great Hoyśāla monarch.

THE RELATION BETWEEN SINGANA DANDANAYAKA AND TIRUVENGADANATHA YADAVARAYA. Of these officers, Perumāḷa Daṇḍanāyaka does not concern us, a very distinguished officer under Vīra Baḷḷāḷa III and his father though he was. His dates were probably in the 13th century, perhaps the last decade of it. His son Mādhava Daṇḍanāyaka has a date about A. D. 1310-11, and succeeded to the position of his father under Vīra Baḷḷāḷa. He acquired the *jāghīr* of Terukaṇāmbi. His sons were two Kētayya Daṇḍanāyaka and Singaṇa Daṇḍanāyaka, both of which names appear in the Tirupati records. From Mysore inscriptions we have dates for both. Of these one record gives Kētayya Daṇḍanāyaka's date as A. D. 1321—22, and another Singaṇa's as A. D. 1338. Without being too precise, we may say that these were both of them officers who succeeded to the position of the father, and were trusted lieutenants of the Hoysāla monarch under Vīra Baḷḷāḷa during the first forty years of the 14th century. Having regard to the dates of the father and the grandfather, we cannot well carry them backward to anywhere near the middle of the 14th century. We have noticed already that the last date we know of for Vīra Narasingadēva is the 12th year of Sundara Pāṇḍya which would mean A. D. 1263—64. Taking that in combination with the date found in No. 90 of the Tirupati inscriptions, he would have had a period of authority extending over 59 years. So a date A. D. 1263—64 should be rather close to the end of his reign period. Whether Tiruvēngaḍanātha Yādavarāya, associated with Singaṇa Daṇḍanāyaka could be an immediate successor of Vīra Narasinga is matter for pronouncing upon on evidence of which we have nothing quite definite. The records in Tirupati referring to this Tiruvēngaḍanātha happen to be the 9th and 12th years of his own reign, which do not lead us to anything definite. But in No. 102 of the Tirupati inscriptions coming from the hill shrine, he is referred to as *Maruhanār* or son-in-law. Whose son-in-law was he ? Sādhu Subramaṇya Śāstri has taken this to mean that his son-in-law was Singaṇa Daṇḍanāyaka, notwithstanding the fact he was a Brahman officer which he apparently does not know and the whole account he tries to evolve in respect of these is confused and contradictory. As the Tamil records read, the term *Maruhanār* cannot apply to Singaṇa, and is descriptive only of Tiruvēngaḍanātha. If that term should be held to describe the relationship between him and Singaṇa, it could only be that he was Singaṇa's son-in-law. But the collocation of words as they occur in this record would not justify that interpretation. Could it be that Tiruvēngaḍanātha Yādavarāya was the son-in-law of Vīra Narasinga? At the worst *Maruhanār* Tiruvēngaḍanātha Yādavarāya could only mean that Tiruvēngaḍanātha was the son-in-law of the ruling Yādavarāya just at the time or before. The known date for Singaṇa Nāyaka is A. D. 1338. That may be a very late date, and it may not be unjustifiable to take the beginning of his activity as a Hoyśāla officer to the commencement of the century while yet the father was wielding his authority as the principal officer under the Hoyśāla monarch. Even so, it is more than 30 years distant from the last known date of Vīra Narasinga. While therefore it would be quite possible he was Vīra Narasinga's son-in-law, it would be difficult to assert it without further evidence. Other possibilities are that he was a son-in-law of an unknown officer of Vīra Narasinga, who still held authority either in the region of Tirupati or round about. This is unlikely as Vīra Narasinga was still in authority. In any case he certainly could not have been the father-in-law of Singaṇa for one thing. That is so far as the personal relations between the two are concerned. But the really more important point for us is the political relationship between the two. Mr. Subramaṇya Śāstri goes the length of suggesting that Singaṇa and his elder brother Kētayya were officers of the Hoyśālas who simultaneously took service also under the Yādavarāyas, which, from all that we know of the matter, seems hopelessly impossible. It cannot be argued from all that we know that even a powerful man like Vīra Narasinga was at any time any more than a feudatory ruler who might have comported himself as an independent ruler. Nowhere does he openly declare himself as such. What indeed was not done by a powerful ruler like Vīra Narasinga, it would be difficult to ascribe to a successor, either immediate or remote, whatever his position, except on the assumption that the higher authority had ceased to exist. The Chōḷa power undoubtedly had gone out of existence, but these chieftains were openly under the Pāṇḍya hegemony. The power of the Pāṇḍyas had not quite gone out of existence, and the last great Pāṇḍya,

Māravarman Kulaśēkhara Pāṇḍya and his lieutenants exercised authority over both the Pāṇḍyan and the Chōḻa kingdoms, though his authority may not have extended to the region round Vēngaḍam in any real sense of the term. But then what had these Hoysāla officers, particularly Singaṇa Nāyaka to do with the region? We have now to go back upon a short retrospect.

THE POLITICAL CONDITION OF SOUTH INDIA—THE MUHAMMADAN INVASIONS. Just a few years after the last year of Vīra Narasinga Yādavarāya, there was a change in the Pāṇḍya succession. Jaṭāvarman Sundara Pāṇḍya, the chief ruler passed away, and his place was taken by a Māravarman Kulaśēkhara, who ruled for more than 40 years, his reign ending in A. D. 1309–10. There were other Pāṇḍyas, who ruled as his lieutenants, and it is just possible there was a Jaṭāvarman Sundara Pāṇḍya II between him and the first Jaṭāvarman Sundara. That is not very material to our purpose. During the period of Māravarman Kulaśēkhara Pāṇḍya, his authority, as the supreme ruler of Tamil India, was recognised both in the Pāṇḍya and Chōḻa kingdoms, and he is spoken of as very often residing in the Chōḻa capital of Muḍikoṇḍaśōḻapuram, sometimes also Jayaṁkoṇḍaśōḻapuram, not far off, during his reign. At least one of his sons, a Vīra Pāṇḍya, was active in the region of Kongu and the parts corresponding farther eastward; and, in his activities, he is reported to have come into clash with the Hoyśālas, and the Hoyśāla army was sometimes drawn towards the Kongu border against him. This would mean that the frontiers of both the powers had become doubtful and frontier wars were not unusual. Vīra Pāṇḍya had been installed in authority in A. D. 1292 or 1293, almost about the same time that Vīra Baḷḷāḷa succeeded to the Hoyśāla throne. The accession of this Baḷḷāḷa brought about a union of the Tamil and the Kaṇṇaḍa parts of the Hoyśāla kingdom which were under the rule of two brothers immediately previous to him, Narasimha ruling over the Mysore country and beyond, and his brother Rāmanātha ruling in the Tamil portions of the Hoyśāla dominions. Rāmanātha claimed two capitals one in the Chōḷa country, the old Hoyśāla capital Vikramapura or Kaṇṇanūr, and the other farther to the north in the Baramahal part of the Salem District, in a place called Kundāṇi or Hesar Kundāṇi in those days. Rāmanātha died, and a son of his by name Viśvanātha after two or three years of precarious existence passed out of view. Thereafter Vīra Baḷḷāḷa stands forth as the one Hoyśāla ruler of the whole of the Hoyśāla empire. This naturally would begin to come into clash with the successors of the Chōḷas, that is, the great Pāṇḍya Māravarman Kulaśēkhara and his lieutenants. This position was complicated by the progress of Muhammadan conquests gradually in the Dakhan which began with an invasion of Dēvagiri by the generals of Allaud-din Khilji in A. D. 1306. This was followed by other campaigns which ended ultimately in the annexation of Dēvagiri to the empire of the Khiljis. Next came the turn of the Kākatīya rulers of Warangal, and that was overthrown after two wars in A. D. 1309. Then it came to the turn of South India. In the course of that South Indian invasion under Malik Kafur, ordered by Allaud-din, a raid on the Hoyśālas was an incident. The invading army encamped itself near Shōlapūr in the *jāghīr* of the Daḷavāy Paraśurām Dēv, General of the Dēvagiri ruler, and from there a raid was conducted up to the Hoyśāla capital, probably a quick cavalry march which succeeded wonderfully as the Hoyśāla armies were occupied on the southern frontier of Kongu against the activities of Vīra Pāṇḍya referred to above. The invasion was so far successful that it plundered the capital of the Hoyśālas after having partly destroyed it, and carried the raid much further to the coast of the Arabian sea. It was afterwards that the armies marched on South India, and, after having plundered the temples of the South, including Śrīrangam, Chidambaram, Madura, and even Rāmēśvaram, the Muhammadan armies retired from the Tamil country. The Muhammadan danger was not altogether over as yet completely. After the raid on the Hoyśāla capital however, Vīra Baḷḷāḷa was made to sue for peace. A representation in his favour was sent up to headquarters with the recommendation of Malik Kafur, and the Hoyśāla prince was sent out on this mission. It was graciously received at headquarters, and the Hoyśāla was accepted as nominal feudatory of the empire; and the prince was sent back with honours. According to a Hoyśāla record,* there were rejoicings on the return of the prince in A. D. 1313. So the Hoyśāla managed to save himself from this Muhammadan danger which threatened his very existence, and, having managed it more or less skilfully, he was reorganising his resources and putting himself in a position of some strength as against future contingencies.

THE REGION OF TIRUPATI UNDER HOYSALA AUTHORITY. It is in the course of his activity in the following years that he seems to have

* *Epi. Car.* VII, Ch. 68, Sewell's *Hist. Ins. of South India*, p. 178.

stretched himself out into the region next adjoining his territory gradually. That must have brought him into the region of Tirupati. The years following the return of Malik Kafur in A. D. 1311 were years of trouble in the capital till Mubarak placed himself on the throne in A. D. 1316. During these five years, the Muhammadan danger ceased to be real in South India. Mubarak's reign proved to be brilliant but very brief; and an invasion that came under his orders to the South met with the success that they looked for, and his general Khusru returned to the capital to play his part in the disturbances that followed and left the Dakhan and South India pretty much to themselves. In Mubarak's reign, the Mahārāshṭra kingdom of Dēvagiri actually became a part of the Mughal empire, and Mubarak tried to strengthen himself by planting Muhammadan garrisons at salient points in the Mahratta country, which, to the Hoyśāla, must have seemed a direct threat against his northern frontier. He had to be therefore alive and active as his northern frontier was in grave and perpetual danger. In the south things were propitious for his activity. The Tamil country suffered from the invasion of Malik Kafur, and an effort made by Ravivarman Kulaśēkhara from the Travancore country, while it just recovered the Tamil country from the grip of the Muhammadans, failed to provide an organisation of any permanence. So the field seemed open to the exploitation of any enterprising neighbour, and the Hoyśāla was the only one in the locality. It was apparently this that made him cast his eyes upon Tiruvaṇṇāmalai as a salient position in which he could place himself with advantage to be in touch with his own kingdom, and, if possible, prevent any advance of the Muhammadans into the Tamil country, should any further effort in that direction be made. That would offer him a safe place of retirement for himself if he should be attacked by the Muhammadans again from the north. The result of this activity on the part of the Hoyśāla is what we see here in the region of Tirupati in the presence of Singaṇa Nāyaka or Singayya Daṇḍanāyaka. As we see it in the records of Tirupati, Singayya Nāyaka is not there in the course of a hostile incursion, nor is he there seeking the hospitality of the local ruler for the time being. We rather see him issuing orders, and being honoured by institutions of festivals and the naming of towns in his name, and of provisions being made for services in the temple for his good. Singaṇa Daṇḍanāyaka is here as the superior authority whose orders the local ruler for the time being felt called upon to carry out. No. 99 of the Tirupati inscriptions is the institution of food services in Tirupati by Singayya Daṇḍanāyaka in honour of another officer Rachayya Daṇḍanāyaka, for which the village of Poṇgaḷūr was to be a *sarvamānyam* gift to the temple, and the order was issued in a letter which conveyed the information that they might indite the grant both in stone and copper as a permanent gift. In No. 102 on the contrary, it is the Tirupati *stānattār* who say that they instituted the festival in the month of *Āḍi*, and a food service named *Sitagaragaṇḍa* both in honour of Singayyadēva. This time the *sarvamānya* village of Poṇgaḷūr is named Singayyanallūr in honour of the officer. It does very many other things all of them intended for his honour. The food services were provided for Vīra Narasingapperumāḷ and Tirumangai Āḻvār in the temple. 32 Vaishṇavas were to be fed in the *Maṭham* or hall of *Sitagaragaṇḍa*, which means that that building, or public hall, must have been constructed either by Singayya, or in his honour by others. There was to be a provision for a flower-garden and a shed for supply of water, etc. Of course the whole of these charities is placed as usual under the protection of the Śrī Vaishṇavas of the locality. Tiruvēngaḍanātha Yādavarāya simply figures here as the officer who did the needful to transform the village completely into a *sarvamānya* village. He is obviously and undoubtedly in the position of a subordinate officer carrying out the orders of a superior in Singayya Daṇḍa-nāyaka. This position would be justified only if this region had been brought more or less under the authority and protection of the Hoyśāla ruler for the time being, and the officers were actually engaged first in the conquest of the district, and then in the maintenance of the authority of their master. This finds the fullest justification in record No. 100, which makes reference to a *Vaḷḷāḷadēvar vari*, a tax or duty levied in the name of Baḷḷāḷadēva, which means a cess or duty collected either for payment to Baḷḷāḷadēva, or for some other use in his name. That could not be unless he were a ruler whose authority they were bound to respect, and this tax could be nothing more than a tribute paid to that authority perhaps to let them carry on their administration as hitherto though under the Baḷḷāḷa suzerain authority.

This position of the Baḷḷāḷa could be understood easily if we remembered that as soon as the Tughlaks established themselves in authority in Delhi in A. D. 1320, their attention was called to the Dakhan, and there was a threat of an invasion of the further south in A. D. 1323 which was saved by the outbreak of cholera in the camp of Muhammad Tughlak. Muhammad Tughlak did not forget it, and was likely to have undertaken an invasion the next year but for the fact that his attention was called to Delhi, where he had to remain when his father was out in suppressing a rebellion in Bengal. It was on his victorious return that he was assasinated, and Muhammad succeeded to the position. Soon after his accession, Muhammad had to come to the south against his cousin who set up in rebellion in what is now the Nizam's Dominions and in the Southern Mahratta country where he held a government. The success that was then achieved would naturally bring him on further. He sent out another invasion in A. D. 1327 which damaged the Hoyśāla capital far more gravely than before, and made the Baḷḷāḷa move into Tiruvaṇṇāmalai, and make it more or less his permanent residence as being a more strategically central position being on the high road between the north and the south, and along the line of communication. It could not be that the Baḷḷāḷa resolved to make Tiruvaṇṇāmalai his place of residence, or an alternative capital of Tiruvaṇṇāmalai town itself, unless he had some hold over the surrounding country and could exercise his authority over the region. The Hoyśāla conquest, the slow and gradual conquest by the Hoyśālas, of these parts seem justified by these documents which bring Singaṇa Daṇḍa-nāyaka into the region of Tirupati.

SRIRANGANATHA YADAVARAYA, SUCCESSOR OF TIRUVENGADANATHA AND CONTEMPORARY OF SINGANA DANDANAYAKA. Without going any further in this matter, we may take the name of another Yādavarāya which figures in the next following inscriptions of the first volume of the Tirupati Dēvastānam inscriptions. No. 103 refers to the 3rd year of Śrī Ranganātha Yādavarāya, which refers to the disposal of certain pieces of land which were forest belonging to Tiruvēngaḍamuḍaiyān, and sold for 200 *paṇams*. Arrangements were made for the irrigation of this land. The next inscription is of the same year and of the same ruler, and refers to this Singaṇa Daṇḍanāyaka, whose father's name is also given by his being called Mādappan Singaṇa Nāyaka with his usual titles. The document seems to refer to his purchase of a *Maṭha* and a flower-garden from certain *Jīyars* (ascetic Vaishṇavas) in management of certain properties belonging to the temple, and making them over to be maintained as the charitable gift of the officer. Further the document seems to refer to his having paid another 400 gold *paṇams* with a view to feeding pilgrims on a certain festival day in one of the *Nandavanas* (flower-gardens) to which the God and the Goddess should be taken on certain festivals. It also refers to the taking of the God to the flower-garden named after Vaṇ Śaṭagōpa, apparently in reference to the Āḻvār for which another provision of 100 *paṇams* had been made. All these were placed under the protection of the Śrī Vaishṇavas. The point calling for notice here is that Śrī Ranganātha Yādavarāya is brought into connection with Singaṇa Nāyaka pretty early in his reign, that is, in his 3rd year. The next one No. 105 refers to the 9th year of this Yādavarāya, but there is no other detail worth our attention. No. 106 comes from the hill shrine as do the previous two documents, and refers to the 19th year and makes provision for the taking out of the god on the fourth day of some festival to the flower pavilion called *Chēdirāyan*, and makes provision for the distribution of food for which money was paid into the treasury. No. 107 is from the same temple and refers to the same Yādavarāya. But very unfortunately his regnal year and the name of the year, both of which were apparently set down in the document, are lost, as otherwise we would have had a precise date for him; but, the other *Panchānga* details given seem to indicate that the year under reference must be either A. D. 1330 or 1333, perhaps the latter better. It is again a provision for some kind of food service. The document is partially gone. This document, even in this imperfect condition, seems to indicate clearly that Śrī Ranganātha Yādavarāya lived some time about A. D. 1330 or 1333 as also Singaṇa Daṇḍanāyaka. From this perhaps we can make the inference that Yādava Śrīranga followed Yādava Tiruvēngaḍanātha, and both of them were contemporaries of Hoyśāla Singaṇa Daṇḍanāyaka. No. 108 comes from the Gōvindarāja shrine and seems to be a record of an agreement between the governing body of the locality and a certain number of other individuals, among whom are the Yādavarāya Viḻupparaiyan, Śōḻa Viḻupparaiyan, Trigartarāya and another Viḻupparaiyan, with the former portion gone, together with the weavers and devotees of Emberumān, which seems here to refer to God: it might also be Rāmānuja who had the name. But the rest of the document is gone. No. 109 comes from the hill shrine and contains a couple of verses glorifying Śrī Ranganātha. It seems to refer to the enemies he conquered, and the 16th year of his reign. No. 110 coming from the same shrine refers to a Śaśikula Chālukki Sangrāmarāma, certainly a Yādavarāya, but we can hardly be certain that it was Śrī Ranganātha Yādavarāya. The date happens to be recorded here, apparently in the Śaka year; but the figures before the 100 are gone, while 181 is left over. It may be 1100 or 1200, or another number of hundreds. But the name of the year *Vikāri* being given, the year under reference seems to be Śaka 1281, which would mean A. D. 1359. It may not be quite too late for Śrī Ranganātha Yādavarāya, but we cannot be quite certain whether it is he that is referred to. Nos. 111 and 112 come from the same shrine and simply put down the name of the *Sitagaragaṇḍan Maṭha* of Singaṇa Daṇḍanāyaka.

OTHER RULERS WHO MAY BE YADAVARAYAS.

No. 113 is of some importance, although the document is gone in vital parts. It refers to Śrī Nāyanār Yādavarāya with obviously Tribhuvanachakravarti going before. But the actual name of the Yādavarāya is not given. All that we can be certain about is it was still a Yādavarāya ruler. The year and month might have been given, but they are gone. All that is left is the month and the date 29, and then follows a reference to a Mahānāyaka Eṟṟamanchi Periya Pammanāyaka, that is the elder (Periya) Pammanāyaka of Eṟṟamanchi. The titles given to him are obviously Vijayanagar titles. He made the donation in cows and bull for one perpetual lamp to Tiruvēngaḍamuḍaiyān. It is stated however that he came there "for the *Vasanta*". Probably he visited the temple during the *Vasanta* (April—May) festival. No. 114 is a similar inscription which mentions a Śrīmān Mahānāyangāchārya with the other attributes of the previous inscriptions and refers to a Bāpu Nāyakar Pemmānāyakar providing for a perpetual lamp. Like the previous document No. 113, this also has the same indication making it perhaps really referable to the next following period. No. 115 merely mentions Yādavanṛpa. Nos. 116 and 117 coming from the hill shrine are of some interest. The first refers to the granting of what is called *Vaikunṭha-Hasta* to the god on the hill by a certain Ahōbalarāya which is in gratitude to the God for giving the people the promise of Heaven by the pose of the hand. The next is a Tamil record to the same effect except that here an Aubalarāya is described as the Yādava ruler of Tañjai (Tanjore). We cannot say what exactly his position was, and whether he was really a successor of the other Yādavarāyas, and why his name gets associated with Tanjore in particular.

OTHER MISCELLANEOUS RECORDS. With No. 118 we begin with a number of miscellaneous inscriptions, all of them being records of gifts of various kinds and institution of certain services in the temple. Most of these inscriptions are too much mutilated to make much from out of them. But some of them that do contain some little information do not admit of the information being properly described for want of full details. The first one of any importance is No. 150 which is a small record and seems to be complete, though the meaning is obscure. It refers to a particular place called the pavilion of *Śēranaivenṛān* the pavilion of 'the person who conquered the Chēra,' possibly in reference to Ravivarman Kulaśēkhara's march up and he is described as one of the lords whose function it was to issue orders or send up communications. Nos. 171 and 172 come from the hill shrine. The first refers to *Uḍaiyavar* and speaks of a certain charitable gift, and in the last line there is the name Anandāḻvān; and the next one refers to a grandson of Anandāḻvān, apparently referring to a service that he arranged for. No. 173 similarly refers to the Āchāryapurushas, and, among them, what seems to be Anandāḻvān Piḷḷai and the flower-garden that he made on the hill. No. 175 refers similarly to the garden, Rāmānuja. It will be remembered that the principal flower-garden laid out and cultivated by Anandāḻvār was called by this name according to the *Vēnkaṭāchala Itihāsamāla*. No. 176 seems to define the boundary between Tirupati and Avulāli, elsewhere called Avilāli. No. 177 refers to a Kāmavilli of Pūvainagar. He is said to have constructed a tank in Tirupati as a charitable gift, as one among the 32 charities that his mother had taken occasion to teach him about. That brings us to the end of the miscellaneous inscriptions, and the records following refer themselves to Vijayanagara rule.

CHAPTER XV.

TONDAMAN CHAKRAVARTI—THE HUMAN FOUNDER OF TIRUPATI.

With Vijayanagara we may regard ourselves as entering, so far as the history of Tirupati is concerned, upon the modern period. Up to that the history of Tirupati would be more or less of the nature of imperfect documents upon which we have had to depend for a regular history of the period, and what we have been able to gather would more or less be of a character almost in keeping with this. We may roughly take the middle of the 14th century as the parting line between the one and the other, and, having come so far collecting and considering all the *disjecta membra* of information so far made available it would perhaps be well to gather together in summary what of the real history of the holy shrine at Tirupati we have been able to gain so far. While the history of the shrine may be said to go back to the commencement of the Christian era, we have no definite information as to who the first human founder of the temple was. It is what is called a shrine self-create *(svayambhu-sthala)*, but, as far as the historical position is concerned, Toṇḍamān

Chakravarti, as he is called in later literature, must be regarded as the human founder. He was by all accounts mentioned as a ruler of the locality having his capital near the hill which could be reached from there even by an underground passage. We must take it, therefore, that he ruled from some place like Nārāyaṇavanam and a few of the other places round about as constituting townships of importance in the locality in later history.

THE VAISHNAVA CHARACTER OF THE SHRINE AT TIRUPATI. Another feature of the tradition regarding him is that he was the son of a Chōḻa ruler by a Nāga princess which we may take to mean a princess, daughter of the local ruler. The Toṇḍamān's arrangements for the conduct of worship in the temple were not anything of his own foundation, as there were already two devotees, a Brahman and a Śūdra who were on their own account engaged in the service, the Vaikhānasa Brahman for the ritual worship, and the Śūdra engaged in the external service necessary to conduct worship, such as the supply of flowers and other things which would be needed for the conduct of the daily worship even according to the Vaikhānasa rites. The period, according to the Paurāṇic sources which are the only source for this period of history, is said to be somewhere between the beginning of the Vikrama era and the Śaka era, that is, in the first century B. C. or A. D. That is as far as the traditional origin of it goes. We find the shrine in Tirupati figuring in the earliest secular sources of information we have for South India, and is already a shrine with arrangements for not merely conducting the daily worship but even some of the more important annual festivals. The earliest writer mentioning this that we know of is the poet Māmūlanār, one of the great celebrities of the Śangam literature. He says specifically that Tirupati was famed for *its annual festivals.* We quoted references to the worship of Vishṇu among the early deities from a poem of Nakkīrar, and a reference to the existence of one of the shrines in Kānchi in the days of Toṇḍamān Iḷam Tiraiyan from the *Perumbāṇ-āṟṟuppaḍai.* It need not therefore be regarded as anything improbable that a shrine should have existed in Tirupati. With these poets and poems we are almost introduced to the first Āḻvārs or the Vaishṇava saints. They are three of them who had the reputation, in the estimation of even the later saints, as writers of classical Tamil (*Śen-Tamiḻ*) Their three centa are regarded by Vaishṇavas as in a way specially dedicated to the Vishṇu shrine in Tirupati. We have collected above all the relevant details, and, on a consideration of these details, we have no hesitation in affirming that the shrine was regarded as a Vishṇu shrine, and the image therein as an image of Vishṇu, notwithstanding features which later on came to be regarded as representing other deities. This peculiarity of features is fully explained not only in the works of these early Āḻvārs but even in some of the later ones. The explanations offered ought to satisfy every one that is a believer in Vaishṇavaic Hinduism as such ; to the outsider who examines it altogether from an extra devotional point of view, these peculiar features would seem strange indeed, as being, more or less, those not ordinarily met with in one's own experience. Assuming for the moment that the image had a human origin and the temple a human foundation, the image representing the deity would be the translation in material form of the ideas that the founder wished should be incorporated in the image representing the deity. Having regard to the circumstances of the time and of the prevailing religious conditions, we can state it with confidence that the period was one in which people were making an effort to provide for worship for the masses of people, possibly with a view to wean them from attachment to, and the attractions of, other contemporary religions such as Jainism and Buddhism. It was therefore a period not so much of distinction, much less of antagonism, between Vaishṇavism and Śaivism ; but it was much rather of Hinduism, a kind of transformed Brahmanism as against the two heretical religions from the point of view of the Hindu. Having regard to this, they would rather lay the emphasis upon the similarities between Vishṇu and Śiva, and the underlying unity, rather than bring into prominence the distinction in character between the two. Hence certain features, which may well form the basis for contention as to the real character of the image, would seem unavoidable. But even so, it is remarkable that, from the earliest times, the shrine was regarded as a Vishṇu shrine and the image that of Vishṇu. Besides the three Āḻvārs, and a fourth, who have to be regarded as coming close after the age of Māmūlanār and Nakkīrar, and Rudran Kaṇṇan all Śangam celebrities, we find Nammāḻvār giving the same character, as also the other Āḻvārs till we come to Āḻvār Tirumangai in the middle of the 8th century. That is not all. Their contemporaries the Śaiva Aḍiyārs and the Nāyanmārs who wrote as largely on their devotion to Śiva and of the places specially dedicated to the worship of Śiva, give no indication whatever of their having felt at any time that the hill shrine at Tirupati was ever a Śaiva shrine. Kāḷahasti not far off, one of the primary Śaiva holy places, has been visited by all these prominent saints, and they celebrate it in their poems. Since they went and visited Kāḷahasti and celebrated the shrine there, we cannot say that they did not know of Tirupati, or hear of it. Nevertheless we do not find them mentioning Tirupati as among their holy places, not to say that they have not celebrated it as a Śiva shrine. We have already noted that there are a few secular references from the Hindu point of view, and they leave it in no doubt and state it, as plainly as language would admit, that Tirupati was a Vishṇu shrine. The author of the *Śilappadhikāram*, who was not a Brahman Hindu, states it in the clearest terms that the hill shrine at Tirupati was a Vishṇu shrine. So does the author of the *Bhārata Veṇbā* at the end of this period, that is, at the commencement of the 9th century; this couples Tirupati and Kānchi as places specially dedicated to Vishṇu. The earliest inscription which refers to this temple belongs to a generation or two previous to the author of the *Bhārata Veṇbā*, and that refers to Tirupati as a Vishṇu shrine. Hence we have to regard it that, whatever the character of the image or the peculiar features that it exhibits, the place passed in the estimation of the people as a Vaishṇava holy place, and the temple a Vaishṇava shrine, during the first eight centuries of its existence.

TIRUPATI IN THE AGE OF THE ACHARYAS: Passing down we come to the age of the Āchāryas who followed the Āḻvārs and continued their teaching, and the accounts of the *Guruparamparas* refer to visits to Tirupati by the first Āchārya Nādamuni. The next important person among this group, Nādamuni's grandson Yāmunāchārya is said not merely to have paid a visit some time in his life but even to have felt, perhaps as a result of the visit, that the arrangements for the flower-service to the God was not satisfactory, and wanted that some stout-hearted person should make up his mind to go and settle down in Tirupati and devote himself to that service. It is as a result of this that one of his grandsons Tirumalai Nambi went and settled down in Tirupati with his father and two young unmarried sisters, from one of whom was to be born later on Rāmānuja, the Vaishṇava teacher. Tirumalai Nambi became a permanent inhabitant of the hill, and some of those that live in Tirupati to-day claim descent directly from him. The fact is therefore confirmed by Rāmānuja having had to go to this uncle of his at Tirupati to learn the esoteric teaching of the *Rāmāyaṇa* as he had received it from his own grandfather Yāmunāchārya. So although tradition is our only authority for some of these specific facts, we can still hold that there is a continuous tradition that the shrine was one dedicated to Vishṇu, that the Vaishṇavas regarded it as a holy place of pilgrimage to which they went on pilgrimage, and certain of the Vaishṇavas came to regard it as their special charge and even made efficient arrangements as far as they could, for the care of the shrine in a locality not as yet well-inhabited, perhaps not quite comfortably habitable as yet. That was the state of affairs regarding the temple till we come to the days of Rāmānuja.

THE ACHARYA RAMANUJA AND THE SHRINE AT TIRUPATI. It was during the life-time of Rāmānuja that a controversy arose which has given rise to different notions regarding the character of the shrine itself. Rāmānuja's was about the age, taking into it a generation or two before him, when the sects were forming distinctly, and even tried more or less to separate themselves into distinct groups in Hindu society. One of the incidents in the course of this development is the natural assertion and counter-assertion of the superiority of Śiva and Vishṇu, in fact the supreme character of the one or other of these. This kind of a contention got set up with impunity, as, at the time the rival creeds of Jainism and Buddhism had not perhaps as great a vogue as in the centuries preceding. Certain other historical circumstances also encouraged a movement like this. Rāmānuja's life was cast in the period when the Chōḷas were the chief power in the Tamil country. The Chōḷa monarchs were most of them Śaivas personally, and some of them very ardent ones. Notwithstanding their personal devotion to the Śaiva faith, as rulers they took care not to become partisan in public matters, and, as far as it came their way, they supported Vaishṇava shrines and the Vaishṇavas as well. In an age of controversy however and contention between the sects, these rulers were bound to be drawn into the struggle, and they might sometimes have let themselves go in support of those of their own conviction to some extent. But the really important feature is the existence of these controversies. We have a tradition that the ruler of Madura invited Periyāḷvār to take part in a controversy raised by a Śaiva divine, and so was Yāmunāchārya, the great-grandfather of Rāmānuja. The advent of the Chōḷas to power gave much support to Śaivism, as in fact it is stated in the records of the Chōḷas that Āditya, the second ruler of the new dynasty, built as may as 300 shrines to Śiva on the banks of the Kāveri. Whether the number was actually 300 or not, he was responsible for a large number of Śaiva shrines. This would mean undoubtedly a rise in the following, and consequently in the influence of Śaivism. The Vaishṇavas were apparently organising themselves also as a sect; but they do not appear to have had a similar influential support to begin with. But still they collected together round important teachers and were gaining in influence also. Matters came to a head at a time when Rāmānuja had to work his way gradually up to a position of influence as the leading teacher among the Vaishṇavas, and the legitimate occupant of the apostolic seat of his great-grandfather Yāmunāchārya at Śrīrangam. Although the ruler contemporary at the time was the enlightened Chōḷa Kulōttunga I, these controversies and controversialists could not be silenced, and it is one of these individual controversies that was responsible for Rāmānuja's exile from Śrīrangam, as was stated already. The period therefore of Rāmānuja's life was one of rising sectarianism and sectarian controversies in which even enlightened rulers were being, willingly or unwillingly, drawn. It was about this time while Rāmānuja was occupying his position as teacher of the Vaishṇavas at Śrīrangam, in considerable influence among his followers, that the question of the character of the Tirupati shrine arose.

ACHARYA RAMANUJA AND TIRUPATI. One of the cardinal facts of Rāmānuja's life, although there is no undoubted evidence of history either from inscriptions or other similar sources, is his having had to go into exile from Śrīrangam as a result of this sectarian animosity. We have discussed the matter in full in the earlier part of the work, and we need not go into details here. Enlightened ruler that Kulōttunga was, his part in the controversy was that of a Śaiva ruler of the locality, and his inviting prominent people to take part in a controversy, not of his own creation. It was purely a question of a challenge by a Śaiva teacher of eminence to disprove his thesis of the supremacy of Śiva in Hinduism; of course on the face of it it was a controversial question. Rulers seem to have felt they were bound to let the disputants come into court and prove their case to the satisfaction of the assembled court. Kulōttunga seems to have had nothing further than this in his mind in inviting Rāmānuja to dispute the Śaiva controversialists. What took place is a result not directly of fanaticism in religion, but of the secular offence that he took at what he might well have considered an irrelevantly impertinent remark by Kūrattāḻvān. So Rāmānuja had to be in exile from his country, and could return to Śrīrangam only after the death of Kulōttunga I. The incident merely indicated the sectarian stir at the time, during the active period of Kulōttunga's life, and even those of his successors. From such evidence as is available in the inscriptions round Tirupati we could infer the favour that had been shown to Śaivism by those Śaiva officers of the Chōḻas who made numbers of donations to the Śiva temple at Tirucchānūr, while we might almost say there were hardly more than a few donations made by Vaishṇava officers or others about the same period to the Vaishṇava temples in the neighbourhood, both on the hill and down below. Even so a record of Kulōttunga in Tirupati itself refers to the god as "Tiruvāyppāḍi Tirumalai Āḻvār" meaning Krishṇa, just as the Mudal Āḻvārs do. It would therefore raise the presumption that, at the time, the Śaiva tide was running strong round the region as a cousin of Rāmānuja himself had become a devotee of Śiva and was living in Kāḷahasti, whom the uncle Tirumalai Nambi could reclaim only after persistent effort. That seems to have been a period unfortunately when, owing perhaps to some calamity or other which might have befallen the few families of Vaishṇavas in Tirupati engaged in the temple service, the temple service had fallen into neglect, and the shrine itself, to some considerable extent, not looked after carefully. It seems possible that this untoward condition was taken advantage of and a claim set up, not necessarily by all the

Śaivas, but by a small but influential body of Śaivas, that the temple was a Śiva temple. The local ruler finding it difficult to decide, on his own responsibility, thought it much the best way to give the very best chance of a final settlement, to invite Rāmānuja as the best exponent of Vaishṇavism to prove the case of the Vaishṇavas if they had a case. It would have been nothing more than a disputation, as in a number of other instances on record, and have no relation to the importance of the issue but for the eminent character of one individual involved. It is given therefore a very exaggerated importance in the Vaishṇava accounts of the locality, and even a miraculous intervention of God himself has been invoked. It will be clear to those who have read the previous pages of this work that the character of the image and some of the features of worship lend themselves to an interpretation different from that actually given, and on the side of the Śaivas therefore there was a plausible case. Rāmānuja found no difficulty in proving it to the satisfaction of the impartial assembly which the Yādavarāya's court provided, and convincing the Yādavarāya himself and the assembly that the shrine was Vaishṇava in character. It would be well to remember in this connection that, in those days, Vaishṇava and Smārtha or even Śaiva did not stand so much apart from each other in social life as now, and hence it would be nothing strange that this matter should have arisen, and in the form in which it actually did. Having given the award in favour of the Vaishṇavas, it would in the ordinary course be only in the fitness of things that Rāmānuja should be asked to pay some little attention and put matters on a proper footing in respect of the Tirupati temple. Rāmānuja did indeed stay in Tirupati, and made the organisation for worship in very many particulars as it is now. That organisation falls naturally in two clear parts, the first one a mere revival of the ritualistic practices of the worship, etc., as they obtained till then; and the second the institution of a number of new services which had not been in existence before. For the former part of it Rāmānuja found authority quite easily in the *Purāṇas*, the *Prabandha* works, and other material to which he has had access, such as some of the Āgamas which may not exist now. The new arrangements took on the character of putting the secular management of the temple on a proper footing, and putting Tirumalai Nambi while he was alive, and Anandāḻvār after him, as guardian advisers in regard to the temple, making proper provision for the temple service by the creation of a certain number of gardens, providing a certain number of additions to the shrine and installing even some other Vishṇu images in the temple. Further the temple management was put on a footing of permanent disinterestedness by the creation of a couple of *Maṭhas* with *Sanyāsins*, or bachelors at their head, and giving them the management. Those interested in the matter will find the details given in the *Śrī Vēnkaṭāchala Itihāsamāla*, which, though compiled later, seems more or less to reflect the actual existing institutions in the temple since then. That Rāmānuja was there as well as Anandāḻvār, and that the principal flower gardens made by Anandāḻvār was given the name Rāmānuja, appear in evidence in inscriptions just a few generations, two or three, after Rāmānuja in inscriptional records. Full provision was made for the recitation of the *Prabandhas*, and the celebration even of an *Adhyayana Utsava* as in Śrīrangam. Some of the details of it such as the *Tiruppāvai Utsava* on the hill shrine, and the shine to Gōdā in the Gōvindarāja shrine appear in inscriptional records of the Yādavarāyas and others. These would be enough to show that Rāmānuja did play an active part in the organisation of worship in the temple, not exactly in the conversion or transformation of a Śiva temple into a Vishṇu temple. We have shown enough evidence of a continuous, and almost irrefutable, character to prove that the temple was intended to be a Vishṇu temple, and had been so regarded throughout up to this particular period. Secular arguments could now be set up against this position, which, in a case like this, are quite out of place. An image of Vishṇu, like the image of any other God, is set up to answer to a particular aspect of the deity as conceived by the individual worshipper or the worshipping community, and not on any absolute pattern for Vishṇu, and after all in a matter of this character traditional evidence is likely to be less at fault than the so-called evidence of reason. Once order had been introduced and an organisation for worship was acknowledged, things went on well with the temple, and we find, in the period immediately following that of Rāmānuja, donations of various kinds were made and the arrangements regulating worship, etc., on the lines said to have been laid down by Rāmānuja himself, continued in force.

THE TEMPLE UNDER THE MANAGEMENT OF THE VAISHNAVA COMMUNITY: It would have been noticed from the summary of the inscriptions given that the management of the temple had been throughout in the hands of those who were devoted worshippers at the temple, and such arrangements as were made were made by those whose religious interests lay that way. Such secular provisions as they did make for various service in the temple were placed under the protection of the Vaishṇava community residing in the locality, but were subject to the control of the popular assemblies which looked after the general administration and ultimately, in case of need, the rulers, kings or governors, according to the period of time to which we make reference. State intervention there was and always when actually needed, and the state did interfere to set matters right and went no further. The state authority withdrew to let the management go on as before, so that, at any rate so far as this temple is concerned—it is in fact true of every other temple that exists—the management was in the hands of the community interested, and the government interested itself in seeing to it that things went on peacefully and satisfactorily from the point of view of the temple management and did not otherwise interfere. For the period of almost a couple of centuries following the active period of Rāmānuja's life, we have only inscriptional records, and the tale that they tell does not differ in the least from this position that we have depicted. That period of a couple of centuries was not uniformly peaceful. The authorities changed, and even the political possession of the locality changed. But the organisation for the management of the temple and the arrangements for the worship went on unaffected by any of these changes. Half a century of confusion consequent upon the incursions of the Muhammadans in A. D. 1310 did introduce a certain amount of confusion; but then it did not reach through the society to affect this organisation in particular in spite of the fact that the temples particularly were exposed to the plundering raids of the invaders. On the whole the shrine at Tirupati, and the shrines dependent thereon, seem to have suffered little scathe, while the temples at Śrīrangam, Chidambaram, Madura and Rāmēśvaram suffered vital injuries. This was due perhaps to the shrines round Tirupati being in a comparatively inaccessible locality, and the invaders perhaps took roads which did not come too near these. When therefore Vijayanagar gets established and the authority of Vijayanagar begins to prevail over these parts, we find the Tirupati shrine well-organised and going on more or less on the set lines of worship and service. This closes the formative period, more or less, of the history of Tirupati from the point of view of the historian, and with the advent of Vijayanagar we are on what might almost be regarded as the modern period of the history of the hill-shrine.

CHAPTER XVI.

TIRUPATI UNDER VIJAYANAGAR.

REGION ROUND TIRUPATI UNDER HOYSALA VIRA BALLALA III. Before proceeding to take up the history of the Tirupati temple, it would be useful to have an idea of the circumstances under which Vijayanagar came into existence, and the character of the change in administration that the advent of this new empire brought about. It would therefore be well to go back upon a slight retrospect, and gather together the details of information that we get regarding the changes that took place in the period ending with the formation of the empire of Vijayanagar. Among the inscriptions collected by the Dēvastānam authorities, the earliest are those connected with the name of Sāḷuva Mangu and Kumāra Kampaṇa Uḍaiyār, the conqueror of Madura; and the dates of the earliest records happen to be about the year A. D. 1359. There is possibly an earlier record in No. 178 of Volume I which just contains the name of Bukkarāya; but such of the titles as precede it in this imperfect record make it doubtful whether it actually refers to Bukka I. It would, however, hardly matter, as the mention of Kumāra Kampaṇa and Sāḷuva Mangu would be about as good as mentioning Bukka I himself, unless we could be certain of the date of this inscription being earlier than the date given above. In the record, as it is available, we have no means of ascertaining that. We may take it therefore that the first Vijayanagar records refer to a period some time about A. D. 1359. By this date we could regard the empire of Vijayanagar as almost well-established, the only enemy that they had to look forward to in the north being the newly established Bahmani kingdom under its second ruler Muhammad Shah, the imperial power at Delhi having almost definitely given up ideas of recovering the southern possessions of the Tughlak empire. We saw already that the last dated record previous to this among the inscriptions of Tirupati were those referring to a Singaṇa Daṇḍanāyaka of date A. D. 1338. We have besides a number of records pertaining to this officer showing him more or less closely associated with the region round Tirupati, and being regarded by the local ruler as an officer deserving of the respect due to an official superior. We have also noticed that this Singaṇa Nāyaka was no other than an officer of the last Hoyśāla ruler, Vīra Baḷḷāḷa III, under whom served not only Singaṇa Nāyaka but even his elder brother, his father and even grandfather. Singaṇa Nāyaka's position in Tirupati therefore gives the clearest indication that the region round Tirupati had passed under the authority of this last Hoyśāla, Vīra Baḷḷāḷa III A. D. 1292 to A. D. 1342. It was in his reign that the first invasion of the Dakhan by the Muhammadans under Alau-d-din took place, and the gradual Muhammadan expansion subsequently. The extension of the authority of Vīra Baḷḷāḷa into the region of Tirupati is directly connected with these Muhammadan invasions, and goes back perhaps a couple of generations earlier when the Hoyśālas were drawn towards the South in support of the last rulers of the Chōḻa dynasty in their struggle to maintain their position. We shall have to make a short review of this period.

THE HOYSALA EXPANSION IN THE SOUTH. It was already stated that the first Hoyśāla intervention was called for in the reign of Rājarāja III, pretty early in his reign, and that Hoyśāla Narasimha II advanced towards the south to assist him, on the one side against the aggressions of the Pāṇḍyas, and on the other the rebellions of powerful chieftains like governors in Toṇḍamaṇḍalam, and even Kōpperunjinga in South Arcot. The declining Chōḻa power under their ruler Rājarāja III, A. D. 1316 to A. D. 1352—53, was harassed within the empire by the rebellions of the Pallava chieftain Kōpperunjinga and possibly others in the neighbourhood on the one side, and the rising power of the Pāṇḍyas in the south whose aggressions were stimulated by a desire for vengeance for all that they had suffered from the Chōḻas, particularly their last great ruler Kulōttunga III. Caught between these two great fires of rebellion in the northern part of the empire, and of the Pāṇḍya aggressions from the south, the Chōḻa power could have sustained itself if it had had at the head of it a powerful and competent monarch who could hold his own against these enemies as several of the great Chōḻas have had to do before Rājarāja III. But Rājarāja III seems to have been a particularly feeble man for the critical position. He seems also to have been troubled by a rival claimant to the throne even at the outset of his reign. In these circumstances, the Chōḻa power could be kept up only if there was a powerful ruler from outside who was interested enough to maintain the integrity of the Chōḻa empire, or even the prestige of the Chōḻa empire for the time being. Family relationship and political consideration alike perhaps prompted the Hoyśāla rulers across the hills to come to the assistance of Rājarāja at a time when he was hard pressed by his rebellious feudatory Kōpperunjinga. In the actual condition of the Chōḻa empire, it was not likely that one intervention, and the setting up of the Chōḻa in power, would put matters on anything like a footing of peace. It was therefore a question whether something more than this occasional interference was not called for. Events showed that more was required to keep the Chōḻas in position. Narasimha II and his son Sōmēśvara who were both of them intimately related with the Chōḻas and the Pāṇdyas, found it necessary to establish themselves in an alternative capital in the south with a view to being ready at hand for the assistance of the Chōḻas. It was therefore that the Hoyśāla Sōmēśvara fortified the village Kaṇṇanūr, four miles away from the north bank of the Coleroon opposite Śrīrangam, and installed himself there in the newly fortified Vikramapura as his capital, which probably proved of some assistance to the Chōḻa, perhaps so far as his feudatories were concerned; but it only aggravated the hatred of the Pāṇḍyas and made them the more implacable as enemies. Sōmēśvara had to exert himself strenuously to keep the Pāṇḍyas from out of the Chōḻa territory, and, in this effort, he strengthened the Hoyśāla position and extended his influence so much that some of the records of Narasimha III claim his having set up a pillar of victory in Rāmēśvaram and making an encircling movement against the Pāṇḍyan territory through the Pudukkōttai State. When the great Jaṭāvarman Sundara Pāṇḍya ascended the Pāṇḍya throne, he carried on a great and successful campaign northwards beating the enemies in the Chōḻa country, among whom the name of Sōmēśvara himself figures prominently as well as that of Kōpperunjinga and others. He anointed himself as a victorious conqueror in Kānchi, and even Nellore farther north, before he celebrated his achievement in crowning himself with the greatest glory both in Śrīrangam and in Chidambaram. This certainly was a crushing blow to the Hoyśāla position in South India; but it also gave some little relief to the Chōḻa by the success that he achieved against the rebellious Chōḻa feudatories further north. But all the same, it did not avail the Chōḻas to regain their lost prestige, much less their territory. We see, however, although it is not clearly stated anywhere in any of the Chōḻa or Pāṇḍya records, that the invasion of Sundara Pāṇḍya I had the effect of putting an end to the Chōḻa empire, as his Pāṇḍya successors are found ruling in the Chōḻa country soon after him. So far as the Hoyśālas were concerned, they had suffered early from Sundara Pāṇḍya and, for the time being, had perhaps been temporarily dispossessed of their territory in the Tamil country. But they were able soon to regain a part of it, as we find two sons of Sōmēśvara succeeding him simultaneously, one, Narasimha III the elder of the sons ruling his ancestral dominions from Haḷabīḍ and Bēlūr. We find another Hoyśāla ruler simultaneously, styled Vīra Rāmanātha in his inscriptions, ruling over the Tamil territories of the Hoyśālas claiming still Vikramapura as his capital and having another Kundāṇi, in the Baramahal parts of the Salem District. Rāmanātha's rule seems to have lasted about a quarter of a century, and when he died, a son of his, succeeded to his territory, and, after two or three years of rule, passed out of view. In consequence the empire of the Hoyśālas was again united under Narasimha III.

EXTENSION OF HOYSALA AUTHORITY INTO THE REGION OF TIRUPATI UNDER VIRA BALLALA III: Narasimha's reign was perhaps more occupied with keeping his northern frontier from encroachment by the Yādavas of Dēvagiri and in bringing as much as possible of the southern part of the empire into his dominions. His period of rule, however, corresponded to that of the great Pāṇḍya Māravarman Kulaśēkhara, the last great Pāṇḍya of Madura before the Muhammadan invasions, and the two powers seem to have been more or less well matched to indulge too readily in the game of war.

Māravarman Kulaśēkhara's activities find echo in the Tanjore District, and the fact that this great Pāṇḍya made Jayankoṇḍachōḻapuram and Gangaikoṇḍachōḻapuram his capitals would indicate that he had to be active on the northern frontier as against aggressions by the Hoysāla, who must have regained his footing in Vikramapura. This interpolation by the Hoysāla between the southern and northern parts of the Chōḻa empire seems really to have been responsible for the falling away of the northern part of the Chōḻa empire from its allegiance, and becoming more or less independent of the empire of the Chōḻas and their successors. If, in the course of these years, this part fell away from the Chōḻa empire, the maintenance of its independence woud have been perhaps rather precarious unless it be under the wings of a greater power than themselves. During a considerable part of this period we find the Yādavarāyas comporting themselves more or less independently after the break up of the Chōḻa empire, but not perhaps without being exposed to the incursions and the influence of a new power; and that power, in the circumstances, must have been that of the Hoysālas. We have already noticed, in our account of the recorded inscriptions in Tirupati and its vicinity, that two Hoysāla generals figure rather prominently with dates well on in the reign of the Hoyśāla Vīra Baḷḷāḷa III, the son and successor of Narasimha III. It fell to this Vīra Baḷḷāḷa to regain the southern part of the empire for the Hoyśālas largely. He had therefore to be very active in this region warring pretty often against the Pāṇḍyas under Māravarman Kulaśēkhara. It is nothing strange therefore that we find his authority in a way acknowledged by the later Yādavarāyas in the region of Tirupati. This becomes the more clear when the family of these officers for three generations held the chief authority under the Hoyśālas as their principal officers, exercising authority no doubt over the whole of the empire, but even holding *jāghīrs* of territory in the southern part of Mysore, which ultimately became an independent division of territory when the Hoyśāla power in its turn declined. Perumāḷa Daṇḍanāyaka was the prime minister of Narasimha III in the later years of his reign, and he continued in that great office under his son and successor at the outset of his reign. He was succeeded in that great office by his son Mādhava Daṇḍanāyaka, and in his turn he was succeeded by two of his sons, Kētayya Daṇḍanāyaka and Singaṇa Daṇḍanāyaka, the names of both of whom and the father occur in the records at Tirupati. It is Mādhava Daṇḍanāyaka that organised his *jāghīr* on the southern frontier of Mysore, and made Terekaṇāmbi his headquarters to develop further and become the chieftaincy of Daṇṇāyakankōṭṭai later. That this was an important frontier and required careful watching is in evidence as the whole of the Kongu frontier was a frontier of contention between the Hoyśālas and the Pāṇḍyas. According to Amir Khusru, the historian of the Muhammadan invasions of South India, on the first occasion of the Muhammadan inroad into the Hoyśāla territory, the Hoyśāla armies were actually on the southern frontier of Kongu operating against Vīra Pāṇḍya, the son of Māravarman Kulaśēkhara, who had a government of his own, and had for his sphere of activity this frontier. That no doubt is one part of the Hoyśāla territory open to attack ; but for any purpose of effective holding of this frontier as against the enemy, the frontier line must have taken the part of Toṇḍamaṇḍalam round the region of Tirupati, and so we find it.

THE MUHAMMADAN INVASIONS OF THE SOUTH: But before proceeding any further, we must consider the Muhammadan irruption into this region with a view to appraising its influence in regard to this frontier in particular. After bringing into well-recognised subordination to the empire of Delhi both the Hindu states of the Dakhan, the Yādava state with its capital at

Dēvagiri and the state of Warangal with its capital much farther east in the Nizam's Dominions first at Hanumakoṇḍa and then Warangal, the Muhammadan general Malik Kafur, the special favourite of Alau-d-din, obtained his master's permission to carry his invasions farther south with a view to acquiring the riches of the temples in South India and gaining possession of a number of the powerful elephants of the south, as they constituted the most efficient arm of the armies of those days. Malik Kafur had really no difficulty in obtaining permission on these terms, and arrangements were made for the march of the army through the friendly and subordinate territory of the Rājas of Dēvagiri. As soon as the army emerged out of the Vindyan Passes of the Narmada and Satpura mountains into the Dakhan, the Dēvagiri government and its army received the invading army, and took them over to Dēvagiri. When after rest and reorganisation, the invasion was ready to start again, the commander-in-chief, whom the Muhammadan historians call Paras Dēvō Dālvi (the corresponding Hindu name would be Parasuram Dēv, the *Dalavōy* or general of the Yādavas) escorted the army to the southern limits of the Yādava territory down to his own *jāghīr* of Shōlapūr. There the army encamped to reorganise itself for entry into the hostile territory of the south. During the period of the halt, what might be regarded as a cavalry raid was undertaken from Shōlapūr into the territory of the Hoyśālas, and that was the first invasion of the Hoyśāla territory in A. D. 1309—10. The main part of the Hoyśāla army was away, but the Hoyśāla did make an effort to stand a siege, in the course of which his capital suffered considerable damage. The invaders were able to carry their raid further westwards to the coast of the Arabian Sea and return with a large quantity of plunder. When, however, the Hoyśāla submitted after the first show of resistance, the Muhammadan general received his overtures kindly, and sent a recommendation to imperial headquarters for the gracious treatment of the Rāja. The mission went under the Hoyśāla prince, was kindly received, and returned with a gracious message from Alau-d-din that the Hoyśāla territory would be respected as under the rule of a subordinate ally. That done Malik Kafur proceeded southwards on his invasion, feeling safe on the side of Hoyśāla in his march to the distant south. The question now arises as to what road this invasion took, and this is of considerable importance to the history of Tirupati especially. If the invasion took the eastern road, it would bring them very close to Tirupati, and Tirupati itself must have figured in the history of this invasion. But it does not, and Tirupati does not appear to have suffered either in this invasion, or even in some of the subsequent ones. We have good reason for believing that the invasion actually proceeded by way of Bangalore into the Salem District, and thence on in the direction of Trichinopoly proceeding therefrom to Madura and Rāmēśvaram. The choice of this road for the march of the army of invasion left the region of Tirupati aside, and saved it from the attacks of this army of invasion. The story of this invasion does not concern us directly. We might note briefly therefore that the army marched south, meeting with comparatively little opposition except for a battle or two when they had to fight against Vīra Pāṇḍya, the more active among the sons of Māravarman Kulaśēkhara, and then marched on plundering Śrīrangam and Chidambaram on the way towards Madura. Having destroyed the capital of Madura, and carrying a further raid forward as far as Rāmēśvaram, the invasion returned to Delhi the following year with something like 350 elephant loads of treasure and much else of warlike material likely to be of value to the emperor. Malik Kafur's return to Delhi was followed by trouble and disturbances at court ending ultimately in the death of Alau-d-din Khilji, and after one or two palace revolutions, Mubarak, one of the sons of Alau-d-din ultimately succeeded to the throne. This new succession was the occasion for the subordinate territories, particularly the new ones. Dēvagiri now under Harpaldēv, a son-in-law of Ramdēv who had submitted to Alau-d-din, showed an inclination to rebel. Mubarak came down upon him, punished Harpaldēv severely, and made the territory of Dēvagiri the first subordinate kingdom in the Dakhan. With a view to riveting his hold on this territory, he sent out a number of Amirs at the head of their troops to occupy salient places in the kingdom with their troops. This made the Hoyśāla realise the danger of his position and prepare himself against eventualities. After Mubarak returned to headquarters, he sent out an invasion to the south under his favourite slave Khusru, a Gujarati-Hindu convert to Islam, who went on this southern invasion and showed an inclination to tarry long in South India. But a palace revolution called for his presence in Delhi, and he went away post haste leaving South India to itself. It was not till the Khiljis were overthrown and the Tughlaks established themselves that they thought of South India again, and an invasion came under Muhammad-bin-Tughlak as a prince in A. D. 1323. It came some way towards the south, and had to turn back from the frontiers of South India owing to an outbreak of cholera in the camp. But Muhammad Tughlak was not the man to forget. After he had placed himself upon the throne securely, he sent out an expedition definitely with a view to the conquest of the south. Naturally the invasion took the course of its predecessors generally, and had to make sure of communications, and the loyalty of those whom they left in possession of power on the route of march. Naturally therefore an invasion had to be sent against the Hoyśālas. Their capital Haḷabīḍ suffered rather more severely this time than before. Having assured themselves of the Hoyśāla remaining loyal by this demonstration of power, the army marched south, and was so far successful in this invasion that Muhammad found it possible to establish a government in distant Madura, the capital of the Pāṇḍyas, under his loyal and doughty general, Jalalu-d-din Āsan Shah, thus laying the foundations of a Muhammadan state ruling in Madura, though only for a comparatively short period of fifty years. Muhammad Tughlak's invasions on this occasion probably came to the south not with the avowed object of conquering the south, but because a rival claimant to the throne had set himself up in rebellion in the south Dakhan as against the claims of Muhammad to the throne of his father. Bahau-d-din Gushtasp or Gurshasp, as the Muhammadan historians name him, was a prince of the Tughlak family, a nephew of Ghiyasu-d-din Tughlak, the father of Muhammad, brought up in the royal family and perhaps with a view to succession as he claimed it. Since Muhammad was suspected of having brought about the death of the father with a view to securing the succession, it seems likely that the nephew put forward his claim and set up in rebellion from his headquarters at Sagar near Gulbarga in the Nizam's Dominions. The invasion came with a view to punish him. But he found asylum first of all in the ruler of Kampli, who, loyal to his promise, would rather lay down his life than surrender a fugitive who sought asylum of him. The valiant Rāja passed him on to the neighbouing Hoyśāla, as being more capable of giving him the asylum that he needed, fought and died, thus putting an end to the kingdom of Kampli. The invasion continued and marched on Haḷabīḍ, and, after destroying the capital partially, it proceeded further south, as was stated already. Jalalu-d-din Āsan Shah, the general ruled in the name of Muhammad-bin Tughlak from Madura, and declared himself independent in A. D. 1335, when Muhammad was engaged in putting down a rebellion of the distant ruler of Bengal, who had already set himself up under Muhammad's father. The opportunity, when yet Muhammad was engaged in his war against the Bengal Sultan, was too good to be lost, and the governor of Madura followed the example of Bengal and set up in rebellion. Madura was too far off for Muhammad's personal intervention, and as Muhammad had to attend to things nearer home, this distant southern rebel had to be neglected for the time. Muhammad's troubles grew so much in volume and variety, that he was not able at any time afterwards to pay his personal attention to this rebel at Madura, and his independence remained unchallenged.

THE HOYSALA REACTION TO THE MUHAMMADAN SULTANATE OF MADURA: The establishment of the Sultanate in Madura under Sultan Jalalu-d-din Āsan Shah marked a stage in the expansion of the Muhammadan power in the South, and the establishment of something like a governorship in Madura which very soon developed into an independent state, was fraught with consequences which might have proved dangerous to Hindu India in the fields alike of current politics and culture. It should have appeared in this character even to contemporaries, and specially to those among them who at all cherished any responsibility in respect of the country round them, particularly in regard to matters touching the religion and culture of the country. At the time to which we have now arrived, say A. D. 1335, the only Hindu power worth the name which could really feel concerned with matters like those was that of the Hoyśāla, the Pāṇḍya and the Chōḻa empires having gone out of existence, and no other state having taken the place of either the one or the other or both. If it is a question of any Hindu state making an effort to set a term to the expansion of the Muhammadan power and keep it within limits, it could only be the Hoyśāḷa state which was at all in a position to do so with any chance of success. It became therefore the special responsibility of the Hoyśāla Vīra Baḷḷāḷa III to exert himself in regard to this matter. But one could appreciate his position which was invidious in the extreme. He had acknowledged himself subordinate to the Muhammadan power at Delhi under the Khiljis. The Tughlak state could claim the same consideration as the political successor of the Khilji empire at Delhi. But the moment that a rebel set himself up against the legitimate authority of Muhammad Tughlak, this consideration would immediately cease to have any value as against this new state. He was not bound by any ties of loyalty to the newly established Sultanate of Madura for one thing. But he saw also clearly that Muhammad took no action against the rebel and showed no inclination to do so in the immediate future. Things across his northern border in the Dakhan were moving fast. Rebellion succeeded rebellion, and a new Mussalman state was in course of formation. While this was not exactly clear in A. D. 1335, indications certainly were not wanting to show that very soon Dakhan would follow in the footsteps of the other Muhammadan states, such as Gujarat and Mālva. So between the nether millstone and the other of a rising Muhammadan state in the Dakhan, if they should ultimately succeed against Muhammd Tughlak and set up in independence, and a Muhammadan kingdom, small though it be to begin with, well established in Madura under a capable governor, the Hoyśāla's position would become precarious in the extreme even though it did not seem likely that the Tughlak sovereign would actively exercise his authority and demand the Hoyśāla's loyalty at the time. If the very Mussalman governorships were in rebellion, Hindu states perhaps might easily follow their example. At any rate, when the empire of Muhammad ceased to exist, such Hindu states as existed need not follow in the trail of any succeeding state in Delhi. What indeed was the course of action that the Hoyśāla was going to adopt was matter which would, to a very great extent, depend upon his own interpretation of the situation, and the courage and capacity with which he could carry out his policy. Notwithstanding the submission that he made to Alau-d-din and the favourable terms that he obtained from him, he suffered badly in the invasion sent out by Muhammad-bin-Tughlak in A. D. 1327, which was so far successful as to partially destroy his capital and otherwise do him considerable damage. Perhaps Muhammad made no secret of his ultimate intention to conquer and annex South India to his own territory in direct contradiction to the policy of Alau-d-din, who made it clear, to his generals at any rate, that he was not anxious to extend his empire to great distances from Delhi, and across the Vindhya frontier particularly. The invasion of A. D. 1327 should have shown clearly to Vīra Baḷḷāḷa that he could not regard his position safe even in his own territory. He must have been driven to take his measures accordingly. From A. D. 1328 he made Tiruvaṇṇāmalai his headquarters, not because his capital of Haḷabīḍ or Bēlūr had really become untenable, but perhaps as providing an important strategic centre from which he could operate advantageously and carry out his policy according to the exigencies of the moment. The advantage of the position in Tiruvaṇṇāmalai would be that it was more or less on the high road to the South by the eastern way, from which he could watch the movements of the Muhammadans even if they should take the further interior central route towards the South. The territory behind Tiruvaṇṇāmalai, and to the north of it was more or less under his authority, and the assistance of its governors and the whole of its resources would be available to him in his operations against the Muhammadans, who had now perhaps fortified themselves in Kaṇṇanūr as an outpost of Madura, and as safeguarding communication with the north for the Muhammadans by the central route. What had been done under Singaṇa Nāyaka, and the strengthening of the Southern frontier under his father Mādhava Daṇḍanāyaka alike would indicate clearly that it was provision made for guarding the Southern frontier from which a Muhammadan attack from the South would be possible now, with a Sultanate established in Madura. That seems to have been the moving consideration with Vīra Baḷḷāḷa in moving out towards Tiruvaṇṇāmalai, and making it more his capital than Haḷabīḍ or Bēlūr. The block of territory extending along the foothills of the Eastern Ghats from the southern frontier of Mysore eastwards to the sea, was a very important salient both for offence and defence against the Muhammadans, and seems to have proved a safe belt of country, if for nothing else, at least for communications from one part of the country to the other. During the seven years following when Madura was only a governorship under the authority of Muhammad Tughlak, he had to be very cautious, and lay his plans secretly and work without causing inconvenient suspicions ; but when once the governor of Madura declared himself independent, and Muhammad showed no inclination to march down with his accustomed speed to bring the rebel to reason, the Hoyśāla could adopt a bolder line of action, and take steps to carry out actively a policy to shut in the Sultan of Madura within narrow limits and bring about the extinction of the Sultanate if possible; if that were not possible, at least to confine it within the narrowest possible limits. He therefore gradually exerted himself to extend his authority over what was the Chōḻa empire, and, through the Pudukkōttai state and through the Rāmnād district, so as to limit the activities of the Muhammadan Sultan to the Madura-Trichinopoly route at the very most, and a comparatively small distance to the north of the Coleroon. When the Baḷḷāḷa carried out these strategic movements of his to a considerable degree of success, it was clear even to the Muhammadan in Madura that he meant nothing less than the extinction of the Muhammadan Sultanate which seemed then possible, as Muhammad's activities were not likely to be of any avail in the distant south, and the state of the Dakhan gave the best guarantee that assistance from the north was altogether impossible. The Muhammadan historians consequently complain that the Hoyśāla was developing a movement to surround and confine the Sultanate of Madura to Madura itself and no more. We find him ultimately carrying out this policy almost to a successful conclusion after seven years of strenuous activity, when, at the head of an army of 1,25,000 troops he placed himself in Trichinopoly, and thus separating the garrison of the Muhammadan cantonment at Kaṇṇanūr from Madura, the headquarters of the Sultan, made an effort to defeat the two parts of the Muhammadan armies in detail and ultimately put an end to Muhammadan power in the south. But unfortunately for the Hindu movement in the south, he fell into the hands of his enemies at the moment of victory, when he had successfully beaten back a desperate attack from the Muhammadans in Madura. He fell into the hands of a raiding party and was put to death, an old man of 80 that he was as stated by the Muhammadan historians. This outspread of the Hoyśāla power is what is indicated in the two or three inscriptions in Tirupati which refer to the Hoyśāla officers Kētayya Daṇḍanāyaka and Singaṇa Daṇḍanāyaka, the brothers, who became afterwards the founders of the family that ruled at Daṇṇāyakankōṭṭai in the Salem District as their headquarters. The unfortunate result of the battle of Trichinopoly should ordinarily have put an end to this Hindu movement once and for all, but for the confused condition of the Tughlak empire, and the almost impossible struggle that Muhammad Tughlak had to maintain for the next ten years against his rebel governors, culminating in his death without achieving the success that he should have under more favourable circumstances. South India was left to itself during all this period, as the Dakhan Sultans, even when they had established themselves into a well-formed kingdom in A. D. 1346, had to be watchful of the activities of Muhammad Tughlak, and could not move freely and actively southwards. That was the saving feature of the situation, and what followed seems to be a concerted action on the part of these officers and governors of the Hoyśāla, continuing and carrying out the policy of Vīra Baḷḷāḷa to success so as to lead ultimately to the establishment of a united Hindu state of the South, which became later the empire of Vijayanagar.

THE REVIVAL OF HOYSALA POWER LEADS TO THE ESTABLISHMENT OF THE EMPIRE OF VIJAYANAGAR: The course of events which culminated in the establishment of Vijayanagar gives indication of a gradual revival and expansion of the Hoyśāla power after the Muhammadan invasions, particularly after the invasion of Muhammad Tughlak in the year A. D. 1327. It is likely that, even this invasion went down upon Trichinopoly and Śrīrangam, as its main objective, particularly the latter, and as such must have avoided the road to the east leaving the region round Tirupati quite clear as it were. This is made very likely by what is stated of the happenings in the south resulting from this invasion. The *Kōvil Oḻuhu*, an account of the history of the temple at Śrīrangam, which records most of the principal events relating to the history of the temple at Śrīrangam, gives a description of what actually took place on this occasion. The inhabitants of Śrīrangam were celebrating one of their famous annual festivals, in which the image of the God is carried to the river Coleroon and set down in the middle of the river bed for getting through a number of items of various acts of worship, till, late in the evening, the God is taken back to the temple in a huge procession. It was in the course of this festivity all unexpectedly that the invading cavalry of Muhammad Tughlak clattered down to the banks of the Coleroon along the road from Kaṇṇanūr. Before the invading forces could come into touch, people immediately in attendance upon the image quickly came to a resolution to save the image of the God, the festival image which was meant for being carried about, and Lōkāchārya, a sturdy man of middle age, carried the image in a palanquin and walked away through unfrequented ways, and escaped through Pudukkōttai avoiding public roads. Taking Tirukkōṭṭiyūr, Tirumāliruṁśōlai, where he made halts, he moved out whenever he heard of the cavalry behind him, to carry the image in safety across into the Travancore country, moving from place to place as each one became untenable. The image was at last taken to safety in Calicut, where it remained for some time. As soon as the imminent danger from these divisions of the invading army was over, they thought it best to bring the image to a place of safety, where it might remain unmolested till the time should come for its being reinstalled in the holy place of Śrīrangam. They thought the best place to go to would be Tirupati, and moved out from Calicut carrying the image with them, reached the place Terukaṇāmbi in Mysore, where they stayed rather comfortably for a while, and proceeded further on their journey till they reached Punganūr in the Chittoor

District on the high way leading from the Mysore plateau into the Madras Presidency. On reaching the place, they discovered detachments of the Muhammadan forces were hovering about, and therefore they resolved to retrace their steps, not being able to reach their destination of Tirupati. As the next best safe place they took the image over to the temple at Mēlkōṭa, where it was kept in hiding for some time, and then, when the roadways were safe, they carried the image over secretly to Tirupati where it was kept in safety in the charge of a worshipping priest, his brother-in-law, perhaps a somewhat younger man, and a young boy of a son. Hearing of the threat of an attack by Muhammadan forces, the priest tied himself and the image to a rope, and asked the brother-in-law to let him slowly down a scarp on the hill, on the western side into a deep glade unfrequented by man generally. There the image is said to have lain under the care of these three till the priest died, followed some time after by the brother-in-law, and the young boy had grown up to be a man of age. When, on an occasional discovery by a forester, the information was carried to Nārāyaṇavaram, the governors of the locality who played a prominent part in the reduction of the Muhammadan garrisons in South India, and in the establishment of the Vijayanagar empire in the army of Kumāra Kampaṇa of Vijayanagar, found occasion, chiefly through the influence of the minister Gōpaṇārya, as he is called, to take over the image and instal it in the temple at Śrīrangam back again. This story throws light upon the general position of the region round about Tirupati and the condition in which that region happened to be at the time. The fact that, owing to the turmoil, they thought Tirupati was about the safest place available and that they could move along unmolested by way of Terukaṇāmbi across Mysore to Tirupati gives indication that the territory concerned was under a state which remained, more or less unmolested, in spite of the Muhammadan invasions, although the roadways were far from being absolutely safe. This must have taken place some years after the invasion of A. D. 1328, which indeed was what set the image of Ranganātha on the move. Perhaps it actually refers to a period when the authority of Singaṇa Nāyaka, or it may be his successors still prevailed over this region, the region round Tirupati extending westwards to as far as Terukaṇāmbi and perhaps beyond, which seems more or less the condition inferable from the account of Ibn Baṭuṭa as well. So during the period of turmoil of the Muhammadan invasions and the years following, Tirupati remained a comparatively safe place to offer protection even to the image of Ranganātha from Śrīrangam. It is perhaps the possession of this region in comparative security and its providing a good place of retreat in times of need, that induced Vīra Baḷḷāḷa to establish himself in Tiruvaṇṇāmalai by preference, a fortified place on the high road leading from the north to the south along one of the well-known highways of the south. Not only did that provide a place of safety with a safe retreat behind for emergencies, but it also proved a convenient centre from which to develop his further movements against the Sultans of Madura as circumstances proved favourable. The establishment of the Vijayanagar empire may be regarded as a fact soon after A. D. 1358 when the coinage of the Sultan of Madura ceases; it would mark one further stage in the growth perhaps in A. D. 1369–70 when the image of Ranganātha was, according to a record in the temple, reinstalled in Śrīrangam. This latter date may be the better date for the establishment of the empire, apart from the date of the foundation of the city. The conclusion of the successful campaign of Kumāra Kampaṇa signalised by the restoration of the destroyed temple at Madura, and the revival of the great temple at Śrīrangam would certainly mark the date of the successful accomplishment of the mission which ended in the establishment of the empire of Vijayanagar. The inscriptional records that we find in Tirupati take us to about this date, and the earliest names of Vijayanagar rulers and officers who find mention happen to be Bukkarāya, posssibly the first of the name, Kumāra Kampaṇa, his son, the princely viceroy of the Muḷbāgal Mahārājya and Sāḷuva Mangu, the first great name in the dynasty of the Sāḷuvas of Nārāyaṇavaram. Bukkarāya must have been the ruler. Kumāra Kampaṇa was responsible for leading the invasion which brought into the empire the rebel Śambuvarāyas of the Pālār basin, and ultimately defeated the Sultan of Madura himself, Sāḷuva Mangu playing the leading part in this South Indian campaign. We shall now take up the tale of the inscriptions at Tirupati during the first century of the existence of Vijayanagar.

THE REGION OF TIRUPATI PASSES UNDER VIJAYANAGAR ALMOST FROM THE BEGINNING: Before taking up the actual subject-matter of the inscriptions of Vijayanagar, some of the features in which these differ from the inscriptions of the Chōḻa and other dynasties must be noted carefully. The first important point is that the dates are marked not in the regnal years of the ruling sovereign as in the case of the earlier inscriptions. They are generally given in the Śaka year with of course details of the date. This, while it makes the dating precise and undoubted, is therefore very convenient; but these inscriptions fall short in historical value as they do not give the historical information supplied in the form of *Praśasti* or *Meykkīrti*. The second point in regard to this is that the date being thus given, the ruler's name generally need not be mentioned unless he has something directly to do with the subject-matter of the inscription. The records therefore would be more or less of a private character except in a certain number of cases where royal personages, or members of the royal family, make the donations. Bearing these limitations in mind, we find that there is a large number of inscriptions in the Tirupati temple itself relating to this period in the first century of the history of Vijayanagar. Actually they extend from No. 178 to 236 of the first volume, and just a small number in the second volume. The first of these records, No. 178, has no date as it has come down to us, and just makes mention of a Bukkarāya, and makes provisions for a daily food-service at the temple on the hill. It probably refers to Bukka I. As we have stated already, the orthodox dating for the foundation of Vijayanagar is A. D. 1336, and that refers to the foundation of the city of Vijayanagar, in its original name Vidyānagara. It would be a date of the foundation of the empire in a sense. But the real foundations of the empire would be somewhat later, and could be marked off in the first years of Harihara II just over fifty years after this date. The actual completion of the operations and the establishment of an empire in the south perhaps may be dated more appropriately somewhere about the year A. D. 1371, when the image of God Ranganātha was reinstalled at Śrīrangam, giving thereby the clearest indication that the first rulers of Vijayanagar felt they had brought the country under their authority, and the establishment of Hindu South India, free of Muhammadan power, had become more or less a fact. But even as early as A. D. 1346, we find inscriptions of the Vijayanagar brothers, Harihara I or Bukka I, extending eastwards as far as Udayagiri in the Nellore District which would mean that the territory with which we are particularly concerned was included in their empire already; and, about this early period, we find their governments at Penukoṇḍa and farther east in the Anantapur District on the one side, and at Muḷbāgal and the roads leading from there into the Madras Presidency on the other, that is the high road leading into Chittoor. We may therefore take it that the territory round

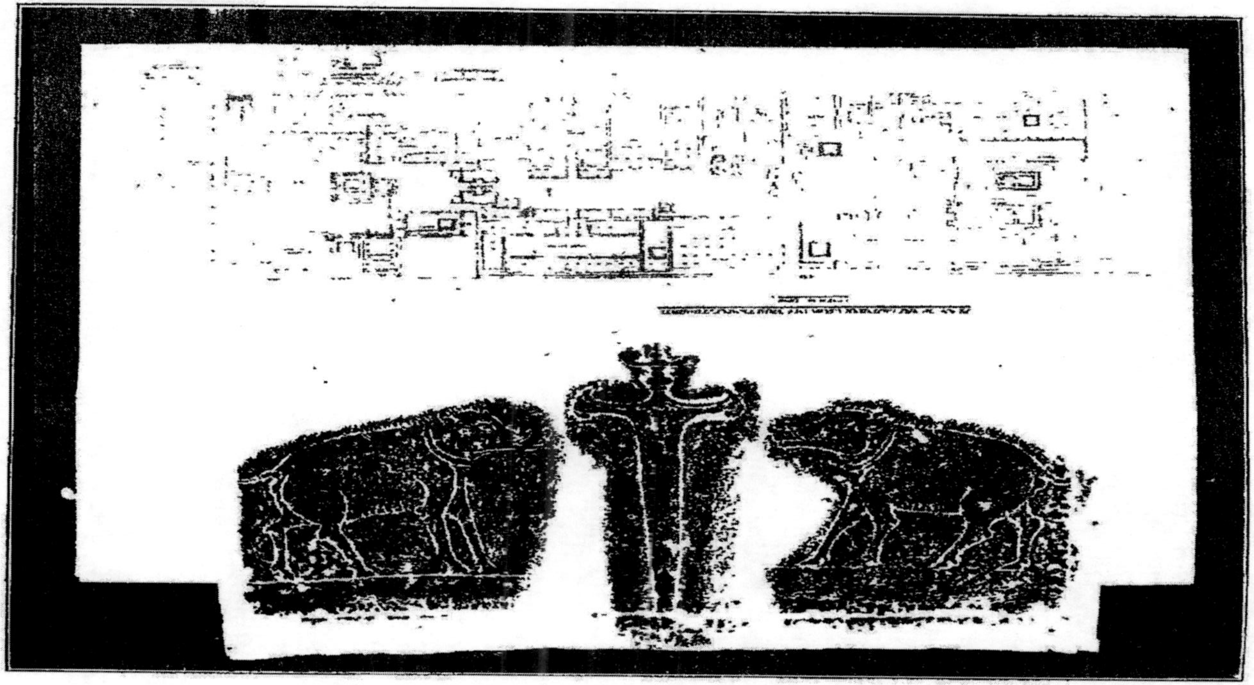

THE EMBLEM OF VIJAYANAGAR

(To face page 425)

Tirupati passed under the authority of Vijayanagar almost directly from that of the Hoyśāla rulers.

THE EARLIEST RECORDS MENTION BUKKA, SALUVA MANGU, KUMARA KAMPANA AND HARIHARA II: Inscriptions 179 and 180 refer to the same matter and recorded in two languages, the first in Telugu, and the next in Tamil. The Telugu part gives the date Śaka 1281, corresponding to 6th July 1359 and refers to the performance of a service by the *Mahāmaṇḍalēśvara* Mangidēva Mahārāja. This apparently refers to, from the partial title given, the Sāḷuva ruler who played a prominent part in the southern invasions of Kumāra Kampaṇa, and distinguished himself in the campaigns which succeeded in bringing the whole of the southern territory under Vijayanagar. He belonged to the Sāḷuva family, of which we shall hear more later, and was one of the earliest chieftains to distinguish himself. His benefaction to the temple consisted in his covering the roofing with gold and setting up a gold pinnacle. The former part of it, the covering with gold is mentioned distinctly in the Tamil record in the expression *pon-mēñju*. Of course, the Tamil expression would be *pon-vēyṅdu*, with also the variant *mēyṅdu*, an expression which is used in respect of similar service rendered to the Śrīrangam temple by

Jaṭāvarman Sundara Pāṇḍya and in similar connections. Among the titles given to this ruler is a Kannaḍa expression *Mīsara Gaṇḍa.* The full expression would be *Mēdinī Mīsara Gaṇḍa*, meaning the man among those in the world with moustaches which means, 'the man among men,' a title which became a peculiar Sāḷuva title, although other chieftains and dynasties sometimes affected it also. No. 181 connects itself with Śrī Vīra Kumāra Kampaṇṇa Uḍaiyār, with various titles generally associated with him. The subject-matter of the inscription is the grant of 28 cows and one breeding bull for lighting a perpetual lamp in the temple. This benefaction seems to have been made by an officer of Kampaṇṇa Uḍaiyār of the rank of *pēkkaḍai*, as it is called in Tamil. This is the equivalent of the Kanarese *Pērgaḍai*, a title of high rank analogous to the Tamil *pēruṁ-taram.* It is noteworthy that the titles given of this Kumāra Kampaṇa should be in Kanarese even in the region of Tirupati. These titles are Mahāmaṇḍalēśvara, *Harirāya (arirāya) - vibāḍa*, and there is a part of the word *Gaṇḍa* with a gap previous which may be filled up from his other inscriptions, *Bhāshegē - Tappuva Rāyara Gaṇḍa.* Of course, the other possibility would be *Mēdinī Mīsara Gaṇḍa*, which is not usually found applied to Kumāra Kampaṇa or other rulers of Vijayanagar. No. 182 seems to be a mere continuation, and contains but one remark. Since the name of the year is given, and we know the period of time, the year Kīlaka would correspond to Śaka 1290, A. D. 1368. No. 183 is interesting, but it is badly mutilated in the form in which it is available to us. It refers to a Śambukula Chakravarti Tiru-Mallinādan Śambuvarāya Perumāḷ, and makes some benefaction in favour of the temple. The intrusion of this Śambuvarāya inscription into Tirupati is indeed interesting as the Śambuvarāyans held rule in the Pālar basin with their capitals at Tiruvallam, and ultimately Vrinchipuram near Vellore, where Kumāra Kampaṇa defeated them, and brought them under the authority of the Vijayanagar empire. But since in this case, we know no date, we could not say anything more about him, nor to what period the record actually belongs, although we are entitled to infer that in the best period of their authority the Śambuvarāyan influence extended as far as Tirupati. No. 184 is of date Ś. 1301 or A. D. 1380. This is a private document more or less, as it refers to a benefaction merely. It makes provision for food-service on the 2nd day of certain festivals in which the image of the God and His consorts are taken to a pavilion called *Aḷahappirān.* In the recorded provision is also included a separate provision for Śrī Varāhanāyanār, that is, the boar form of Vishṇu, whose shrine is on the west bank of the Svāmi Pushkariṇi tank. The capital of 450 gold pieces was deposited by a Vaishṇava Kalikaṅṛidāsa, son of Aḻahappirānār. The expenses of the service were to be met from the interest on this capital deposited, and was accepted by the Śrī Vaishṇavas. The document was committed to writing by the temple accountant, Tiruniṅṛavūr Uḍaiyān, which would mean the lord of the village of Tiruniṅṛavūr, now Tinnanūr. In a number of documents following, this accountant's name occurs, and he is the responsible author of all the documents in the temple, and was under the supervision of the Vaishṇavas of Tirupati. In regard to the donor, his name has one of the titles of Tirumangai Āḻvār, and he was one of the leaders among the Vaishṇavas of Tirupati.

OTHER DOCUMENTS OF HARIHARA'S REIGN: The next one No. 185, which is on the north wall of the Varadarājasvāmi shrine in the temple, is of great interest, and gives the name of the year. From this detail and further attendant circumstances, the date would work out to the 18th of January 1388. It refers to the deposit of 100 gold pieces into the treasury by Mullai Tiruvēngaḍa Jīyar in residence in his Maṭha in one of the flower-gardens apparently. From the income of this deposit, service had to be made on a particular festival day as is generally done on other festival days in the shape of food, etc., and this was made in the name of Harihararāya obviously Harihara II. The donor's name is, not actually mentioned; but the donation is entrusted to the care of the particular Śanyāsin, one among the managers of the temple. The same accountant, Tirunin̄ṛavūr Uḍaiyān, put the document in writing. No. 186 seems to be a continuation of this document. No. 187 refers to Ś. 1312, and would correspond to A. D. 1390. It is an agreement between the *stānaṭṭār* (people of the locality) and Mullai Tiruvēngaḍa Jīyar, supervisor of the flower-garden Ariśāṇālaiyam. This makes provision for a food-service during the *Mārgaḻi* (December—January) festival, when through the whole month the God and His consorts listen to the recital of the *Tiruppāvai* from the *Prabhanda* works. This makes provision for distribution of food during the middle ten days, and on the concluding day, for the God at Tirupati, and similar provision is also included for Gōvindarāja Perumāḷ in Lower Tirupati. The amount of deposit was 1,200 gold pieces from the interest of which the expenses of the provision have to be met. There are also details as to the distribution of the food, and there is the interesting remark at the end that, when

Tiruvēngaḍa Jīyar should die, his successor in the office should hold himself responsible for seeing to the working out of this provision, and be entitled to the privileges that it carries along with it. It is noted that his successor should be an *Ekāngi* (a single man) like himself. No. 188 is an imperfect document, and contains only a detail in regard to the distribution of food. The inscriptions so far are all of them from the hill shrine. With 189 we come to the Gōvindarāja temple. It is on the south wall of the Pārthasārathisvāmi shrine in the temple precincts, and is the same document as No. 187 that we discussed before, where the provision made is a joint provision for the temple at Tirupati and the temple of Gōvindarāja. No. 190 again is in the hill shrine and refers to Ś. 1314, corresponding to the 25th February 1393. It is again an agreement between the *stānattār* and the Jīyar referred to above, and makes provision for certain services to the God on the day following the conclusion of the festivals throughout the year. For doing this, 600 gold pieces were deposited in the treasury, and the service was to be conducted as described. The same accountant reduced the document to writing. No. 191 is outside the temple in a building on the road leading from the hill shrine to Chandragiri. It refers to the Śaka date 1326 corresponding to

18th December 1404. It refers to an agreement between the *stānattār* and one Giridēvappa, who was a younger brother of Sāntappa Nāgapaṇṇa who was himself the son of Sāyaṇṇa of the Ātrēyagōtra. This Sāyaṇṇa apparently was a member of the ruling dynasty from the *gōtra* which is the *gōtra* of the family. It makes provision for a service on the 7th day festival in a *maṇṭapa* constructed in the midst of a garden in a locality some little way from the temple, and from the locality it seems to refer to a place near Lower Tirupati.

DEVARAYA II AND THE INSTITUTION OF VEDA CHANTING IN TIRUPATI: No. 192 is an important document in the hill shrine. It refers to the year Ś. 1351 corresponding to 5th December 1429. It is a benefaction by the great Vijayanagar emperor Dēvarāya, the second of the name. It seems to refer to the grant of land in certain villages to the temple, taking into it certain parts already given to the God. From the income out of the land, or villages belonging to the Chandragiri treasury thus given, provision had to be made, in the name of the king, for certain services of food, etc., on certain festivals. The document is broken up and the full meaning of it cannot be made out. A certain number of villages are mentioned paying revenue into the treasury at Chandragiri, and it is those that are made over to the temple from out of which the provision was to be made. The village Iḷamaṇḍaya figures in this group. No. 193 belongs to the Śaka year 1352, corresponding to 1st July 1430. It is in the Tirupati temple, and is a Sanskrit verse and refers to the grant of a gold *paṭṭa* (a plate for wearing on the face) by prince Śrīgiri, the son of a Bissaṇṇa Dēvarāya. The next one 184 also comes from the hill temple and refers to Ś. 1330, with details of date corresponding to 13th March 1409, and is an agreement between the *stānattār* and a certain Mallaṇṇa, otherwise Mādhavadāsa, a disciple of Gōpināthayya. This is provision for a food-service and the burning of a perpetual lamp. The really interesting part of the document consists in this, namely, that the donor repaired the irrigation channel from the river at his own expense, leading it into the tank near the village Avilāli, and thereby bringing the lands below the tank into cultivation. Of this 5,000 *kuḻi* of hitherto uncultivated land was to be reclaimed and brought into cultivation at his expense, and, from the income therefrom, the expenses of the food-service should be met. He made separate provision for the lamp by presenting 82 cows including calves. The repairing of the channel, the making of the tank serviceable for agriculture, the reclaiming of the lands hitherto uncultivable, were all made at the expenditure of the donor, and then made over for the temple service. No. 195 conveys the same information without any detail in a Sanskrit verse. There Mallaṇṇa is described as *Amātyaśēkhara*, the chief of the body of ministers. No. 196 is of date Ś. 1339 corresponding to A. D. 25th August 1417. The same Chandragiri Mallaṇṇa repaired from the base to the top a pavilion in the temple. No. 197 belongs to Ś. 1366 equivalent to 2nd October 1444, and is an agreement between the *stānattār* and a Mallāṇḍaiyār of Chandragiri son of Dēvarasa, and is a provision for a food-service like those mentioned in Nos. 194 and 195, and even the terms are similar, the construction of a canal, the bringing of land into cultivation etc. No. 198 refers to the repairs carried out to the *Ānandavimāna*, that is, the tower over the sanctum of the temple by Mādhavadāsa, a disciple of Gopināthayya. We cannot be positive, although it seems likely, whether this Gōpinātha is not the same as Gōpaṇārya, who was responsible for the administration of the territory under the rule of the Sāḷuvas in the early years of the Vijayanagar empire. The next following group of documents, Nos. 199 to 202, are all from the hill shrine at Tirupati and relate to one particular subject, the institution of Vēda-chanting in the temple.

They are all of Śaka 1355, although the figure for fifty is damaged in the first record. Therefore the date corresponds regularly to 22nd November 1433. The interesting part of the document is that a *Vēda-pārāyaṇa* (chanting of the Vēda) by a number of Brahmans in the temple itself should be made at stated times, and along with the processions when the image of the deity is being carried round on festival occasions. The chanting of the Vēda was instituted in this case in the name of the ruling sovereign Dēvarāya and came about as follows. The leading Srī Vaishṇava Brahman Aḻahappirānār, son of Tiru Kalikanṛidāsa made a representation to Dēvaṇṇa Uḍaiyār in the following terms. He pointed out that, for the God, Tiruvēngaḍamuḍaiyān, there were already provided all the features of greatness, and the one desideratum was *Vēda-pārāyaṇa*, and suggested it would be well if this could be instituted in the name of the ruling sovereign Dēvarāya Mahārāja, who must be the great Dēvarāya II of the first dynasty of Vijayanagar. As the text words it, this leader of the Vaishṇava community in Tirupati pointed out actually, to the local ruler apparently, that, for the God in the temple, everything that constituted features of greatness was provided for, and that this one only was not, and that it would be well if this defect also should be remedied, and in case the governor agreed to do it, that the institution may be introduced in the name of the reigning sovereign. These statements arise clearly from the language. The Dēvastānam translation leaves much to be desired. The part is translated that the chanting of the Vēda 'ceased to be conducted,' which would mean that the *Vēda-pārāyaṇa* was being conducted, but it was given up at some time or other, and what was done now is but a revival of the institution. The terms of the original records* give no authority for this statement. On the face of it, the language would simply mean the Vēda-chanting was not there, and the request was that it might be provided for. The arrangement made was that the governor ordered one half of the revenue of a village called Śittakkuṭṭai, which was being paid into the state treasury (*Rāja Bhanḍāra*), should be set apart for this service; and the subsequent documents mention it that, as this provision was found inadequate, the other half of the revenue of the same village, which was paid into the temple treasury (*Śrī Bhanḍāra*) be also appropriated for this particular purpose; the temple treasury

* "திருவேங்கடம் உடையானுக்கு ஸகலமான வைபோகங்களும் உண்டா[யிரு]க்க வேதபாராயண[ம்] நடவாதிருந்தபடி ஆலே."

Dēvastānam Ins. Vol. I, No. 199.

being compensated by the other *Dēvadānam* villages round about, which are named, agreeing to pay quotas to make up the sum, into the temple treasury itself. The document as it has come down to us here is an agreement between the *stānattār* of Tirupati, and the *Mahājana* of Śrīnivāsapuram, otherewise Śittakkuṭṭai, which is said to be the *aharam*, the village in the enjoyment of Kalikaṅṛidāsar, the first (*Mudaliyār*) among the Śrī Vaishṇavas in Tirupati. This institution is a matter of considerable importance, and the question arises whether in Tirupati there was no *Vēda-pārāyaṇam* at all down to the Śaka year 1355, when it was actually instituted as stated in these records. On the authority of the record we have to take it that *Vēda-pārāyaṇam* did not form a part of the institutions in the temple. We have so far not come upon any records that makes any mention of it, although we cannot very well point out specifically where exactly it might find mention. For one thing in all the arrangements that Rāmānuja is said to have made in the *Śrī Vēnkaṭāchala Itihāsamāla*, this does not occur, as it might well have, had it existed. This does not mean that *Vēda-pārāyaṇa* was not usual in temple service, or even in Vaishṇava temples. The way that this is mentioned on this particular occasion presumes that it was one of the usual adjuncts, and the absence of it in Tirupati was the really remarkable feature. The chanting of the Vēda is well known in the Tamil country, as the Maduraikānji makes pointed reference to "the excellent Vēdas being illuminatingly chanted." It is also under reference in a poem which glorifies the excellent chanting of the Rig-Vēda as constituting one of the essential qualifications of a good Brahman. The poet and critic Rājaśēkhara, who lived at the commencement of the 10th century, states it in clear terms that, for excellent Vēda-chanting, one ought to come all the way down to the Drāviḍa country in the whole of India. The absence of a *Vēda-pārāyaṇam* therefore must have been peculiar only to Tirupati. It is just possible that it was absent in Tirupati, because we have had occasion to notice that Tirupati proved a place which did not provide the conveniences of life, and therefore there were comparatively few people that actually lived on the hill. The complaint had been that even such essentials as the supply of water and the supply of flower proved unsatisfactory from time to time and had to be arranged for specially, both in the days of Āḷavandār and subsequently in the days of Rāmānuja. It may be therefore that in Tirupati, the chanting of the Vēda was not usual, although it seems very strange that Rāmānuja should not have provided for it as he was so careful to provide for so many other things of even lesser importance in respect of the Tirupati shrine. Record No. 200 contains the latter half of this agreement. No. 201 begins with the same introduction referring to Dēvarāya's reign, giving the Śaka date 1355, and is an agreement by which the villages belonging to the temple both in Tirukkuḍavūr-nāḍu and Vaikunṭhavaḷa-nāḍu entered into an agreement with the *stānattār* that they would see to the incidence of revenue being paid to the 24 Brahmans, so that they may render the service of chanting the Vēda without interruption for all time, and the signature of a number of leading villagers is given as authority for this document. This puts the institution of Vēda-chanting on a footing of permanence. No. 202 continues the details of the agreement in this behalf, and fixes the amount payable by the various parties to the agreement. No. 203 similarly is an agreement signed on the other side for the same purpose.

OTHER RECORDS OF DEVARAYA II: No. 204 also from Tirupati is one which seems to refer to Dēvarāya II also and bears date Ś. 1358. It is an agreement by Śaḍagōpanambi Aḷahappirāṉār Gōvinda selling a house to the temple treasury for 1,000 gold pieces. The name Dēvaṇṇa Uḍaiyār occurs in the middle, and refers to the property as acquired by this Gōvinda as the property of a lady who had no children, apparently some relation of his. Then follow the usual conditions in regard to sale of property. No. 205 seems to be a similar document, a similar deed of a house sold to the temple treasury from out of the money received from Dēvaṇṇa Uḍaiyār. The amount involved was 4,200, the value of two and three fourths of a ground including the building, followed by signatures of this Gōvinda, the temple accountant and a number of Āchārya Purushas of the locality. No. 206 is a document belonging to Dēvarāya's reign. The date is gone, and even otherwise, the document is too far gone to be intelligible. No. 207 from Tirupati also is of date Ś. 1356, and does not make any reference to the ruler. It is an agreement between the *stānattār* and the first among the Śrī Vaishṇavas of Tirupati, namely, Kalikanṛidāsa Aḷahappirānār. The latter paid 4,000 gold pieces to the temple treasury for a festival to be celebrated at break of dawn during the six months of the *Dakshiṇāyana* (October—March). No. 208 is a document too far gone. No. 209 relates to Ś. 1368, and is a document in Kanarese. It refers to the gift in charity by Teppada Nāgayya Nāyaka, son of Muddayya Nāyaka, of 3,000 gold pieces. The amount has been entrusted to the *stānattār* to arrange that this service was rendered regularly. No. 210 comes from the hill temple, and is of date Ś. 1368. It is an agreement between the *stānattār* and Periyamalladēva, son of Eṛṛakkampayadēva Mahārāja with the titles *Mēdini-Mīsara-Gaṇḍa-Kaṭṭāri-Sāḷuva.* It relates to the payment of 1,000 gold pieces from the income of which a food-service was to be rendered to the God for all time. It was put on record by the temple accountant as usual. Record No. 211 refers to the Ś. year 1364, and is an agreement between the *stānattār* and one Karuṇākaradāsa a *Śāttāda* Śrī Vaishṇava of Tirupati for food-service to Gōvindarājapperumāḷ in Lower Tirupati in the name of this Dāsa. He paid 100 gold pieces from the income of which this was to be conducted. No. 212 coming similarly from Lower Tirupati is an agreement between the *stānattār* and four people apparently Vaishṇavas, namely, Āḷvār Mudaliyār, Ulahuḍaiyaperumāḷ, Tiru Anandāḷvār and Nārāyaṇa Perumāḷ. It is of date Ś. 1367 (13th December 1445). It makes provision for festivals on certain days in the names of the first two, and on certain other days in the names of the next two, for which they paid different sums, and stipulates the details of, how, after food-service to the God, it was to be disposed of. No. 213 is from the hill shrine and is of date Ś. 1367 (15th December 1445). It is an agreement between the *stānattār* and one Ananta-śayana, son of Rāmānujadāsa, a member of the Tirucchānūr *Sabhā*. It makes provison for some kind of food-service for the flag-hoisting of the seven festivals in the hill shrine, and two festivals of the shrine in Lower Tirupati. The details of the food-service are given as usual, and the agreement had been put on record by the temple accountant. No. 215 comes from Lower Tirupati, and is of Ś. 1368 corresponding to 23rd November 1446. It is an agreement between the *stānattār* and a member of the Tirucchānūr *Sabhā* whose name is given as Vaḍamāmalaidāsar Aḷahar Appiḷḷai Tiruvanandāḷvār Periya Perumāḷ. It is a provision again for some kind of food-service on the nine flag-hoisting festivals as in the previous document. No. 216 similarly comes from Lower Tirupati and is of date Ś. 1368 corresponding to 14th November 1446. It is again an agreement between the *stānattār* and Aḷahiya Perumāḷ, son of Rāmānujadāsa, a member of the Tirucchānūr *Sabhā*. This records a payment of 200 gold pieces into the temple treasury, and makes provision for a food-service during the 30 days of the month of *Mārgaḷi* (December—January) of the year.

RECORDS OF THE REIGN OF MALLIKARJUNA DEVARAYA: The inscription No. 217, is outside the temple on a slab at the end of the Sannidhi

Street in Lower Tirupati. It refers to the reign of Vīrapratāpa Mallikārjuna Dēvarāya, and is dated Ś. 1371 corresponding to 4th March 1450. It is an agreement between two Śri Vaishṇava Brahmans of Tirupati, Āḻvār Mudaliyār and Ulahuḍaiyaperumāḷ Mudaliyār for the sale of a house in the hill-town of Tirupati, belonging to Tirukkuḍavūr-nāḍu to a resident of Chandragiri in Vaikunṭhavaḷa-nāḍu, a *Nīyōgi* by name Lāsamālikam Chennappa Uḍaiyār. The next one, No. 218 comes from the hill shrine and is of date Ś. 1372 (31st August 1450), and does not refer to the ruler. It is a record of an agreement between the *stānattār* and Śirumallaiyadēva, son of Malagangayyadēva Mahārāja with the titles *Mahāmaṇḍalēśvara Mēdini-Mīsara-Gaṇḍa-Kaṭṭāri Sāḷuva.* He paid 1,200 gold pieces into the treasury for a daily food-service in his name. No. 219 from the hill shrine refers to a date Ś. 1367, although the latter part of the date is gone, corresponding to 13th December 1445. This is an agreement between the *stānattār* as usual and one Emberumānār Jīyar for two food-services in his name for which he paid 2,000 gold pieces into the temple treasury. The detailed provision for this service is recorded. The interesting point in this record is that this Emberumānār Jīyar is said to be the owner or resident of the flower-garden *Pankayachelvi* on the hill, and he is also described as one who supervised the affairs of the temple (*Kōil Kēḻvi*), thus giving us indication of one of the items arranged for in connection with Rāmānuja's organisation. No. 220 is also from the hill-shrine and is of date Ś. 1367 (17th February 1446). This is an agreement between the Jīyar and the *stānattār*, and provides for food-service in the name of the Jīyar on the nine flag-hoisting festivals, seven in the hill shrine and two in Lower Tirupati, and two other festivals, one on the hill, a flower-service (*pushpayāga*), and on the day of the concluding festival of Gōvindarāja. He paid 1,000 gold pieces into the treasury. Another detail of importance in this is that, on the day of the *pushpayāga*, the God and His consorts come to the pavilion named *Malaikkiniyaninṛaperumāḷ* and listen to the recital of the *Tiruvāyoḻi*, Nammāḻvār's portion of the *Prabhandha*, and then the usual provision for the distribution of food follows. After the usual distribution of food the remaining part was to be given over to the Jīyar who was in charge of the flower-garden, *Pankayachelvi*, and the *Maṭha* should receive it. The Jīyars are described as *Ēkāki*, that is, single Vaishṇavas. They must be unmarried men and should be entitled to receive this part of the food in succession. No. 221 also from the hill shrine is a similar provision for certain other festivals along with the nine flag-hoisting ceremonies. The provision is 1,000 gold pieces and the details of distribution of service, etc., are the same as before. It is of date Ś. 1368 (27th January 1446). No. 222 from Tirupati is a similar provision. It is only the name of the year that is given corresponding to 17th July 1447. In addition to the usual nine festivals, certain other festivals are included. No. 223 is from Lower Tirupati and refers to date Ś. 1378, (21st February 1457). It is an agreement between the ***stānattār*** and the Emberumānār Jīyar, who paid 5,000 gold pieces for certain daily services to the temple of Gōvindarāja in the temple. But the interesting point of the document is that the 5,000 gold pieces made over to the treasury, should be applied to the digging of the tank in the temple village of Avilāli, and, from the income derived therefrom, the provision for the service should be made. Similar provision for distribution of food is made as in previous cases. No. 224 is a particularly interesting document throwing light upon certain important matters of internal administration. It refers to the year Ś. 1372 (1450–51). It was provision made by a certain Channakēśavadāsa for taking out a canal from the boundary of Baiṇḍapaḷḷi to the village Śittakkuṭṭai, and taking out a canal from that of a different character, perhaps from percolated water called *Kaśakkāl* to the tank at Avilāli wherefrom water should be carried to cultivate lands that had not been brought into cultivation in the Śittakuṭṭai village. The Baiṇḍapaḷḷi people objected that, if this irrigation work should be carried out, their lands were likely to suffer, and lands under cultivation would go out of cultivation. The matter therefore was taken to the notice of the officers responsible, and an arrangement was made by which the land was made over to the people of Baiṇḍapaḷḷi, enjoining upon them the specific purpose for which this project was made. They are said to have made satisfactory arrangements for carrying a canal through another part and altogether in another way to serve the same purpose successfully, but without detriment to their own properties. The food provision that was intended to be made to Vīra Narasimhapperumāḷ of Śrīnivāsapuram was made successfully in consequence. The food remaining after distribution to those entitled to it, was to be utilised for feeding those who were in residence at the *Rāmānujakūṭa* of the village. No. 225 is from the hill shrine of date Ś. 1376 (7th July 1454). It is an agreement between the *stānattār* and Rāmānujadāsa, who was maintaining a flower-garden at Pāpanāśa. This Dāsa paid into the treasury 1,000 pieces of gold, and the necessary arrangements were made for carrying this out. The available food after distribution was to be given to the Śrī Vaishṇavas who were engaged in maintaining the flower-gardens. No. 226 merely records this piece of charity in a Sanskrit *Ślōka*.

OTHER RECORDS OF THE PERIOD: No. 228 comes from the Pārthasārathi shrine within the precincts of the Gōvindarājasvāmi temple in Lower Tirupati. It is of date Ś. 1308 which would mean A. D. 24th March 1387. It is an agreement between the *stānattār* and the head among the Vaishṇavas in Tirupati by name Kolli Kāvalidāsa, the first part of the name being one of the titles of Kulaśēkhara Āḻvār. It is a daily food-service for which he paid 1,000 gold pieces into the treasury. The service was to be conducted perpetually, and the part of the food given to him should be continued to his descendents. As usual, the record is set down in writing by the temple accountant. The remaining seven or eight records are too far gone and too imperfect to make anything out of. It is only two or three documents of Volume II that fall within our period. The first has reference to Ś. 1367 (13th December 1445). It is an agreement between the *stānattār* and Dēvaṇṇa, son of Periya-perumāḷdāsa Aruḷāḷadāsa of the Bhāradvāja *gōtra.* It is a provision for a food-service on the nine flag-hoisting days as usual. The usual provision was made therefor. The next one No. 2 of Volume II is in the Gōvindarāja shrine in Lower Tirupati and is of date Ś. 1376 (25th August 1454). This is an agreement between the *stānattār* with one Hariyappa of Chandragiri. He is described as the son of a Gauraṇṇa, who was a *Rig-Vēdin* of the Dananjaya *gōtra* in Āśvalāyana Sūtra. He paid 3,000 gold pieces into the treasury for provision for food-serviee, to be used for feeding 12 Brahmans in Tirupati. The 3,000 gold pieces were to be applied for digging irrigation channels where the water supplied comes from springs or percolation, and the water should be made use of for purposes of cultivation; the income from this was to be utilised for carrying out the terms of the provision. The next one from Lower Tirupati is of date Ś. 1379 (A. D. 1457) and is an agreement between the *stānattār*, and the temple accountant Tiruninṛaiyūruḍaiyān. He paid 100 gold pieces for a festival to be celebrated in his name by taking God Gōvindarāja to a flower pavilion, which he himself constructed on the bank of a new tank Śrīnivāsaputtēri. This work of charity should be conducted by all his successors for all time.

THE FIRST CENTURY OF VIJAYANAGAR RULE IN TIRUPATI: We may take it roughly that we have so far covered the first century of the history of Vijayanagar, as far as it comes from the records of Tirupati. We see that almost the first record in Tirupati makes a reference to Bukkarāya, although the reference is imperfect and to a great extent the record is unintelligible. But it certainly does relate to something that was done in the name of Bukkarāya or in his honour. The last record chronologically takes us to the reign of Mallikārjuna and to the date A. D. 1457. That is pretty well on in the reign of Mallikārjuna, while he actually died in A. D. 1465, and was succeeded by a brother by name Virūpāksha who is referred to by historians as Virūpāksha III of Vijayanagar. With this change the actual character of Vijayanagar history changes in many ways, more particularly in Tirupati. But before proceeding to that question we may note here that the region round Tirupati had been under rulers who were subordinate to the empire, but carried on the administration with a freedom which would perhaps justify an inference that the control exercised by the empire was not so close. This need not necessarily be the case, as we have already explained that the change in the manner of dating, and therefore the omission very often of any reference to the reigning monarch consequent thereon, need not be due to want of control. The dates being given in the Śaka era, it does not necessarily involve introducing, as a matter of necessity, the name of the ruler for the time being, as in the case of inscriptions of the period anterior to this, where they had necessarily to mention the name of the ruling sovereign, as the dates are marked in the year of the reign of the monarch for the time being. It is clear, however, that this region forming a part of the empire had a distinct character of its own. We see, among the names of royal personages, those of Bukkarāya, the first of the name; his son Kumāra Kampaṇa, Dēvarāya II and Mallikārjuna figure, though indirectly, the indirectness being due to the manner of dating, as explained above. The names of these monarchs figure because the benefactions made to the temple in each case happens to be in honour of the sovereign or prince concerned. As in the period preceding, the temple management had remained altogether autonomous, and under the control of the Śrī Vaishṇavas of the locality. The features of temple organisation show this more clearly, and a number of details appear in respect of it which seem quite reminiscent of the various items of organisation that Rāmānuja is said to have actually carried out in the place. This is made certain by references to a certain number of festivals which were all his introduction. One particular feature to be noticed is that while, on the basis of Rāmānuja's arrangement, almost the whole of the *Prabandha* seems to have been recited on festival days, a special provision was made for the chanting of some of these, such as the *Tiruppāvai*. There has so far been no reference to the chanting of the Vēda in front of the God, either in the shrine itself, or when the image of God is taken out in processions, or, as the record words it, that "while Tiruvēngaḍamuḍaiyān had all other attributes of greatness, the chanting of the Vēda was the one item wanting." We find provision made here for the recital of the Vēda *(vēda-pārāyaṇa* as it is called), and that happens to be done by the most prominent Vaishṇavas of the locality bringing it to the notice of Dēvaṇṇa Uḍaiyār who set apart some of the royal revenue, one half the revenue of Śittakkuṭṭai for the purpose; but, as suggested by Kalikanṛidāsar Aḻagappirānār, under the name of and in honour of the sovereign Dēvarāya II, Dēvarāya Mahārāya, as he is called in the record. There are a large number of benefactions to the temple, several of them from officers of importance, while some of them are from people associated with the management of the temple such as the heads of some of the *Maṭhas* in the gardens round the temple, where resided the bachelors or *Sanyāsins*, who had the management of the various institutions attached to the temple. One noticeable feature of these benefactions is that while the smaller of them are of the ordinary character, the larger benefactions take on the character of investments of money being made for irrigation and other facilities for the lands already under cultivation, or bringing uncultivated lands into cultivation, and making the income therefrom serve the purpose of the benefactions. This gives clear indication of a double purpose; the acquisition of the religious merit of a benefaction in a holy place, and making this benefaction serve at the same time the secular useful purpose of benefitting those who lived upon the land by providing them facilities, and really bringing more land under cultivation. This would be immediately for their benefit, so that what was intended for the spiritual merit of the individual donor proved of benefit not only to the God or the temple, or the Brahmans dependent thereon, but also served equally to benefit the other communities concerned. Direct state control, or of benefactions by the state as such, we have not come upon so far, and even where royalty and important officials made these benefactions, they were intended for their personal spiritual benefit, and therefore were provided for from out of their own funds rather than from the funds of the state. The contributions therefore of the state as such may so far be regarded as almost non-existent, and the properties attaching to the temple are entirely, at any rate, so far as this shrine is concerned, the result of private benefactions for the benefit of the temple itself.

CHAPTER XVII.

TIRUPATI UNDER THE SALUVAS.

THE SALUVAS, THEIR ORIGIN AND EARLY HISTORY.

In the inscriptions so far considered, we have come upon rulers of Vijayanagar belonging to the first dynasty, of whom the latest to be mentioned is Mallikārjuna with dates going as far down as A. D. 1457. Mallikārjuna died in A. D. 1465, and was succeeded by Virūpāksha, generally taken to be his brother, which seems to be made certain almost by the Śrīśailam plates of this ruler. His reign continued for twenty years almost, and then came a change of dynasty, when the new ruler, a member of the famous Sāḷuva family, called Sāḷuva Narasinga, placed himself on the throne of Vijayanagar. But long before he became emperor, he had become so influential in the state that the whole period since A. D. 1450 may be regarded as, in a way peculiarly, connected with him; the more so in the region of Tirupati, because this family was early associated with this region with their headquarters at Chandragiri. In dealing with the period therefore following the year A. D. 1457, we find that the inscriptions in Tirupati seem to refer more or less entirely to members of this family and their benefactions to the shrines. This is rightly so, for two valid reasons. The first of them naturally is because that the Sāḷuvas, who played a distinguished part in the very foundation of the empire, were allotted this region for their government. We mentioned already an inscription of Sāḷuva Mangu, recording his benefaction to the temple of the covering of the roof of the *Vimānamaṇṭapa* with gold and the mounting of a pinnacle on the top of it, in obvious imitation almost of what had been done by other rulers before in temples like Śrīrangam and Chidambaram. Mangidēva was one of the generals who played a distinguished part in the campaigns of Kumāra Kampaṇa, the son of Bukkarāya I. The principal achievements that he claims are the defeat and re-establishment of Śambuvarāya, and the defeat of the Muhammadan Sultan of Madura, achievements both of them ascribed generally to Kumāra Kampaṇa, the prince in chief command of this expedition. So the Sāḷuva family comes into fame almost at the beginning of Vijayanagar history; but even so, it is not clear why they should be associated with this particular region as we find them already there. In the period anterior to this, families connected with the government of this region were certainly many; but none of them seems to be associated with the Sāḷuvas. We have heard of the Telugu Chōḷas in the locality, of the Telugu Pallavas, of the Yādavarāyas related to the Chāḷukya family. But anything like a Sāḷuva family had not been heard of. In fact the family name Sāḷuva, for this dynasty, was one of comparatively recent acquisition. In fact it was acquired by Mangi by his own achievements, and therefore we cannot well expect this name to occur in previous records. But even so, there is nothing obviously to connect them with any of those families except a stray reference in which among the titles of the early rulers of this family, occurs the title Chāḷukya Nārāyaṇa. This title is given to an ancestor of the family by name Guṇḍa, who is said to have killed in battle 'the Sultan who had got ready for the conquest of the world', and he is said to have been in residence in his capital Kalyāṇapura, the name by which Kalyāṇi in the Nizam's Dominions, the capital of the later Chāḷukyas, is generally known. On the basis of these stray facts we may perhaps surmise that they were members of the Chāḷukya family like the Yādavarāyas, and became early associated with this locality. If the associations of this family with Kalyāṇi should be correct, it may be that that was their original place, and they must have moved from there, because of the conquest of the

Dakhan by the Muhammadans, and the foundation of the Bahmani kingdom. Whatever it is, they seem to have been members of the Chāḷukya family who migrated southwards, and early settled in the region round Tirupati with perhaps their headquarters at Chandragiri, which, at that time, was probably unoccupied country requiring to be brought into civilisation by various acts of reclamation, which we shall find prominently to be a feature of even the various grants made in this period to the temple itself. A long genealogy is given of this family in the work *Sāḷuvābhyudhayam*, which has come down to us in a single manuscript, a poetical work celebrating the exploits of Sāḷuva Narasimha written by the court poet Rājānātha Diṇḍima. There is another work ascribed to Narasimha himself; but seems to be more or less a work of this Rājānātha Diṇḍima called *Rāmābhyudhaya* which is a *Kāvya* written relating the story of the Rāmāyaṇa. The first name of any historical importance even in this is that of a Mangi or Mangidēva who played an important part, as was stated above, in Kampaṇa's southern invasion. Mangi had one son, among many, by name Gautama or Gauta, one of six sons; but of whom we know very little. This Gauta had four sons, of whom the first was Guṇḍa, the third of the name in the family, who had two sons, Timma the elder, and

Narasimha, better known as Sāḷuva Narasinga. He had another son by name Tippa, who had married a sister of the great Dēvarāya II himself, whose son Gōpa proved to be a distinguished ruler about the time when Sāḷuva Narasimha was rising into importance. Gōpa had two sons, Timma or Tirumalaidēva, and Tippa or Tripurāntaka, both of whom were governors in the southern provinces of the empire. Narasimha had two sons both of them very young, and of whom we shall have to speak later on. There was another brother by name Sāḷuva who had a son Parvatarāja, whose name also appears in the inscriptions as governor. This is the distinguished family, which, from the surname or title Mangidēva acquired, has got to be described the Sāḷuvas more or less as the name of the family.

VIRUPAKSHA'S MISRULE THE OPPORTUNITY FOR SALUVA NARASIMHA: The advent of the Sāḷuvas to power coincided with a period of new trouble and confusion in the history of Vijayanagar, and this it is that provided an opportunity for the rise of Sāḷuva Narasimha to supreme power as we shall see. It is the prominent position that they occupied among the feudatories of the empire that gave them the title Sāḷuva, which became the name of the family or the dynasty, as we have already seen. They were content to be the feudatories of Vijayanagar from the date of its foundation to the death of Mallikārjuna without any trouble. The death of Mallikārjuna seems to have introduced a certain amount of disturbance, which seems to have been caused more or less by an act of usurpation by his younger brother, who followed Mallikārjuna in A. D. 1465. He had to set aside two boys, sons of his brother, and, in bringing this about permanently in the interests of his own children, he seems to have perpetrated a massacre of the members of the royal family, and made himself unpopular even otherwise. It is this that ultimately brought about the usurpation of Sāḷuva Narasimha. The succession of rulers of this first dynasty may be set down as below, taking only the names of those that ruled :—

Harihara I A. D. 1336—1355.
Bukka A. D. 1355—1377.
Harihara II A, D. 1377—1404.
Bukka II A. D. 1404—1406.
Dēvarāya I A. D. 1406—1422.
Vijaya Bhūpati A. D. 1422.
Dēvarāya II A. D. 1422—1449.
Mallikārjuna A. D. 1449—1465.
Virūpāksha A. D. 1465—1485.

The foundation of Vijayanagar was followed soon by the establishment of the Muhammadan

Bahmani kingdom in the Dakhan, and, from the circumstances of its very foundation, it became more or less a matter of necessity for the rulers of Vijayanagar to guard the northern frontier against the aggressions of this new power. That was more or less the preoccupation of the rulers of Vijayanagar under the first dynasty, nay almost throughout its whole period of existence. The first rulers, Bukka and Harihara, and those associated with them had, of course, to carry on campaigns elsewhere also to bring about the establishment of this new power. Once that was done, and the fact was more or less recognised with the accession of Harihara II, their whole attention had to be paid to the northern frontier. Invasions were usual, and Vijayanagar had to be constantly on the defensive. This became so regular and so irritating a feature that the great Dēvarāya II carried out a regular reorganisation of the forces of Vijayanagar in such a way as not merely to keep back the aggressions of the Muhammadans, but even turn the tables upon them by carrying an invasion or two successfully against them, so that, by the time that the reign of Dēvarāya II came to an end, the power of Vijayanagar had become well-established, and even their Bahmani neighbour showed an inclination to respect it.

THE ADVANCE OF ORISSA DOWN THE COAST DISTRICTS: THE OPPORTUNITY FOR SALUVA NARASIMHA: Just at the moment, a new state in the north was coming into existence in Orissa under a new and vigorous ruler Kapilēśvara. The advent of this ruler coincided almost with the accession of Mallikārjuna who had, almost as the first act of his reign, to stand a siege in Vijayanagar under the combined forces of the Bahmani Sultans and the ruler of Orissa. He managed to come out successful; but the aggressions of the Orissa Hindus continued nevertheless. They managed gradually to extend their territory and take possession of the coast districts of the Bahmani kingdom as far as the Gōdāvari river, and, placing themselves there, they carried further aggressions southwards to secure possession of some of the main fortresses along the lower course of the Krishṇa, such as Koṇḍapalli, Koṇḍavīḍu, and places like that. From there again, they advanced further south into the territory of Vijayanagar, and at one time were in possession of Udayagiri in the Nellore District and carried their raids much farther, and deep into the South Arcot District as well. So the period of history with which we are concerned was one which called for great activity, along this coast region, to keep back the aggressions of these Kalingas, or Orissa rulers, within bounds. This position of affairs would give to any ruler, placed in Chandragiri and regions in the immediate neighbourhood, the chance of distinguishing himself by loyal service to the empire, and thereby becoming powerful for good or for evil, and, if the governor happened to be a talented man, he could certainly turn all this to his own advantage. While apparently serving the interests of the empire after beating back the first combined invasion, Mallikārjuna had to be constantly active, and we have a record which states that Mallikārjuna and his minister were somewhere in the eastern borders of the empire attending to the affairs of the territory under Narasinga.* This gives clear indication that the anxiety of the rulers was in respect of this activity of the Orissa rulers. That was the opportunity, for Sāḷuva Narasinga and he used this opportunity to purpose.

THE COURSE OF SALUVA NARASIMHA'S RISE TO POWER: The Sāḷuvas beginning with Sāḷuva Mangu were associated with the region round Tirupati, and their capital is clearly stated to have been Chandragiri. For all historical purposes, it was the Chandragiri province that fell to the government of these rulers, however actually it came about. It might be that the

* *E. C. III* Nos. 12, 59. Sewell's *Hist. Ins.* under date 1459.

Sāḷuvas were somehow related to the rulers of the locality that preceded them, say, for a possibility, the Yādavarāyas ; or it may be, that they came newly into power in the region which may be as the result of Vijayanagar coming into authority over the region superseding the previous rulers. There is nothing so far that gives us a clear indication as to how exactly they came to be there. Sāḷuva Mangu and Gōpaṇārya are stated to be the ruler and the minister of Nārāyaṇavaram in the *Kōvil Oḻuhu* (the history of temple organisation at Śrīrangam). That certainly would take in the territory under the Toṇḍamāns of old, and, if they became ultimately rulers of Chandragirirājyam, it would be nothing unnatural. Of course during the period of activity of Sāḷuva Mangu and his successors, it would have been a governorship, the governors of which bore their part and shared the responsibility in the conquests which culminated in the establishment of the empire of Vijayanagar. Of course, so much is made clear even in the one record that has come down to us of Sāḷuva Mangu from Tirupati itself. But as we advance in Vijayanagar history, we find the province continuing its normal course till the end of the reign of Dēvarāya II. It is the death of this great monarch, and almost the simultaneous rise of a new dynasty in Orissa, that altered the political situation. Till then it was only the activity of the Bahmani Sultans that had to be provided against efficiently, and that was done more specifically under Dēvarāya II. It is Dēvarāya's military equipment and the improvement in the military efficiency of Vijayanagar that made the Bahmanis feel the need of an alliance, just when Kapilēśvara of Orissa had satisfactorily established himself, and was quite inclined to pursue a policy of aggression on Vijayanagar territory. Dēvarāya's reign would not be suitable for any attacks on the empire with impunity, and it seems likely that his death might cause disturbances in Vijayanagar endangering the succession of the prince, although we do not know positively of any such disturbance having taken place. But the succession of a young ruler like Mallikārjuna was the opportunity for the united enemies, the rulers of the Bahmani kingdom and the new ruler of Orissa. So in A. D. 1450 we are told of an attack upon the empire of Vijayanagar, Mallikārjuna having had to stand a siege in the capital itself. He managed for the time to beat back the enemy. But that only gave indication of the actual danger in the northern frontier. The rulers of Vijayanagar therefore had to provide efficient defences against the aggressions from the coast side on behalf of Orissa even more urgently than aggressions from the Bahmani kingdom itself. It is this that gave the opportunity for a talented governor of Chandragiri to make for himself a position many ways unique among those of the governors of the empire. Sāḷuva Guṇḍa himself has had to bear a part. Either while he was yet alive or subsequently, the activities of Orissa became real, and then advanced into the territory of Vijayanagar on the eastern side rapidly from step to step till they could occupy a considerable part of the coast districts on the east and go forward against Koṇḍavīḍu, Udayagiri, and further down into the districts of the Tamil country. It is this activity of Orissa that caused anxiety and brought about the emperor Mallikārjuna and his minister going towards this frontier with a view to organise the defences of the kingdom. Sāḷuva Narasimha placing himself across the way of this advance of the Orissa rulers was able to use his position gradually and effectively against this. Marching from place to place, and pressing back the enemy back from one place after another, he managed to drive the enemy from the territories immediately dependent upon him in the region south of the Nellore District, and then over Udayagiri Fort and places dependent upon it. That done he could put the southern border in some safety, and march northwards to be on the watch both against the king of Orissa and against the Bahmani Sultans. These latter were occupied for some time with their own internal difficulties, and, with the accession of Muhammad Shah III, they were in some position of safety in their own territory to think of an aggression eastwards. When therefore in A. D. 1483—84, Muhammad Shah advanced towards Rājahmundry and encamped himself on the banks of the Gōdāvari, he found Sāḷuva Narasimha in power there with a large army well posted. This indicates to us clearly how it was that Narasimha was able to build a peculiar position for himself, by rendering valuable services to the state as against its enemies.

EMPEROR VIRUPAKSHA'S ACTS STIMULATED NARASIMHA'S COURSE TO POWER: In the latest stages of the operations connected with this move, Vijayanagar was under the rule, not of Mallikārjuna, but of a brother of his, who might perhaps be regarded as having usurped the throne of Vijayanagar if not to begin with, at least soon after, and made himself unpopular as a consequence. Virūpāksha, brother of Mallikārjuna became ruler about the end of the year A. D. 1465, following the death of Mallikārjuna somewhat earlier in the year, and thereafter Sāḷuva Narasimha conducted himself as if he were independent of the headquarters, although there is nothing done openly or formally to assert this independence. In the years immediately following we find Narasimha himself, or his generals, active, all over this region and in the southern districts next across. The names of Īśvara, and his son Narasa, of Āravīṭi Bukka and even Nāgama Nāyaka, figure in the transactions of the period, so that about the time that Sāḷuva Narasimha had to fight against Muhammad Shah III, he had gradually brought under his control, all the territory extending from Rājahmundry southwards well into the South Arcot District and further stretching westwards deep into Mysore as far as Śrīrangapaṭām itself. His authority and influence would be nothing objectionable so long as he conducted himself as a valiant and powerful governor under the empire. That is almost the position that he maintained, although the emperor does not appear to have attempted to exercise much control, or Sāḷuva Narasimha to submit himself to such. Virūpāksha's administration, apart from the initial difficulties of the situation, did not improve with years; much rather it seems to have grown from bad to worse, and, from all the information that we have, it would appear as though Virūpāksha's mismanagement went all round to make his own position really difficult. His unpopular and incompetent rule showed itself even on the west coast where the Portuguese speak of his perpetrating a massacre of the Muhammadan horse traders in Honovar (Onore), and throwing them into hostility to them. In this condition of affairs, Virūpāksha seems to have made an effort to set aside his nephews, and secure the succession to his own sons, which brought about dissatisfaction in the empire, and provided a splendid occasion for Narasimha's usurpation. The position of the empire was such that it required a watchful and capable ruler to keep the empire intact. Emperor Virūpāksha was not the kind of ruler, and his acts only made matters worse. When the moment arrived, Narasimha was able to set aside the unpopular princes, the successors of Virūpāksha and occupy the throne himself as offering the best guarantee for the successful maintenance of the integrity of the empire. It would be clear from this that from A. D. 1450 to A. D. 1485, Sāḷuva Narasimha was left more or less to himself, governing the provinces under his control and extending his authority gradually to become really the most powerful man in the empire. We shall now proceed to the inscriptions of this period in the temple of Tirupati, and see how far this position of his is reflected in his records there, and what he actually was able to do for the temple itself.

End of Volume I.

INDEX

A

INDEX

Printed at the Ananda Press, Madras.